D0933619

BASTARD FEUDALISM
AND THE LAW

BASTARD FEUDALISM
AND THE LAW

J. G. BELLAMY

Professor of History, Carleton University, Ottawa

AREOPAGITICA
PRESS

Portland, Oregon

Richard H. Jones, Ph.D., General Editor

First published 1989
by Areopagitica Press
9999 S.W. Wilshire, Portland, Oregon 97225

© 1989 J. G. Bellamy

Typeset by Input Typesetting Ltd
Printed in Great Britain by T. J. Press (Padstow) Ltd,
Padstow, Cornwall

ISBN 0 918400 10 4

CONTENTS

INTRODUCTION

The study of the secular history of late-medieval England has flourished in the last fifty years. Once a period relatively neglected by historians, the later fourteenth and the fifteenth centuries have attracted since the Second World War more than their expected share of research interest. While this *floruit* is in part explicable by the 'swing of the pendulum', a compensation for the earlier overemphasis on preceding centuries, other factors were quite as influential. One was a technical one. The calendaring of the rolls of chancery, which was nearly complete by the 1920s, provided historians with a research tool whose importance to this day is often underrated. The calendars offered for the later medieval period source material which had great prosopographical value, especially in regard to the gentry and the middling classes of men. In that such men were often office-holders, examination of the calendars fostered the study of administrative history at both the national and local levels.[1] In addition, the chancery rolls, particularly the close rolls, provided information about the landholding of the upper classes. This made practical the closer study of noble and gentry families, the study of the latter in turn promoting the study of parliamentary history from a new perspective since from the gentry were drawn the knights of the shire and indeed some of the 'burgesses' who sat in medieval parliaments.[2]

The ready availability of such material was, in time, bound to engage the attention of researchers and draw them to these topics, but the attraction was probably the sooner and greater because of one of the small number of professional historians who pioneered the late-medieval secular field. This was K. B. McFarlane. McFarlane was blessed with a personality his students found both

1

sympathetic and stimulating. He had a way of imparting his views on historical problems to them and other historians in a manner and with a mystique which commanded wide admiration. In his writings and even more noticeably in his lectures, he demonstrated an ability to stand back from the scene he was examining so as to address the reader or listener and that person's experience of life directly, in some ways not unlike Maitland had done.[3] Above all, it was McFarlane's main topic of enquiry, the English nobility and the world of bastard feudalism in which it lived, and his method of approach that won him renown and a devoted following. It was he indeed who popularized the term 'bastard feudalism' and gave it definition: a late medieval society where the features of feudalism still subsisted, though only superficially, and where the tenurial bond between lord and vassal had been superseded as the primary social tie by the personal contract between master and man. His was a fresh field at a time when the study of constitutional history was approaching the final period of its long and glorious reign. In that kingship and royal power, although not omitted from consideration by McFarlane, were given a lower profile, there was something novel here, as indeed there was in the fact that the object of his investigations was a whole and dominant social class. He was particularly concerned with the basis of the nobles' power, their land, and he paid especial attention to their financial records. He was in this way in harmony with the rising discipline of economic history, but at the same time his work maintained strong connections with an older school of history because he was involved with what he jokingly termed 'disreputable occupations', specifically the study of heraldry, genealogy, and the descents of manors.[4]

McFarlane's writings on bastard feudalism were a compound of economic (financial), family, and political history, with a dash of inheritance and land law added. It was a blend particularly attractive in that it cut across the rigid time frames and divisions, which were until so recently such an established part of English historiography, and it was made even more enticing by his habit of interpolating perceptive biographical capsules on noblemen or their lines in order to exemplify major trends. The study of the later medieval upper classes and their land, and of the administration (central and local) which was the backdrop to bastard feudalism, was the preferred area of investigation for several whose doctoral studies were supervised by McFarlane, and indeed of some of their own research students an academic generation later.[5] The quality of the debate engendered, and the incontrovertible fact that so many aspects of late-medieval English life were intertwined with bastard feudalism, drew in other historians and has produced over the last thirty years a cohesiveness in investigation and a level of academic writing which can be regarded as a particularly creditable episode in English historical scholarship. Significantly, neither the researches of McFarlane and his pupils nor those of the other investigators in the field have given rise to fundamental differences of opinion, although there have been minor disagreements in interpretation where politics and government were concerned.[6]

The investigators are to be the more commended because of the nature of the sources. There survives a fairly wide range of material superficially relevant but only a small amount with any real depth. There is no particular record source, apart from the relatively small amount of contemporary correspondence extant, which can be labelled the quintessence of bastard feudalism. As a result, we have been told a fair amount about the phenomena of bastard feudalism, the families, circles, and affinities of the upper classes, the extent of their property and the nature of their politics, but relatively little about the prime causes of human activity in that milieu and the actual mechanics of behaviour. There is a need to put together some form of 'model' which demonstrates the interlocking nature and functioning of the component parts of bastard feudalism, the suits, entries into land, maintenance, retainers, patronage, and property settlements; and to find which parts were central, which peripheral, which stimulated the development of which others and in what manner.

Perhaps the greatest single lacuna in the corpus of scholarship concerned with bastard feudalism is the legal aspect, although that is not to suggest there has not been some valuable work in that area. McFarlane's own comments on the operation of the criminal law, and on the lawlessness which should have been its target, although few, were very much to the point. He argued that the increased outcry against the lack of public order, which was typical of much of the fourteenth and fifteenth centuries, was caused by a rise of sensitivity among the populace rather than by the malfunctioning of the legal system or any sort of crime wave. He held that from as early as the reign of Edward I private warfare was giving way to seeking satisfaction, albeit with the employment of legal guile, through the courts. He was clearly in disagreement with Maitland, who held that the fifteenth century, 'the time of . . . private wars', was 'at least as lawless as the thirteenth'. There was, as McFarlane saw it, no real threat to public order in the late-medieval period, a position much in accord with his basic tenet of England at that time being a society with few, if any, grievous problems.[7]

If McFarlane's comments on the topic were perfunctory, so also have been those of other contributors to the debate, and it is important to understand why this should be so and why historians have not benefited from evidence from the rolls and files of the courts which handled criminal cases. The chief reasons are the value and extent of those records. Few of the records of the sessions of the justices of the peace, who handled most of the relevant cases in the first instance, have survived from the medieval period, and very few indeed from the period between the early fifteenth century and the middle of the sixteenth. Thus we have no way of ascertaining accurately how great was the incidence of the different offences (maintenance, embracery, forcible entry, riot, illegal retaining, and the giving or taking of livery) which were an integral part of bastard feudalism, or at least how many of these misdeeds led to indictments. Such misdemeanours were also tried by periodically appointed commissions of oyer and terminer, and some of their records from the period are still extant. They are of value and have been utilized by a few scholars. However, since most owe their survival to the fact that the cases recorded were moved or were being moved by writ of *certiorari* into the king's bench so that those indicted (usually gentry and their associates and followers) might in the interim arrange the purchase of pardons, we may doubt if they provide any acceptable indication of the general incidence of offences connected with bastard feudalism, although they do offer valuable insights into feuds, methods of doing justice, and the range of crimes imputed. The list of offences typical of the world of bastard feudalism does not include felonies. Certainly there occurred the occasional (and apparently regretted) homicide, but the upper classes in their land wars did their best to eschew hanging offences like the slaying of men and serious theft, and victims were reluctant to bring charges of felony for what on the face of it appears to have been just that. Thus it appears that the loss of the vast majority of the records of the gaol delivery sessions of the period *c.* 1420–1560 is no great impediment to the investigation of the subject. The lack of fifteenth-century conciliar records of the judicial variety, on the other hand, is a serious handicap, bearing in mind that council was specifically given authority over riot cases by statute in 1411 and later.

The value to the historian of bastard feudalism of the records of the courts which entertained private suits is somewhat greater than those of the criminal courts but not exceptionally so. They provide us with the basic information about what land or money was at issue and between whom. There is virtually nothing in the records themselves (apart from suits of attaint and error) suggestive of corruption of jurors or witnesses or of other efforts to interfere with the doing of justice, behaviour that was typical of the times. Nor do the suits over entry, disseisin, or riot, as they are recorded in the court rolls, usually tell us such things as the place of the action within a feud or land war (if indeed it was part of such) or what was really behind it. A recent study of a series of Bedfordshire suits in the period c. 1260–1380 has argued that there is little evidence that litigation was preceded by violence or disorderly conduct or that violence was used as an auxiliary to aid litigation: therefore there was little interference with actions over land.[8] To this thesis the immediate answer is that should we study the suits of those whose feuding is described in the fifteenth-century correspondence of the Paston family, but only through reading the plea rolls, we would probably come to the same conclusion. When, however, there is contemporary comment available on suits where such an important thing as title to land was at stake, either in letters or (more rarely) in governmental records or chronicle sources, we see quite clearly that few litigants merely handed their cause over to an attorney and went hunting. Rather they spent a great deal of time and money preparing the ground. They did not merely consider the actions and the procedural moves available but sought the good offices of the sheriff, undersheriff, and bailiffs, 'laboured' court officials, justices, clerks, jurors, and witnesses, and had a word in the ear of magnates whose influence was dominant in that region. It was a matter, to use modern terminology, of leaning on those who could make things happen and of calling in one's markers. They might also, if they were not seised there, take possession of the land in dispute as a tactical manoeuvre. Tremendous effort and substantial amounts of cash might be expended on acquiring or defending a few acres of land, the relevant entries in the plea rolls telling us the absolute minimum. What is lacking for our proper understanding of the lawsuits of the late-medieval period and the quarrels which lay behind them is information about what happened out of court, information which only becomes available (and then in very limited amounts) from the second half of the fifteenth century. Mostly it is to be found in correspondence of the gentry, but we are extremely fortunate to have preserved for us a unique autobiographical account of a Lancashire gentleman's long-lasting suit and land war over title to land, which dates from the reigns of Edward IV and Henry VII. As an example of what the land wars were about, especially the mentalities of the contestants, it could hardly be better.[9] From around 1500 onwards there survive substantial numbers of bills, answers, replications, rejoinders, and so forth from the suits heard before the king's council, which, where the exaggerations can be gauged and the contradictions resolved, provide valuable insight into the activity behind the suits.

The sources from which my conclusions have been drawn are mixed and the material is scattered. As well as in the autobiographical account just mentioned, there is much relating to the law in the correspondence of the Pastons, Plumptons, Stonors, Willoughbys, and other fifteenth- and sixteenth-century families, although the majority of it is not specific but suggested or implied. It has happily been possible to supplement some of the Paston correspondence by examination of relevant files of oyer and terminer commissions of the mid-fifteenth century. Also essential to any investigation of bastard feudalism is an understanding of the land law and the changes it underwent in the period under consideration. Fortuitously, the Year Books (Edward I to 1536) and the law reports and legal collections of the early Tudor period, a large part of whose contents concerns the holding of land, have recently been scrutinized by scholars in some depth for what they can tell us about aspects of the land law. The state of the latter, it must be emphasized, was quite crucial in sustaining many of the elements of bastard feudalism. The statute and parliamentary rolls are a very necessary recourse for the historian working in the area of bastard feudalism. Lawyers were continually seeking ways round the letter of the law, and many possessed their own collections of statutes and had read them thoroughly. A new Act was not just the passing whim of one parliament, not just a token response to a petition and something which would soon be forgotten by contemporaries as some twentieth-century historians would have us believe. Legislation, then as now, was a matter of precision both in regard to the criminal law and to property. Most Acts embodied remedies which were eminently practical and dovetailed in neatly with other statutes and the general tenor of the law in their area. When it became apparent that one line of attack on the many-faceted problem of bastard feudalism was not working, then other legislative approaches were tried. There was little inertia on the part of governments, nor a lack of imagination. Indeed some of the procedural and judicial remedies stipulated were startling in their severity, even if we can appreciate how they were developed from notions and practices already part of the common law. Kings, ministers, and parliaments worked repeatedly, if not persistently, towards the eradication of the evils attendant on bastard feudalism but, because these were an integral part of the very structure of society, progress was necessarily slow.

The criminal law as it affected bastard feudalism was concerned with the duties of law-officers and jurors and how malfeasance could be restricted, which was a difficult proposition given contemporary attitudes to office-holding and contemporary belief in suitor/defendant participation in the legal process. The criminal law was also necessarily concerned with the definition and scope of the misdemeanours in the bastard feudalism orbit (riot, forcible entry, illegal retaining and livery, maintenance, embracery, conspiracy) and the process by which the perpetrators were brought to trial and adjudged. While there is not much difficulty in discovering the history of the scope and definition of these offences, we are handicapped in judging the effectiveness of the different types of criminal procedure by the loss of court records already noted. We do have, however, the writings of a number of Tudor legal commentators, some of which throw light on how the criminal law functioned in the fifteenth century as well as in their own period. Riot and armed entry into land in the bastard feudalism context bring to mind the king's council in the Star Chamber. Forcible entry and riot do indeed figure prominently in Star Chamber records but the cases were private actions: the Star Chamber was not, strictly speaking, a criminal court, that is to say one where accusations/complaints were frequently made for the benefit of the king. We are lucky in that the cases which came before the court over various periods of time during the Tudor period have been analysed in respect of the main matter at issue, although the social and legal significance of the findings have not been examined. I therefore provide some commentary on this issue, and I also address the question of why and how quarrels over land came before the Star Chamber.

If the land law and attitudes towards land are of great importance in the study of bastard feudalism, then especially so are the rules prevailing in regard to entry into land. Maitland drew attention to the custom of the twelfth and thirteenth centuries which allowed a man to expel by his own force or that of his friends someone who had ejected him from his land, provided he did so within four days of being ousted; for in four days the ejector could acquire seisin. The design behind this rule was not that a man should be expected to use force to protect his property but rather the reverse. The intention was to protect possession (seisin), even 'untitled' and 'vicious possession', against ownership. There existed, argued Maitland, 'an extremely rigorous prohibition of self-help' which necessitated a 'system of possessory remedies'. These worked well at first but unfortunately 'fell to pieces in the course of the fourteenth century'; by the fifteenth century, so he believed, the law allowed more self-help than in the twelfth century and protected possession as against ownership in a mere two particular situations.[10] Recently D. W. Sutherland, in his study of the assize of novel disseisin, has argued to good effect conversely that the lawful occasions for the employment of self-help actually diminished rather than increased in the later Middle Ages, and where self-help did occur a gentlemanly standard of behaviour was expected.[11] Such conduct as the bearing of arms by entrants or the taking of personal property was forbidden; usually the party ousted was allowed to take away his horse, wardrobe, and cash-box.

Yet contemporary comment suggests that it was illegal entry which was the great exacerbator of disputes over land in the later Middle Ages, and I pay particular attention to that phenomenon. There is also the matter of the best way of approaching the world of bastard feudalism. I have chosen to view the struggles over land, the 'gentlemen's wars' as I think they should be called, from the viewpoint of the contestants rather than to centre investigation on the operations of the courts.[12] This pursuit of land-war participants and their strategies necessitates a detour away from the law and its administration in order to study their activities at the fount of influence and patronage, the Court. While much bastard feudalism activity was intended to outmanoeuvre opponents so as to be able to take the maximum advantage of the law, we should not fail to notice the contribution made by political manoeuvre, even if it was usually at the lower rather than at the higher level. Indeed, it is quite possible that one type of court may actually have been intended to provide justice of a political flavour. One final comment is necessary. My observations about the criminal law suggest that so intractable and so enduring were the problems created by bastard feudalism that the government was forced increasingly into developing that law in a direction which was quite distinct from what had obtained before the later fourteenth century. Particularly at risk for a time, in regard to a fairly extensive list of misdemeanours, were the two types of criminal jury. Whether this legal development, ultimately largely abortive, can be construed as a borrowing of foreign judicial procedure and something akin to the sixteenth-century 'reception', which Maitland believed he had detected, seems doubtful, but that there was a novel impulse in the development of the English criminal law for a time seems certain.

I commence this study by examining the nature of judicial administration in the milieu of bastard feudalism particularly in regard to the roles of the sheriff, justices, and jurors. For this it is necessary *inter alia* to unravel and analyse the significance of the welter of relevant legislation from a period of over two centuries. Only by undertaking this long neglected and somewhat onerous task is it possible to reach a conclusion on whether the evils which have at various times been attributed to bastard feudalism were created, fuelled, or even perhaps kept within reasonable limits by the administrators and the administration of the law; and whether this dark side was, as has sometimes been implied, the result of an ill-conceived, malfunctioning, or corrupt legal system.

Chapter One

SHERIFFS, JUSTICES, AND JURIES

A sheriff, Sir John Fortescue tells us, shall be chosen in the exchequer on the day after All Souls by the council, the lords spiritual and temporal, the judges of the two benches, the barons of the exchequer, and the clerk of the rolls. These nominated for each bailiwick three knights or esquires of better repute and disposition of whom the king then chose one.[1] An appointee was supposed to hold his post for only a single year at a time (14 Edw. III st. 1 c. 7) and there must be three years between terms (23 Hen. VI c. 7). Who had the greatest influence on the selection of the three candidates and the final choice of one of these (for the king must usually have acted on advice) must have been dictated by the politics of the time. A dominant monarch, who took a personal interest in legal administration, would have some idea whom he preferred, but rulers of a different disposition or occupied with more pressing matters would probably leave it to the council, or more likely to the minister or ministers who dominated there. Since it is the nature of man to be political, there can have been few occasions in the centuries under review when there were no factions within the council and when one of these factions did not have the king's ear and confidence to a greater degree than its rivals. This dominant Court faction, probably headed by the king's favourite minister of the time, would normally prevail in the sheriff's appointment. However, there may well have been times when one or several of the dignitaries who had a voice in the nomination were willing to cede their rights to members of the local nobility or gentry, perhaps to settle political debts. There is one such reference in the Paston letters but how frequent such aberrations were we cannot tell. The local gentry may also have been successful in having sheriffs they found obnoxious removed during their term of office.[2]

At the level of council at least, and very probably among the nobility and gentry at large, men knew what they wanted in a sheriff. This is clearly displayed to us in sixteenth-century correspondence and there is no good reason to doubt that similar views obtained in Lancastrian and Yorkist times. It was reckoned essential that the sheriff should have property in the bailiwick in which he would serve. He should possess a reasonable amount of land overall but he must not be litigious, at least he must not be engaged in more than a minimum number of lawsuits when his name was being considered. Nor must he be involved in any bitter factional dispute in the area or be known to have received substantial benefits in the recent past from one of the contesting parties. On the personal rather than the political side, youthfulness or a large family to provide for were definite disadvantages. On the other hand, it was considered meritorious to have been a regular member of the local peace commission (though one could not, of course, be a justice of the peace while sheriff), to be without debts, and not be a castle keeper. That he should not be the steward of a magnate was not a desideratum but a rule. Ideally, because it would mean he had fewer enemies in his bailiwick, the candidate for the shrievalty should hold land there but have his main residence outside it.[3] Like the vast majority of justices of the peace, the sheriff was a member of the gentry and thus himself a part of the world of bastard feudalism, even if temporarily charged with authority over it.

The reason why the magnates and gentry with land in a particular county took interest in the personal qualities, territorial possessions, and political affinities of a candidate for the shrievalty was his future power, if chosen, as an officer of the central government to aid or hinder their ambitions or interests in that bailiwick. The aspect of the sheriff's authority with which they were most concerned was the administration of the law both on the criminal side and in the field of private suits. Twice a year, even into the seventeenth century, the sheriffs held tourns in each hundred in the month following Easter and Michaelmas. There they enquired by a free-holder jury of presentment of felonies and trespasses (homicide and other sudden death excepted), the indictments subsequently being forwarded to the justices of the peace for determination (1 Edw. IV c. 2) or for later handling at gaol delivery sessions.[4] Once a month the sheriff was also responsible for holding a session of the county court to hear pleas of debt where the sum involved or the damages claimed was under 40 shillings. The sheriff and his officers (the undersheriff and the hundred bailiffs), men whom he himself had appointed and whose time in office could not exceed his own, had the power to arrest persons appearing suspicious or travelling armed.[5] Under fourteenth-century statutes the sheriff took part in the examination of 'roberdsmen' and 'draghlatches' (5 Edw. III c. 14) and of vagabonds (7 Ric. II c. 5). By the Act 1 Ric. III c. 3 he was given authority to bail those who had been arrested for felony. The sheriff also had the power to order any person to find surety of the peace and it was he who frequently had the right to appoint the keeper of the county gaol, a task he would take care over since escapes from custody could cost him large sums in fines to the king.[6] He also had the duty of certifying the names of the prisoners to the justices of gaol delivery when they held sessions. Another vital task of the sheriff concerned the property of those who came before the courts on criminal charges. From the fourteenth century, when a suspect had been indicted or on receipt of the second writ of *capias* (arrest), it was up to the sheriff to take into his keeping his goods; after the suspect was arraigned and convicted, the sheriff then took possession of the guilty person's lands as well. A change in practice was instituted by a statute of Richard III's reign: thenceforward goods, like lands, were not to be taken into the sheriff's hands before the suspect was tried and convicted.[7]

These shrieval duties of a legal nature might be performed in ways either detrimental or beneficial to particular members of the upper classes and their households and clients. The full force of the law might be used quickly and heavily against one group but the misdeeds of another ignored or the normal peace-keeping procedures implemented but slowly or slackly. This was clearly most important to the nobility and the gentry, but what concerned them perhaps even more than maintaining public order directly was how a sheriff conducted himself in the world of the 'gentlemen's wars', the struggles for aggrandisement by litigation and self-help which characterize upper-class and even national society better than anything else over a period of at least three centuries. In this world felonies were rare but trespasses (of the non-commercial kind) and private actions numerous. A duty closely connected with these 'wars', and indeed the activity for which the sheriff was mentioned with great frequency in contemporary records, was the execution of writs, an essential feature of any litigation and a shrieval monopoly. The control of writs gave the sheriff considerable influence in local politics, for without proper communication justice could not be done since men would not know they were summoned to court nor, if a trial did occur, would the judgment of the court be implemented. By failing to serve writs a sheriff could get men into great legal danger and even cause them to lose their lands. The sheriff had it in his power to delay suits greatly and in so doing he was sometimes in covin with one of the contesting parties. From the fifteenth century there is evidence that, despite his oath on taking office, a sheriff might demand a substantial bribe before he would serve a writ or implement its instructions when the matter was a suit between parties.[8] Particularly was this the case when the writ was a distringas (distraint) or a replevin (restoration) whereby a defendant's goods were seized or returned.

The area where it lay in the sheriff's power to affect the world of the upper-class feud the most was that of juries and their empanelling. Of the many aspects of litigation and criminal process which gave rise to concern and argument in the centuries under review, there was none which caused emotions to run higher than the selection of jurors and their potential for corruption. Although in practice jury panels for both personal actions and criminal cases were empanelled by his officers rather than by the sheriff himself, no panel was in fact supposed to be returned without his approval.[9] All knew that a single jury verdict could lead to a person losing his whole inheritance once and for all because the opportunity to appeal the verdict to a higher court was very limited. A very good legal case indeed had to be made by the defeated party to the justices before they would countenance such a request. Those who knew the legal system well would advise a friend, when his suit was to be tried, to 'labour' immediately the sheriffs of those counties where the land in dispute was located.[10] To 'labour' in this instance meant seeking to influence the sheriff's supposed neutrality in a particular direction, and it was usually accomplished by paying that official a bribe in cash. Fifteenth-century correspondence refers to this as though it was considered somewhat bold but not uncommon or truly reprehensible. The examples we possess show bribery in operation in private actions rather than when prosecution was at the king's suit, and the design was that the sheriff in return for the bribe should install on the jury kinfolk, friends, associates, tenants, or former servants of one of the parties involved. In these actions, where possession of land was frequently at stake, much store was set on the obtaining of the jurors' names before the court sat.[11] In theory (under the Act 42 Edw. III c. 11) the sheriff was obliged to array panels of jurors four days before the suit came to trial. This was so that the parties should have time to acquaint the jurors with their 'evidences', which were usually deeds demonstrating their claim to the property. Because over 90 per cent of lawsuits and quarrels among the upper classes from the fourteenth to the sixteenth centuries must have involved claims to land, and because these were settled by juries which were empanelled under the sheriff's supervision, it is clear that the sheriff's favour was essential if one was to be a frequent winner in litigation.

On the criminal law side the situation was not dissimilar. The person against whom complaint was made endeavoured in the first place to ensure that the bill of assault, forcible entry, trespass, or even homicide, did not gain the approval of the grand jury and so become an indictment.[12] To achieve this the sheriff had to be persuaded, as in a private action, to load the jury with men who had an affinity with the person complained against or were persons at his command (baliffs, clerks) as the statute 23 Hen. VI c. 9 noted. If the bill of indictment was found to be true, then the petty jury had to be embraced (as the contemporary term was) in a similar manner and again it was the sheriff who could do it. For the complainant the problem was the same. He must try to arrange for sympathizers, relatives, or tenants to serve on the grand jury and the petty jury. If the criticisms of sixteenth-century legal writers about the shortage of actual indictments at that time reflected the situation in the fifteenth, we may conclude that complainants pestered sheriffs over empanelling of jurors somewhat less than did the accused and their associates.

The sheriff was also involved with bastard feudalism in a judicial or quasi-judicial capacity. It was a feature of the English criminal law, one relatively unnoticed by historians, that in the fifteenth century officials were on several occasions invested with the power to do summary justice against those suspected of offences connected with bastard feudalism such as riot and forcible entry.[13] The recipients of these powers were primarily the justices of the peace yet the sheriff was also given a role. It is worthy of note that he had been allowed to do justice without the need for a formal enquiry by jury even in the fourteenth century. The Ordinance of Labourers (1349) stipulated that labourers who refused to work at the wage rates of 20 Edw. III for those who required their services should go to gaol until they gave sureties to so serve if their refusal was proven by two witnesses before a sheriff, constable, or bailiff. In 1383 sheriffs were given authority with justices of assize and justices of the peace to examine vagabonds and compel them, if in default, to find sureties for their good behaviour, or if they could not do this to put them in gaol.[14] The first occasion the sheriff was given a role of this type which involved offences connected with bastard feudalism was under the great riot statute of 1411 (13 Hen. IV c. 7). This commanded that, when a riot was reported, two justices of the peace and the sheriff, with the posse, were to go to the scene of the offence and arrest the miscreants. If the three law-officers actually found the riot in progress on their arrival, their record of this was to be sufficient to convict the rioters who were to be lodged in gaol until they paid a fine. What catches the eye in this statute is the manner in which the sheriff was given the same powers as the justices of the peace. It did not occur in other statutes which provided members of the peace commission with authority to use judicial process of an abbreviated character. Nor did the sheriff appear in the most important of the Acts on forcible entry, 15 Ric. II c. 2, the procedure in which served as a model for the designers of 13 Hen. IV c. 7. In the early Tudor period, however, the sheriff made one appearance in criminal law legislation which was comparable with his role in the statute of 1411. The Act 19 Hen. VII c. 13, which also ordered the fifteenth-century riot statute to be enforced strictly, stipulated that, where in cases of forcible entry the jurors would not find a verdict of 'guilty' because of interference and pressure by the parties accused, the sheriff might certify the names of the maintainers, which would have the effect of a conviction. This was power indeed, but it was soon lost. The Act ceased to be operative with the accession of Henry VIII and there were no similar windfalls for sheriffs in the remainder of the Tudor period.

It would have been remarkable had there been no laws enacted in the centuries under review to control and remedy the misbehaviour of so vital an officer to the doing of justice as the sheriff. In regard to his duties relating to bastard feudalism, there were between the reigns of Edward III and Elizabeth I at least seven statutes. The Act 20 Edw. III c. 6 set justices of assize to enquire into and try cases of the taking of gifts by sheriffs and other officials and the illegal making of panels of jurors. The Act 4 Hen. VI c. 1 provided for private suits with double damages against sheriffs extorting from those whose writs they were serving. The Act 8 Henry VI c. 9, designed primarily to provide remedy for those evicted from land by force or kept out by force, gave authority to justices of assize to try sheriffs accused of defaults. Charges were to be laid either by indictment or by the relatively new method of information, a process which would provide the informer, if successful, with half of the convicted sheriff's forfeiture in addition to costs and expenses. The Act 23 Hen. VI c. 9 forbade the putting of sheriffs' officers on inquests and the taking of anything to their profit 'for ease or favour' from those they had arrested; enquiry into these abuses was to be by justices of assize, of the peace, or of the two benches, but suit could also be brought by the victim (who could win treble damages). By the statute 11 Hen. VII c. 5 it was provided that two justices of the peace might examine sheriffs accused of mis-entering in the records plaints made in their tourns, while under 11 Hen. VII c. 24 justices of gaol delivery and justices of the peace were empowered when the suit was the king's to remove unsuitable jurors from panels made by sheriffs and others. By the Act 27 Eliz. I c. 12 the rule was made that undersheriffs should swear an oath not to empanel corrupt juries; furthermore, justices of gaol delivery and justices of the peace might, without opposition from the sheriff, remove jurors and install new ones. Again complaint could be made by either bill of indictment or information. These Acts do not seem to have diminished shrieval authority and activity markedly but they demonstrate that the sheriff had come in time squarely under the supervision of the justices in regard to duties connected with bastard feudalism. This legislation cannot have done other than diminish the prestige of the shrieval office. It goes without saying that sheriffs were never empowered to investigate the behaviour of any justices.

The picture which emerges of the shrieval office in the years between c. 1350 and 1600 is not therefore one of marked decline or supercession. The sheriff may not in his duties relating to public order have been the great power he was at times in earlier centuries but the position, which still provided the holder with a number of judicial duties, was certainly quite crucial in the quarrelsome world of bastard feudalism. This was particularly through the authority to empanel the jurors who produced the formal charges and the verdicts. These verdicts could mean the loss of land and the substantial, even perhaps the total, impoverishment of one of the parties involved. The hostility we detect in contemporary correspondence to the local occupant of the shrieval office appears to have arisen from trepidation that he was empanelling a jury which would prove hostile to the writer; also from distaste for another aspect of the sheriff's duties, namely the execution of process, be it the seizure of the chattels or land of those whose arrest had been commanded, the incomplete restoration of seisin, or the too efficient implementation of a court judgment. Where the law fell fairly but heavily on an individual, he was likely to view the agent of the legal system with hostility.

The law-enforcement official who had most to do with the illegal aspects of bastard feudalism was undoubtedly the justice of the peace, and indeed the rise of that social phenomenon in the fourteenth century was contemporaneous with the rise of that class of law-officer. Justices of the peace, whose domain in fact was the criminal law, not the field of private actions, were appointed by the king on the advice of the chancellor, the treasurer, and the council (2 Hen. V st. 2 c. 1).[15] In practice, local politics and the connection of local magnates with their peers who were on the council must have played a part in the selection. The Paston family's letters suggest the more powerful of the local gentry also played a part in the process. Sir John Fastolf and the first John Paston were able at various times to veto a candidate, secure the selection of another, and to negotiate with the chancellor for their own reappointment and that of their friends. At the end of the sixteenth century we hear of justices of the peace appointed by the chief justice of the king's bench and by the attorney-general.[16] There were several statutes which barred men in various categories from the office. A justice of the peace, who ought to be a man of good name, should not be a barrator (i.e. persistently involved in legal suits) nor a maintainer of anyone who was (1 Edw. III c. 1); he should not be the steward of one of the nobility (12 Ric. II c. 10); he should hold land or tenements worth £20 a year for the purposes of prestige and so that he would not be tempted to extort (18 Hen. VI c. 11); if he was a member of the gentry, but not if he was a lord or a justice of assize, he ought to live in the county on whose bench he was to serve. How stringently these rules were applied before the sixteenth century there is little evidence to indicate, but in 1595 Queen Elizabeth ordered the removal of those JPs who lived outside the county whose bench they adorned and those who lacked the required amount of property.[17]

We know for sure that justices of the peace were just as quarrelsome as their neighbours who did not sit on the bench and that a good number gave support to miscreants. Indeed, many must have sought the office in order to assist a county faction and to protect their own dependants, friends, and servants from legal action. There was never a law that justices of the peace must not be the retainers of others, although in June 1561 it was apparently the intention of Sir William Cecil, Elizabeth's chief minister, to remove such men from the commission.[18] It was governmental policy from as early as Edward II's reign to exclude the sheriff. In the size of their membership, peace commissions during the later fourteenth century and the fifteenth century tended to increase relentlessly. There were as few as six JPs per county being appointed at each turn in the 1380s, over a dozen in the early fifteenth century, thirty or more in some counties by the early sixteenth, and double that by the end of Elizabeth's reign.[19] In the early years of the peace commission's existence, those on it, while they usually possessed the authority to determine trespass, might not be allowed that power in regard to felony. There seem to have been occasions, furthermore, when the determination of the crimes in each of these categories was reserved to particular members of the peace commission, no doubt those with some degree of training in the law. In 1394 it was enacted that two such justices of the peace might deliver gaols in their county. This provided them with authority to arraign those indicted of felony, a power being lost to the peace commission as such, for although its members might enquire into felony, they were being forced to yield the right to try it and were being restricted in their arraignments to a diet of trespass.[20]

In the world of feud among the members of the upper classes threats and hot words were frequent. It was the justices of the peace, both in and out of their sessions, on whom the king relied above others to defuse these potentially explosive situations, and their chief instrument was the surety of the peace. Marowe, who expounded on the peace commission in the later years of Henry VII's reign, held that the JP's power to order the giving of this surety was virtually unlimited. Lambarde, writing on the same topic eighty years later, argued that any person could ask for and secure it against anyone else, even a wife against her husband and vice versa. The cause would very likely be a fear of personal injury or damage to property, but whether justices investigated the request to see if it was based on actual danger we cannot tell.[21] Fitzherbert stated that no surety should be given unless the party asking for it first took an oath to the effect that he was not prompted by malice. If the person reckoned to be endangering the peace refused to find sureties, then the justice of the peace could command his arrest and committal to gaol until he would comply. The sureties, of whom there were normally two, were men of substance who, by the late sixteenth century at least, must provide pledges in the order of £20 leviable on their goods; these could be released by the man in danger or the justice of the peace at their discretion but no later than the day set when the pledges were taken. The pledges were forfeit should the peace be broken by the party pledged, even if he did so only by threatening words or by carrying a weapon.[22]

The justices of the peace began to make their mark as judicial officers immediately before the time certain aspects of bastard feudalism became so obnoxious that they had to be proscribed by law. Probably because they had insufficient professional judges, perhaps because they were pushed into it by the Commons of Parliament, the kings of the fourteenth and fifteenth centuries decided to utilize the justices of the peace to operate the statutes against this class of misbehaviour. Thus in the fields of the illegal giving of livery or retaining, the statute 1 Ric. II c. 7, which was directed against those who gave livery and made covenants with the recipients so that they should maintain each other in their quarrels, was left to the justices of assize to administer, yet the commission of the peace of 1380 empowered JPs to hear and determine offences of livery and maintenance. The important statute of 1390 (13 Ric. II st. 3), which defined what retaining was to be lawful, gave in contrast no indication who was responsible for trying offenders, but the Act 20 Ric. II c. 2, which forbade a yeoman or anyone below the estate of an esquire from bearing livery unless he was a household servant in the continuous employ of a lord, was given to the justices of the peace to enforce by their enquiry and by punishment at their discretion.[23] In the first parliament of the reign of Henry IV there was passed an Act (1 Hen. IV c. 7) which forbade lords giving livery of company to any knight, esquire, or yeoman. By the statute 7 Hen. IV c. 14 private suits of the *qui tam . . . quam* variety (i.e. the complaining party sued both for himself and for the king, which later became known as a penal action) against such miscreants were countenanced, but these were to be brought before the justices of assize. These procedures cannot have brought satisfactory results, for the Act 8 Hen. VI c. 4 said that the two above-mentioned Acts were not being operated because of lack of indictments on account of maintenance (i.e. pressure on victims and jurors by someone not personally involved in the case). Thenceforward, therefore, justices of assize and of the peace were empowered to attach (arrest) suspects as though they had been indicted for trespass; then they could examine them and, if they were found guilty, punish them by a fine of 100 shillings, the examination apparently serving as both indictment and a form of trial.

Here, then, we have justices of the peace as associates of the professional judges administering justice on the errant nobility and furthermore doing so in summary fashion, the noble suspect being neither indicted (which was impossible because of his maintenance) nor arraigned before a jury. This was to be a salient feature of legislation against bastard feudalism for a century. Yet the statute 8 Hen. VI c. 4 was also unsatisfactory, at least it was considered so in Edward IV's reign. Therefore by 8 Edw. IV c. 2 it was forbidden to give livery to anyone save household officers, servants, or legal counsel. Procedure against offenders was to be by the laying of information in the king's bench, the common pleas, or at sessions of the peace. The justices in those courts were empowered, if they preferred to proceed without normal arraignment, to try the accused by mere examination. This tradition of employing justices of the peace to deal with livery-giving offences and allowing them to exercise summary justice continued into the reign of Henry VII. The statute 11 Hen. VII c. 3, noting that the Acts concerned with riot, unlawful assembly, illegal retaining, the giving and taking of livery, maintenance, embracery, and excessive wages could not be executed because of embracery, maintenance, and corruption, provided for justices of assize and JPs on information received to proceed against those named as if they had already been indicted. We notice that the procedure envisaged in this Act was not quite as abbreviated as in 8 Edw. IV c. 2 in that trial was probably (it was not stated) to be of the normal sort and not by examination.

In regard to livery-giving and retaining, the statute 11 Hen. VII c. 3 was no great success and therefore the very detailed 19 Hen. VII c. 14 was designed to remedy matters. This it did by a system of fines, by seeking to ensure better evidence about these offences came before the courts, and by encouraging accusations made by information laid before the chancellor, the keeper of the great seal, the king's bench, or the council. These dignitaries and courts were empowered to dispatch privy seal or subpoena writs and then examine the suspects summoned, the examination serving as a full arraignment under the common law. At the lower level it was provided that justices of the peace should enquire at quarter sessions by means of a jury of twenty-four substantial men about illegal retaining and livery-giving in their counties. They were to order the chief constables and bailiffs of the hundreds and the constables of vills to appear at the sessions and give evidence about the offences on oath. The suspects reported were to be examined by the JPs at the sessions or at any convenient time or place and the names certified to the king's bench, the certificate taking the place of an indictment. The 1504 Act, we may say, dealt with illegal retaining much as 8 Edw. IV c. 2 dealt with livery-giving. Indictment by jurors, it is true, was allowed a certain role but most reliance was placed on accusation by means of information. The suspects were to be tried by examination by great officers of the realm, by the king's bench, council, or justices of the peace. The effect, if they were convicted, was to be 'as though [they were] condemned after the course of the common law'. Once more the JPs were the category of justices entrusted with the administration of the law at the lower level and indeed they were the only common element envisaged in the operation of 8 Edw. IV c. 2, 11 Hen. VII c. 3, and 19 Hen. VII c. 14.

Legislation which accentuated the role of the justice of the peace in regard to bastard feudalism was also forthcoming in the field of riot and forcible entry during the same period of time. What may be taken as the first statute against riot was 2 Ric. II st. 1 c. 6. This provided for lords, when 'credibly certified' of a riot, to arrest those involved without waiting for any indictments and commit them to gaol for trial by the justices of assize. On the grounds that it was too severe, this Act was annulled at a later date by the very parliament which passed it. The next statute on riot, 13 Hen. IV c. 7, was very probably the most important of them all. It gave power to arrest rioters to justices of the peace and the sheriff instead of to lords. If these officers arrived at a riot before the rioters had dispersed, they could seize the offenders and put them into gaol as convicted by their record.[24] If the rioters had dispersed, the justices were to enquire of the facts by means of a jury, but if they could not get at the truth that way, maintenance perhaps intervening, they were to certify their own beliefs about the miscreants (which cerificate was to have the force of an indictment) into king's bench or to the council, where the matter was to be tried.[25] There was no other statute which substantially affected the law of riot until 1495. Then the Act 11 Hen. VII c. 3, as we have seen, permitted accusations in regard to a good range of offences connected with bastard feudalism, including riot, to be made not by indictment but by means of information laid before justices of assize and justices of the peace.[26] Again the use of a jury for laying charges was absent and the normal procedure was therefore abbreviated.

In regard to the crime of forcible entry, which first made its appearance as an indictable trespass in 1381 (5 Ric. II st. 1 c. 7), the justices of the peace were given a major role by the two most important statutes. 15 Ric. II c. 2, which seems to have been the archetypal Act in the matter of truncated process where offences touching bastard feudalism were involved, stipulated that on receiving a complaint of forcible entry into property a single or several JPs, probably with the sheriff attendant on them, might take a posse to the scene of the misdemeanour and, if they found any person holding a place forcibly after entry made, they could put the miscreants in gaol as convicted by their mere record. There the offenders were to stay until they made a fine with the king. What is particularly noteworthy is that all this might follow from the simple word of a single justice of the peace. In 1429 there was passed a second forcible entry Act, 8 Hen. VI c. 9. This one was to deal with instances where entry was made peaceably but the property was subsequently held by force, where forcible entrants fled when a justice of the peace arrived, and where an entrant had made a gift or feoffment to a lord so as to have his maintenance in the enterprise. In regard to the last, if the party put out could prove it by a private action, the feoffment was to be void. No doubt because a justice of the peace could not 'record' an entry by force which he did not see, it was provided that he should enquire about the entry from the entrants themselves and from the people of the county. The latter sounds like enquiry by a local jury rather than plain examination, although the former suggests interrogation. Here the rules laid down are strongly reminiscent of those for riot as set out in 13 Hen. IV c. 7, enquiry by jury being resorted to when no 'recording' was possible. If the justices of the peace could not behave in a summary fashion under 8 Hen. VI c. 9 as they were able to under 15 Ric. II c. 2, they were nevertheless entrusted with an authority which put them in a potent position to discipline nobility and gentry in their land wars. The only other statute on riot and forcible entry before the death of Henry VII was passed in the Parliament of 1504 (19 Hen. VII c. 13). Although the Act rehearsed 13 Hen. IV c. 7 and ordered its proper enforcement, it provided that, where a jury was used (i.e. because the rioters had dispersed when the JPs and sheriff arrived at the scene) and it failed to find a true bill on account of maintenance or embracery, the justices and the sheriff might certify the names of the offenders and this was to work an instant conviction.[27]

After the accession of Henry VIII nothing truly similar to these summary statutes on riot, forcible entry, livery-giving and retaining was promulgated, and most certainly nothing of the type which gave summary authority over those offences to justices of the peace. Indeed, in the rest of the Tudor period there was but one new Act touching procedure where offences were of the bastard feudalism type (33 Hen. VIII c. 10) and one which affected the technical scope of riot.[28] The Act 19 Hen. VII c. 14 contained a clause which cut short its operation when that king died, but the other statutes in the group theoretically continued in force. The evidence of plea rolls in regard to the utilization of these Acts by the Crown and where indictment and jury trial were used is unfortunately rather scanty. The extant records of the Hampshire peace commission for 1474–5 show two indictments for forcible entry (probably under 15 Ric. II c. 2), one for riot (under 5 Ric. II st. 1 c. 7 or 17 Ric. II c. 8), and one for the illegal giving of livery (under 8 Edw. IV c. 2) out of a total of thirty-seven.[29] The records of the Norfolk JPs for 1532–3 which survive provide eleven cases of forcible entry and seven of riot out of a total of some 250. The Essex quarter sessions records of July 1565 to April 1566 contain five indictments for forcible entry out of a total of about fifty-four.[30] Privy or special sessions held by justices of the peace seem to have had a special connection with these two types of offence. Of the eleven privy sessions known to have been held in Staffordshire between 1581 and 1597, five were concerned with forcible entry and riot and were summoned under 8 Hen. VI c. 9 and 19 Hen. VII c. 13.[31] These totals, which show forcible entry and riot still to be relatively common offences in the sixteenth century, probably represent something considerably less than the actual incidence.

The charges appearing in the records just mentioned were brought for the most part by means of indictment, the most common manner, not by the truncated methods provided in statutes like 15 Ric. II c. 2 (forcible entry), 13 Hen. IV c. 7 (riot), 8 Edw. IV c. 2 (illicit livery and retaining), 19 Hen. VII c. 13 (maintenance and embracery), and in the similar Acts we have noticed above.[32] These each provided for a method of trial quite different from that used in regard to virtually all other offences. Essentially the justices of the peace by their record could report the offenders and that record would have the force of an indictment. In the case of 15 Ric. II c. 2 the JPs record could also work a conviction, while under 8 Edw. IV c. 2 a justice of the peace could examine a suspect and that simple examination, if it were unfavourable, would count as a conviction. This was power indeed, even if the punishment meted out could not endanger life and limb.[33] The majority of cases under 13 Hen. IV c. 7 and 8 Edw. IV c. 2 must have gone before courts other than those of the peace commission. In the case of illicit giving and taking of livery, and retaining contrary to statute, many cases probably went into king's bench or before general commissions of oyer and terminer, while where the offence was riot they may have gone for the most part before the king's council. The power of the justices of the peace in cases which fell under the Acts 13 Hen. IV c. 7 and its improver 19 Hen. VII c. 13, as well as under 15 Ric. II c. 2, was such that those who caused a riot or entered forcibly might never come before the courts and still less be punished, provided the JPs who viewed the riot or entry chose not to record what they had seen or summon a jury to enquire. This situation, which cannot have been infrequent, made for one good reason why the upper classes were so keen that they themselves or their clients should be members of the peace commission. To what degree parliamentary pressure by the nobility and the gentry was responible for obtaining this great authority over land-war offences is not clear. If the king favoured the provisions legislated because it saved him from having to employ more professional judges, the members of the upper classes must have approved of them out of a desire to preserve their property and a mistrust of the traditional procedures.

Another facet of the authority of the justices of the peace was their ability to interfere in the selection and the work of juries. Despite the popularity of truncated process and the use of record, examination, and information to circumvent the employment of jurors, they were still necessary for the presentment and trial of a number of offences directly connected with bastard feudalism. Thus the many trespasses of the assault variety had to be handled by juries, as did all the relatively few felonies committed in the land wars. Jurors were also essential, of course, when the matter at trial was a private action, as for example of trespass or novel disseisin. The same was also true in regard to most of the actions brought by informers under the many laws which provided a share of the forfeitures, and even costs and rewards, to the successful suitor. Information, it is worth noting here, was allowed as a method of accusation in a good number of statutes against crime which had a direct connection with bastard feudalism.[34]

In theory, the indicting or 'grand' jurors were picked through the bailiff of each hundred choosing two lawful men who in turn performed the actual selection. In practice, by the sixteenth century at least, the justices of the peace recommended the jurors to the sheriffs who then empanelled them.[35] By Elizabeth's reign there were instances of the sheriff needing to have the approval of the justices of assize for his selection. The *Articuli super Cartas* (1300) stated that jurors ought to be 'next neighbours, most sufficient and least suspicious', but it is uncertain whether this referred to all juries or only to those used in private suits. Fortescue, referring to practice in Henry VI's time, mentions the grand jury as being twenty-four men of the township where the misdeed was done, with no affinity with the accused and each worth 100 shillings a year in land or rents, a substantial sum. Lambarde refers also to another jury, one 'from the body of the shire' comprising the constables of the hundreds, which produced indictments for crimes missed by the hundred juries; indeed it might indict those juries for concealment. The 'body of the shire' jury in the mid-fifteenth century was composed of proven and lawful men not constables. The number of such jurors as were actually sworn in order to indict was usually around fifteen at that time. In 1572 and again in 1583 the Crown asked the justices of assize to make sure no retainer sat on any jury. Grand jurors were loath to accuse their social superiors, Lambarde tells us, and were still in his time much too easily influenced by the sight of livery.[36]

The indictment process was where factions sought to interfere in order to protect their members from criminal charges and also to try to get their own accusations accepted as true bills. This we can tell from court records and contemporary correspondence. Great efforts were made to install one's allies, relatives, servants and tenants, and those of friends, on the jury, and with good reason. We hear of bills of indictment being rejected because the foreman of the jury was cousin to the person accused, or because the sheriff's servant or those of gentlemen of the opposing faction were jurors. We hear of the widow of a murdered man being allowed to name the jurors. No rank in society seems to have failed to interfere; even an archbishop would use pressure to ensure his bills became indictments.[37] In the fifteenth century grand juries, according to Fortescue, were happy to investigate crimes because the jurors of that period were sheep farmers. They thus had a certain amount of spare time denied to arable farmers. Yet it seems likely that although grand juries might enquire, there was a reluctance, if the misdemeanours involved great men or their clients, to find a 'true bill', to bring in an indictment. Sir Thomas More tells us this was particularly true of his time in regard to three crimes, one of which was riot; furthermore, grand juries were known to him to have rejected many charges where there was good evidence to support the bill.[38] Lambarde noticed the same thing in the later years of that century.[39]

Although in theory grand juries scrutinized any bill brought to court by an individual, there seems to have been some attempt by justices of the peace to monitor this process. By his day, Lambarde tells us, the grand jurors were only allowed to pronounce on bills already seen by JPs. This practice he justified as a method of ensuring the form of the bill was legally correct, but we may suspect that there was an element of censorship which again made the role of those justices quite critical. We should remember, however, that grand juries were not always under the JPs' eyes directly. More tells us they were entitled to hear evidence before they came to the sessions and could keep secret the names of those who told them.[40] Justices of the peace were known to tamper with accusation procedure in another manner also. This was by persuading an informer to allow his information to become a bill of indictment and then go before the grand jury to give evidence in its support.[41] Grand juries, except for a short period, were not immune from legal action by those who believed they were corrupt. Edward I laid down that those who had suffered by the procuring of a grand jury might obtain a writ of conspiracy against the suborner. A little later, by an ordinance of 1305, conspiracy was specifically defined as including allying together by covenant or bond in order to indict or acquit falsely. Such charges were apparently common at trailbaston proceedings in the earlier fourteenth century. Suits of conspiracy against suborners of grand juries are to be found among the pleas before the king's bench in the fifteenth century, but how frequent and how successful they were at this time is not known as yet.[42]

The type of trial jury which was perhaps most affected by the pressures of bastard feudalism was not that used where prosecution was at the king's suit but rather the variety which decided private actions. These jurors were expected to have a reasonable but not necessarily a substantial amount of wealth. The statute 2 Hen. V st. 2 c. 3 set the qualification for jurors giving a verdict in private suits over land or involving debt or damage of more than 40 marks at the same level as that demanded of a member of a petty jury deciding a case of murder, i.e. having land or tenements worth at least 40 shillings a year. By the Act 27 Eliz. c. 6 this requirement was raised to £4. The reason given was that jurors of the 'poorer and simpler sort' were 'the least able to discerne the causes in question' (i.e. appreciate the legal arguments); also they were unable to afford to attend the sessions. Only in regard to jurors in party suits were there limitations as to old age and bad health: from Edward I's time it had been the rule that jurors in petty assizes (i.e. actions of novel disseisin, mort d'ancestor, and such) should not be over seventy years of age or be continually sick. Nor ought they to live outside the county where the case arose.[43] By the statute 35 Hen. VIII c. 6 on every jury panel which was to decide a private action in the king's courts of record there had to be six jurors from the hundred where the matter at issue originated.

To attempt to bribe or pressure jurors in a suit of party so as to influence their decision was embracery, the investigation and punishment of which by the Act 20 Edw. III c. 6 was allotted to the justices of assize, although complaint could also be made to the treasurer and the chancellor. From 1361 such offences were punishable by a fine ten times the size of the bribe.[44] For a juror to be convicted of taking a gift from a party would result in imprisonment, a fine, and future omission from jury service (5 Edw. III c. 10). However, seeking in the course of a private action to convince the jurors of the rightness of one's case before it came to actual trial in court was considered much less blameworthy. We read of litigants who sent their evidences in regard to the land in dispute to the jurors-to-be, or who wrote to each of them, or, being of high rank, sent a messenger to tell them how they felt about the case. The third John Paston, we know, used his chief witness in the forthcoming trial to get hold of certain evidences pertaining to his title and to labour the jurors about them.[45] This was considered acceptable, if rather sharp, practice in the fifteenth and early sixteenth centuries, but by Elizabeth's reign it had become much less acceptable, even if there were no laws specifically forbidding it. Hudson, the historian of the Star Chamber, for example, states clearly that a plaintiff or defendant ought not to labour jurors about the 'state of the cause'.[46]

After labouring, the next concern of a litigant was that the jurors with whom he had communicated should actually attend the trial, for there was a high level of absenteeism. Many of the delays which beset private actions were caused, as one statute of Henry VIII pointed out, simply by the shortage of acceptable jurors at the sessions.[47] This was the result partly of challenges but largely of maintenance and embracery, that is to say pressure by one party or by those of his faction or affinity to dissuade them from being at the trial. To ensure the jurors whom he had laboured did attend, a party might help them with their travel expenses by, for example, paying for their lodging in the town where the court sat.[48] This practice continued into the sixteenth century. As with juries of indictment, the juries which sat to decide private actions were frequently packed with men who had connections with one or other of the contesting parties. Robert Pilkington tells us in regard to what seems to have been an action of novel disseisin that his adversaries packed the jury with the kinsmen, 'sibmen', old servants, tenants, and allies. Robert Plumpton was told in regard to his suit at the Yorkshire assizes of February 1498 that he should obtain a copy of the panel for purposes of challenge and check if any men 'syb or allied' to his adversary William Babthorp were included. To challenge any juror who was 'alied, feed or servant to his adverse partie' or a personal enemy, as Thomas Smith pointed out in the mid-sixteenth-century tract on the English legal system, was quite proper but whether the litigant was able to do so with total success seems doubtful.[49]

Any plaintiff or defendant in a private action who felt that the jury which had given the verdict was corrupt might seek the attainder of the jurors for perjury ('the greatest mischief which can beset the realm', as the Act 15 Hen. VI c. 5 put it) through the decision of another jury, this time one of twenty-four men. Should the accused be found guilty, they could suffer total forfeiture. Thomas Smith implies that by the mid-sixteenth century the use of juries of attaint was infrequent and that when they were used the cases rarely proceeded to a verdict; instead, they were settled out of court.[50] In Henry VII's reign two statutes were promulgated which were designed to provide a more satisfactory procedure. The so-called 'Star Chamber' Act (3 Hen. VII c. 1) set up a court of great post-holders to examine complainants who put in a bill or information about illegal livery and retaining, embracery, and the taking of money by juries. This was, however, designed primarily to improve the criminal law. To extend this statute to private suits, there was passed 11 Hen. VII c. 25, the 'Perjury Act', as it has been called. Under this a complainant about a corrupt verdict was to have his bill passed to the chancellor, who would then summon the accused jurors to appear before a court comprising himself, the treasurer, the two chief justices, and the master of the rolls. The court was to examine the accused and punish them at discretion, which meant that it was to serve as a court of summary justice.[51] If he did not include sufficient evidence in his bill or he non-suited, the complainant was liable for costs and damages.

The Act by its own wording ceased to be operative when the Parliament of 1504 met, while the other court, the one established in 1487, does not seem to have functioned after 1495. Cases involving corrupt juries were certainly dealt with by Wolsey's court of Star Chamber but the number, if we judge by recent research, was never high or even substantial. Guy found six cases concerning maintenance, five involving corrupt verdicts, and five of embracery or perjury out of a total of 473 cases where the records were full enough to reveal the type of crime at issue. Apparently the number of cases of this type which came before the Star Chamber increased in the 1530s and 1540s, a trend which became more pronounced still under Elizabeth.[52] How many of these cases involved juries deciding private actions and how many were those dealing with the king's suit, we are not told. Sir Thomas More, Sir Thomas Smith, and William Hudson each refer in their writings to errant juries in both private suits and those of the king having to appear before the council. More implies that the practice of being called to the Star Chamber or before the privy council was not infrequent, Smith that it was, whereas Hudson in his Star Chamber treatise states that from 1485 a grand or trial jury was fined there for its verdict virtually every law term.[53] Overall, the evidence of decisive action being taken against corrupt jurors is not impressive. Probably few cases came to trial and convictions were fewer still, which of course was a major reason why the evils of bastard feudalism were so long-lived.

If some jurors were punished for their corrupt behaviour, very few sheriffs or justices of the peace can have been. The extant records of medieval commissions of the peace provide few instances of indictments for that purpose. Indeed the only example they contain of a substantial investigation into shrieval malfeasance seems to have been one in Devon in 1352, whereby two ex-sheriffs, William Auncel and Robert Hacche, were indicted of extortion in regard to the return of writs and the detention of beasts, levying fines illegally, allowing bail contrary to the law, placing men of bad fame on juries in return for money, failing to make an arrest because of a bribe, and taking payments from parties in return for maintaining them in their quarrels.[54] Each of these categories of offence was, of course, intimately connected with bastard feudalism. They were very similar to those attributed to sheriffs in *Britton*, the late thirteenth-century legal treatise and by the 'rules for sheriffs' of 1516.[55] Responsible for the prosecutions of 1352 seems to have been Chief Justice William Shareshull, who served on the Devon peace commission at the time and appears to have been a major driving force behind the attempt in the mid-fourteenth century to make the criminal law more effective.[56] Because there are no other similar indictments in these records from the later fourteenth or the fifteenth centuries, we must assume that those of the gentry who served regularly as sheriffs and justices of the peace had a tacit agreement amongst themselves never to seek the indictment of each other for malfeasance of office in the period of the land wars and that they resisted any suggestion from the centre that they should do so. This seems to be confirmed by extant fifteenth-century correspondence, which makes no reference to the prosecution for malfeasance of these officials in regard to their legal duties, although there remains the faint chance that such does exist in the files of some unexplored general oyer and terminer commission.[57]

We must also consider whether the puisne justices in their capacity as justices of assize and of oyer and terminer were tarred with the same brush as the justices of the peace. Were they totally above the county feuds over land, or did they occasionally give favour to particular suitors, complainants, and accused? That in the earlier fourteenth century they accepted fees and robes from magnates is not in doubt, but it has been suggested that an ordinance of 1346, and perhaps the punishing of judges who were particularly errant in this respect, resulted in the later limitation of the practice and its probable elimination by 1500.[58] If this was so, there is nevertheless good testimony that the judges were regarded in the early sixteenth century as still being far too easily influenced. Edmund Dudley, Henry VII's unpopular minister, writing in 1509, suggested that the king should encourage judges to guard against being affected by the fear of great persons or of incurring the displeasure of the king's councillors or servants.[59] Dudley's tone is that such interference was common in his day and that the judges sometimes tilted the scales in the influential person's favour. He does not mention actually bribing a judge and the implication is that if there was any reward for the latter it took the form of a favour for a favour. The Paston correspondence suggests upper-class women might achieve the same by personal supplication and by means of their charm, and might even obtain helpful legal advice from those who were later to try their cases.[60]

The superior justices, there is evidence to suspect, were most affected when they were trying private actions and it was probably not entirely their own failing. There are indications that litigation in its course and outcome was much influenced by court officials and judges' clerks and servants. These had the power to cause endless delays unless their support was obtained, delays which might cause plaintiffs to abandon their suits or affect more directly one side's chances of winning. The 'Song on the Venality of the

Judges', a thirteenth-century satirical poem on the law, provides an instructive picture of clerks and servants of judges actually touting for business for their masters' sessions and promising the prospective plaintiff success in his suit if he was willing to hand over half of his winnings.[61] The 'Song' advised would-be litigants over land that their chances of success were small unless gifts were made to these minions and officials. The private records of Sir John Fastolf show him to have made payments for, or in anticipation of, favours by the clerk of the petty bag, a clerk of the exchequer, and the clerk to Sir William Yelverton, justice of the king's bench.[62] Robert Pilkington in his narrative of a long-lasting lawsuit says that his adversary, William Ainsworth, went as far as to retain the second prothonotary of the king's bench as his second attorney.[63]

Although we hear of Sir John Fortescue, the chief justice of the king's bench, being given a robe by Sir John Fastolf, there is no evidence of substantial bribery of the professional judges in fifteenth-century correspondence or even for that matter of justices of the peace.[64] It seems to have been considered that the way to success with a judge who was serving on a commission of oyer and terminer or was on the assize circuit was to seek him out before he set out from London and explain to him informally one's forthcoming suit and perhaps the current state of relevant local feuds and politics. An incident reported in the Paston correspondence shows that the king or his close advisers, when in 1451 they sought to influence the outcome of a general oyer and terminer commission, tried to put pressure on the local sheriff rather than interfere with the judges. The first John Paston, the opponent of the party whom the Crown supported, acted similarly and tried to persuade the Norfolk sheriff to accept a *douceur*.[65] The absence of references to attempts to bribe judges probably reflected reality: men knew they had only limited ability to affect verdicts which in any case they were reluctant to do. Nor is there evidence from the fifteenth century to suggest that they overawed jurors, as they are supposed to have done in Tudor times, or that they interfered in a suit in such a way as to give one party an advantage in procedure or in pleading; nor do there survive reports, as there do from the sixteenth century, of their browbeating justices of the peace.[66] Certainly the Pastons do not appear to have thought of attributing any sharp practice to Sir William Yelverton, the puisne justice with whom they had a serious quarrel in the 1460s. It is additionally noteworthy that they were able, although hard-pressed at times, to weather Yelverton's hostility relatively unscathed.

The tale, then, that the laws and the behaviour of those involved in administering justice have to tell us is of a judicial administration under great pressure from society at large; furthermore, they tell us that there were a good number of sensible attempts to support and improve the legal apparatus, notably the efforts to diminish the role of the two types of jury. It is also fairly evident that although the failures in legal and judicial administration played an important part in fuelling the disruptive side-effects of bastard feudalism they were not the only causes of those maladies. To approach closer to the other major causes, we must now investigate the errant behaviour of the upper classes, namely the endemic land wars which they waged so persistently.

Chapter Two

THE LAND WARS

Very few indeed of the men and women of gentry status and above, who lived in the England of the later Middle Ages or the Tudor period, did not appear as either plaintiff or defendant in the courts of assize, common pleas, or king's bench at some time in their lives. For those who were politically active and held local administrative office, appearance in private actions was virtually certain. Many gentry and nobility sued or were sued in the course of their lives not once or twice but on dozens or scores of occasions. Thus Henry, Lord Berkeley in the course of a single regnal year (22–23 Eliz. I) had no fewer than thirteen suits in the Star Chamber and twelve in king's bench or common pleas. Elizabeth, widow of Robert Poynings and sister of the first John Paston, was noted in 1461 as having as many as a dozen actions in progress in her name in the courts at that time.[1]

The prevalence of the litigious spirit in the period under review has been commented on frequently by historians, but the causes for its existence have only been mentioned in the most general terms with emphasis even being laid on such variable human qualities as shortness of temper, contentiousness, and pride.[2] Some men and women, indeed, were 'mervelously geven to vexation and trouble in the lawe', and we read of a mere slight, an insult, or even a physical confrontation between the female members of two families leading to extended litigation. John Smyth, the historian of the Berkeley family, states, in what appears to be well-considered post-scripts, that the many legal actions between William, marquess of Berkeley, and Margaret, countess of Shrewsbury, and her successors in the later fifteenth century and sixteenth century sprang from Margaret's spilling of the blood of William's mother Isabel in an altercation in 1454. The suits at law in Elizabeth I's reign between Lord Henry Berkeley and the earls of Warwick and Leicester Smyth attributed to the slights offered to the latter when they tried to secure the marriage of their nephews Sir Robert and Sir Philip Sydney to the Berkeley daughters.[3] Yet, despite such colourful evidence, we should put aside the notion that litigation of any extended nature, and the feuds behind it, could be sustained by personal animosities alone.[4] Nearly always there was an underlying economic cause, a cause which in nine cases out of ten concerned the possession of land.

Virtually non-existent by the later Middle Ages were instances of sheer freebooting, that is to say the suing for or seizure of land by a person with no legal claim to it at all. Litigation concerning land, and entry into land, was based in the aggressor's eyes at least on a claim of substance. It seems that those of gentle blood were accustomed to keep to hand a list of their claims to various manors whilst awaiting an opportune time to sue at law or make an entry.[5] The great interest in genealogies which manifested itself in the fifteenth century was derived as much from the search for land, which ancestors or family members had once held or had a claim to, as from the desire to increase social respectability. The plausible tale that a gentleman wished to check his ancestry in another's genealogies seems to have been used not infrequently to gain access to a muniment room so as to seek evidence supporting the investigator's land claims, and even to examine the strength of the host's own titles to various manors.[6] Suing for land and seizing land were common practices of the upper classes from the fourteenth to the sixteenth century but, since men only acted thus when they thought they had a reasonable claim, we must ask if there was a factor operating which encouraged, or at least facilitated, the holding of such beliefs. The answer is in the affirmative: there was indeed such a factor. It was the complex state of the land law, particularly those of its rules which governed inheritance.

Recently a number of historians have drawn attention to changes in the way land was passed by members of the upper classes to their successors, and to the side-effects of the rules which controlled inheritance. Saul has argued that feuds among the gentry became more common in the fourteenth century because of the increasing complexity of land settlements; the employment of entails, uses, and jointures in particular being the cause of much 'confusion and entanglements'. In fourteenth-century Gloucestershire the histories of the Cardiff, Basset, and Langley families demonstrate, he suggests, how most vicious feuds were the result of disputed inheritances.[7] Coward has noted the ambiguous nature of the land law at the end of the period under review, the later sixteenth century. He has argued that because of the Statute of Uses of 1535 and the inconsistent interpretation of its rubric by the courts, particularly over the matter of whether uses for terms of years fell within the Act, no settlement of land between that Act and 1620 'was certain of being upheld'. The result was that disputes between heirs general and collateral heirs male were common in the 'chaotic legal situation' which was engendered.[8]

Of particular relevance to the history of inheritance and therefore to quarrels over land was the rise of the 'use'. Conveying the title to land to feoffees, who then gave the use of that land back to the donor (the *cestui que use*' as he was called), was a legal device which was in existence by the earlier fourteenth century.[9] The intention was in part to avoid the necessity of the heir having to pay a relief on the death of his ancestor, the holder of the land. It also allowed the family to escape the tribulations of having an heir who was under age when he inherited and therefore subject to the twin burdens of wardship and the arranging of his marriage by his feudal lord. The use, furthermore, protected the *cestui que use* from forfeiting land if he committed felony or treason. The establishment of a use was often accompanied by the making of a will, the instrument which actually instructed the feoffees as to how the feoffor wanted his land to be dealt with.[10] Not until 1540 was the will recognized by the common law; prior to that date it could not be used (outside towns) to devise lands by itself.

From a study of several fourteenth-century Berkshire families, Jefferies has demonstrated that the use, in conjunction with the will, was employed, additionally to the purposes just mentioned, in order to divide the estate. This was not, however, so as to provide for younger children by alienating property from the heir.[11] Perhaps we should add to this assessment the words 'in the long term', for certainly uses provided for dependants (and even dependants' children) other than the heir and sometimes for the period of their lives. Thus, often these settlements by use and will were designed to give the feoffor's widow substantial lands for her lifetime, lands considerably more extensive than her dower.[12] Employment of the use was not without its hazards. Feoffees could and did refuse to carry out the instructions given by the feoffor. They might enfeoff someone other than those they were instructed to, or, more rarely, not enfeoff at all. Sometimes they had to consider whether they ought to ignore their instructions, as when the whole intent of the use, to escape the financial burdens of a minority, was ruined by the death of the young heir, an occurrence not infrequent in the later fourteenth and early fifteenth centuries with the recurrent outbreaks of plague. Although uses were not protected by the common law, should a feoffee act against the intent of the feoffor he could be made to answer before the chancellor or in court ecclesiastical.[13] Whether, however, the penalties there inflicted were sufficient to deter malpractice seems doubtful. Another way by which the normal workings of the law of primogeniture might be circumvented was the entail. This was less flexible than the use. Whereas the role of the latter was frequently to provide for dependants for a limited period, the entail was normally employed to settle a substantial estate on a son (or daughter), who was not the heir by primogeniture, which he (or she) could not alienate until after the third heir had entered.

The employment of these legal devices, the entail and the use coupled with the will, often resulted in what amounted to the disinheriting of the heir in the short term. Almost inevitably this must have created disharmony in the family. As K. B. McFarlane has pointed out, a beneficiary under an entail or a use, if he is sensible, would offer the party 'disinherited' some form of bribe not to bring suit against him in the courts.[14] A reasonable appreciation of human nature tells us that anyone failing to inherit all he believed should have come to him was likely to be exceedingly bitter, the more so if, because the use was controlled by a will made just before death, the details of the settlement were unknown until after the demise. To receive or fail to receive a large share of a father's lands because of accident of birth was accepted; to benefit unduly because of a carefully constructed settlement or one reflecting death-bed supplications was likely to cause much resentment. Legal actions, entry into land, and even the ouster of those currently seized were the inevitable result.

Possessing a good claim supported with legal 'evidences' (as they were called) to a piece of property would not usually propel the claimant into litigation the moment he inherited the claim or acquired the evidences. All members of the upper classes, and probably even lesser men, knew the time had to be propitious for such a serious enterprise: therefore they awaited their opportunity. Not even an entry by adversaries into what a man firmly believed to be his land by right would necessarily lead him to seek remedy in the courts immediately. Thus Osbert Mundford, the Normandy veteran, who was entered on in 1452 whilst in the king's service and thus while under royal protection, planned first to seek assistance from his patrons (his 'gode lordes') before he had recourse to actions of forcible entry, trespass, and novel disseisin.[15] What in fact propelled men into bringing a suit in the courts at one point in time rather than at another were circumstances in the widest sense of the word, not necessarily or even mainly legal ones. Such circumstances could well include what was happening in national politics or at Court, although quite as important were a man's relationships with his lord, his friends, his clients, his tenants and servants, the possibility of outside backers, and the disposition of such important local officials as the sheriff.[16] How politics at a national level might persuade a man to litigate is well brought out in the history of the Berkeley family. We are told that when Elizabeth died and James I ascended the throne Lord Henry Berkeley 'to the utmost of his Strength pursued his Westminster hall warrs, hoping to change his fortunes with the change of time and persons'. He believed, and with cause, his Catholicism would be less of a handicap than it had been in the previous reign. He therefore sued out straightaway no fewer than three writs of right against Viscount Lisle. His boldness was rewarded: he was able to force his adversary to make an accord. In his account of his great legal cause, Robert Pilkington mentions he undertook a suit at Westminster at Michaelmas term 1496 against his enemy, John Ainsworth, because the latter had brought actions of trespass against seven tenants in Tideswell manor court.[17] For having to commence suits late in Elizabeth's reign both Lord Henry Berkeley and his adversary Sir Thomas Throckmorton were inclined to blame the 'provocations' of their servants. Sir Thomas also noted that Berkeley's friends brought suits of their own against him in support. As for the sympathy of local officials, it is hard to imagine that the first John Paston, when embroiled with Lord Moleyns in the spring of 1452, would have been seeking the attaint of a jury were it not for the fact that the current sheriff of Norfolk and Suffolk was on the best of terms with him at the time.[18]

Although men might delay in suing those who infringed their rights or entered their lands they were ready to make legal moves of a sort. To ensure a claim to a disputed piece of land did not lapse it was held wisest to enter the property and thereby preserve one's right of entry, which was an integral part of possessing title. This could take the form of a mere technical entry, a visit to the land in dispute in daylight and a public announcement of one's claim coupled with a demand that the occupier should withdraw. Right of entry, although from 1340 it could not be lost through time alone, could be 'tolled' (extinguished) should the occupant of the land make a feoffment whilst seised or should he die ('descent cast') and his heir inherit. The rule that 'feoffment over', as it was called, should toll entry was abandoned in the 1380s but the threat of descent cast remained. Cases in Edward III's reign showed that the plaintiff must have raised contention up to the time of the occupant's death if he was to preserve the right, and a case of Henry IV's reign demonstrated such an attempt must be made in the year preceding the occupant's death.[19] Not until the statutes 32 Hen. VIII cc. 7, 28 and 33 was the would-be plaintiff allowed to be less active. From that time, one which was of great importance to land wars and litigation, the plaintiff's right of entry, if he had one, remained intact so long as he had tried to enter at some point in the five-year period prior to the late occupant's death.

The token or technical entry was also utilized in order to bring the matter of title to the land in dispute to trial. Even if the entrant had himself never been in possession before his entrance, if his opponent refused to let him in or in any way obstructed him there was provided grounds for the bringing of an action under the assize of novel disseisin or, from the late fourteenth century, an action or trespass or forcible entry, either of which could decide title. This procedure had developed by the late fourteenth century out of legislation and judicial decisions intended to bring an end to the earlier practice of entering with a number of men in support so as to damage the tenement or throw the adversary out by force, or both. An important Act of 1381 (5 Rich. II st. 1 c. 7) made all entry by force illegal. Nevertheless, despite these advances in the law, contemporary correspondence and legal records indicate that entries with force and the ejection of the occupant were frequent phenomena from the late fourteenth century and for the next hundred years at least, and we must consider why this should have been so. It seems unlikely, on the face of it, that the reason lay in the lack of success which those who made a merely token entry and then sued in the courts enjoyed in their lawsuit. Plaintiffs at the assize of novel disseisin, up to the middle of the fifteenth century at least, appear to have been victors in a high percentage of instances (perhaps between 65 and 75 per cent), although it is possible that some of these victories were gained by the adversary (the party entered on) who, recognizing what was happening and knowing the plaintiff had the advantage, took the assize first.[20] The percentage of successful plaintiffs in actions of trespass and forcible entry is as yet unknown, nor do we have any inkling whether being in occupation of the land in dispute at the commencement of the suit influenced the jurors towards favouring the occupier in their decision. It is possible that a demonstration of the ability to take and hold the land in dispute proved to the jurors, some of whom were drawn from the locality where the land was situated, that the entering party was a force to be reckoned with in county politics and not to be crossed lightly. Such a demonstration might perhaps gain a verdict against the prevailing trend.

The early seventeenth-century legal treatise writer Ferdinand Pulton noted that those who made entry intending to eject their rivals and keep them out were often motivated by rage having themselves been put out by their adversaries earlier on. Pulton suggested further, however, that in entering they believed they would be able to avoid the penalties for forcible entry, but he did not elucidate. Presumably they were so convinced of the validity of their own claims to title that they believed they would win any suit brought against them and thereby escape the heavy damages losers could incur.[21] Often, however, it appears the motivation behind an entry was very rational, as for example when the entrant set about collecting rents in the land in dispute. In that way he would remind the tenants (who were potential jurors) of his claims and his power, and at the same time increase his liquid assets against the expense of lawsuits in the future. There were many other reasons for entry. We read of the duke of Suffolk in the summer of 1465 entering the manor of Drayton with the intent, as the first John Paston, his adversary, saw it, of forcing him 'to show his evidens or tytill' to his land there. On another occasion the duke, so Paston believed, sent a servant to enter Drayton in order 'to cause me to loose my labor ayens him for Dedham'.[22] If Paston's interpretation was correct, the duke was entering one manor in order to counter pressure of the land-war sort by his opponent elsewhere. The design in these two cases was not to make a claim and withdraw. In the first the duke presumably intended to remain if Paston's evidences did not, on inspection, override his own. In the second he or his representative again intended to stay, at least until he was assured Paston would not continue his legal or extra-legal manoeuvring. The most obvious and probably the most common circumstance where entry was made with intention to stay rather than retire involved an entrant, claiming good title no doubt, who believed he was considerably more powerful than his adversary or that the latter for some reason could not use force in response.[23] Such entrants calculated that the adversary they ousted could not hurt them by direct action. They might intend to stay in possession indefinitely, although it is not unlikely that they hoped in the not too distant future to bargain with or compel the party evicted to accept his discomfiture in a treaty or agree to the matter of title being tried in the courts.

The actual event of property seizure tells us much more about the conventions of the land wars and something about the law as well. The number of followers whom the adversaries employed in their feuds varied enormously, even when it came to such vital undertakings as entry or permanent occupation. The force utilized might comprise between six and ten persons, or it might contain several hundred; a total of between twenty and forty was probably most common. The wealth of the party involved, rather than any legal rule about how many men there could be in an upper-class entourage, was the deciding factor.[24] The first objective of entrants determined to remain was to clear the manor of the opponent's followers and family servants. If the manor had been held against the entrants, the garrison was usually to be found in the manor house or where the occupant's steward resided. Resistance was sanctioned by the statute 21 Edw. III c. 34 which stipulated that the party entered on might use force in defence of his goods, including the company he had in the house, if he had been in quiet possession for at least three years.[25] It was, of course, impractical to think of defending the perimeter of the manor, while to offer battle in the open (if one had the men) was recognized as likely to lead to a good number of injuries and even death. The members of the forces opposing each other in the land wars were certainly not intent on such heroics if they could possibly be avoided. The battle of Nibley Green on 30 March 1469, a day 'of knighthood and of manhood', in which William, Marquess Berkeley with 1,000 men met Thomas Talbot, Viscount Lisle, with probably a similar band in a set-piece confrontation, was by the later fifteenth century a unique event and one occasioned by the disarray in governmental circles at the time. Few men seem to have been severely injured when entries were made and adversaries ousted. Deaths appear to have been rare. Robert Pilkington in his account of his great quarrel makes no reference to such, while in the Paston letters there is only a handful of instances where homicide figures in land wars. The uncommonness of the occurrence was demonstrated by the legal proceedings resulting: appeals of homicide were made by two widows which caused great concern to the Pastons and their men for more than two years.[26] Generally injuries were few because, where there was resistance to ouster, one side was ensconced behind manor-house walls which the other besieged from a polite distance. Warfare seems to have taken the form of exchange of missiles whether from guns or bombards or from long-bows and cross-bows. There was little zeal to get into combat at close quarters.[27] The party entering seems to have tried to raise the largest force he could so as to overawe the defenders and thereby lessen the likelihood of actual conflict and injuries. Therefore to know how many men the garrison numbered was rated a high priority.

The party entering was not by law allowed to seize the personal property of the adversary who was ousted.[28] Thus Margaret Paston was apparently in a bitter mood when she told her husband about the devastation done by the duke of Suffolk's men in October 1465 in their attack on Hellesdon, which had been manned by the Pastons on the advice of legal counsel. The intruders had gone beyond the normal bounds of entry practice in actually looting before breaking down the walls of 'the place' and the lodge; they also ransacked the church. At the same time the duke had entered another manor, Drayton, which the Pastons then held. His men drove off 1,300 sheep as well as other beasts. John Paston was able in the latter instance, however, to get the king to intervene directly and order their restoration, which suggests this pillaging was considered most unacceptable.[29] Both the party in occupation and the would-be entrant usually avoided using the tenants of the manor in their forces, generally preferring men from outside. Quite naturally the locals feared damage to their property should their side lose. One of the few references to an occasion when they did take part is to Hellesdon in 1465. There they were compelled to join in demolishing the walls of the 'place' and the lodge.

When entry had been accomplished and the adversary, if he was in the manor, ousted, there remained the problem of how to deal with occupied land over the longer term. Now the previous holder had been antagonized he would quite likely be looking for an opportunity to re-enter. Thus the entrant must quickly address the problems attendant on successful entry. The first was the establishment of seisin, a vital task given the great likelihood of future litigation over the land which was the cause of the quarrel. Proof that seisin had been established, so we are told, amounted to keeping the manor court, the selling or burning of woods, the taking of fealty, the letting of farms, dismissing the bailiff, and, in the fourteenth century at least, freeing unfree tenants.[30] What we find is that the party making the ouster sought first and foremost to hold a sessions of the manor court. The necessary warning to the tenants was probably given by the parish priest in his pulpit. There is reference to the necessity for the party entering to have a good number of men on hand when the day of the court's meeting arrived, but the exact purpose is not apparent, even if we suspect that there was some attempt to overawe the jurors so that no charges were brought against those of the tenants who favoured the new regime. There is some evidence that tenants who sided with the entrants were encouraged to bring suits in the manor court against supporters of the party ousted.[31] One purpose of the court's summoning may well have been to have the tenants attorned (give their fealty) to the new occupier. If they refused, they may have been deprived of grazing rights and suchlike. Nevertheless the rival parties were inclined to treat the tenants on the land in dispute with respect and to avoid recriminations. Although the threat of eviction was not entirely absent from quarrels over land it was not used by the upper classes as a tactic against freemen, who were by the fifteenth century the vast proportion of villagers. On the other hand, tenants might sometimes decide such land wars were a burden not to be tolerated and so would quit their holdings.[32] It seems not unlikely that those who wished to enter land and oust the occupant made their entry, if circumstances allowed, just before the rents of the tenants were due. The collection of the rents provided additional proof that the party who collected them had seisin. Rents were particularly valuable because it was an age when actual coin was not readily available even for a family of substantial wealth. A letter to Sir Robert Plumpton in 1501, when he was to visit lands in Nottinghamshire which were about to be entered by two adversaries of his, advised him, 'Sir, bryng with you money convenient for your expenses for as yet . . . here be now rent teyned' (i.e. no rent obtained).[33]

To regard the tenantry as mere pawns in the land wars of the upper classes would be wrong. Rather they were visited, talked to, and considered with the utmost diligence, since not to do so could mean a hostility which might encourage any part wishing to enter. When he who had seisin of a manor recognized that an entry was in the mind of an adversary he had to seek to make certain of the tenants' hearts and minds. He could not, however, by the later Middle Ages prevent similar activities on the part of his adversary. Thus, in the late summer of 1461, William Yelverton visited the Paston manor of Cotton and, while there, he flattered the tenants, promised that they should have restitution for losses earlier, and asked them to pay their money (rents) only to him. 'Because of such tales,' said the first John Paston's informant, 'your tenunts owe hym the better will.' So Paston sent his servant Richard Calle to Cotton where he 'walked about' and spoke with the farmers and tenants 'to undrestande her disposessyn' as well as to receive their money. Although he was unsuccessful in the latter quest, he got them to promise to pay no man but Paston as long as he would protect them.[34]

More valuable in such situations than the presence of a servant or a bailiff was that of the party seised himself or his wife. The tenants of Cotton, so the first John Paston was told in October 1461, 'specyally desyr to have zowr owne presens and they wold be of gret cownfort'. When, in June 1465, the duke of Suffolk was threatening entry into his manors of Hellesdon, Drayton, Costessey, and Sparham, John Paston thought it wise to send his wife Margaret to comfort the tenants there, to show them that the Pastons had no intentions of yielding to their great adversary and were determined to collect rents as they had in the past. Margaret was even instructed to explain to the tenants that the Pastons' titles to the land were legally impregnable.[35] Similarly Sir Robert Plumpton, when his lands in south Nottinghamshire were threatened with entry in 1501, was advised to 'come yourselfe and be sene amongst your tenants and frynds the which were to them a singler pleasure and comforth, and to yourselfe a great strength'. Even a nobleman would visit those he considered tenants. In March 1449 Lord Moleyns, who had entered Gresham the previous year, wrote to the tenants there to say he would declare his title to them soon, and would be with them when parliament ended.[36] A bold front, the exudation of self-confidence, and regular appearances by the lord and his family in the manors where entry on the part of others was feared, coupled perhaps with a readiness to talk to the tenants and listen to their complaints, were very important. This was for both short- and long-term reasons. In the short term the presence of the party seized might ensure the payment of rents, while for the long term a convicting explanation on his part of the nature of his title might well be of value through its effect on jurors and 'treytors' (the go-betweens in arbitration and out-of-court settlements) in later litigation.

If we examine the matter of entry from the viewpoint of the party entered on, it is clear that unless he was a landholder of magnate status defence of the land in a military fashion was rarely a possibility. Unless he could be present in person, the party seised had usually to settle for a garrison of only one or two men to maintain a presence and to ensure the legal niceties of manorial life were attended to. They did little to discourage would-be entrants, who must in any case have often sought to avoid confrontation so that the entry could be called a peaceable one and therefore not be a criminal offence under the statutes 5 Ric. II c. 7 and 15 Ric. II c. 2. Once within the manor the entrant would probably seek to communicate directly with the tenants in order to advise them of the rightfulness of his claim as he saw it. This might well be followed by an attempt to summon the manor court, then to appropriate the profits of that court, and subsequently to collect rents. Such a situation as this was in fact one of double occupation since the party seised or his followers were still on the manor. Some odd scenes were the result. We are told of the third John Paston in 1472 attending a manor court sessions held by the entrant into his brother's manor of Saxthorpe, and seeking not only to stop the proceedings but also to have his presence recorded in the rolls. He sat down by the steward and blotted his book with his finger as he wrote, 'so that all tenants afermyd that the coort was enterupte by me . . . and I reqwered them to record that ther was no pesybyll coort kept, and so they seyd they wold'.[37] As soon as he was aware of the attempt to oust him, the party entered on would probably instruct his tenants to make sure that they had paid their rents to him, their rightful lord, and not to the intruder. Had they already made payment to the latter but under duress, they might be excused penalties. If they had paid voluntarily or entered into a bond to pay and the party entered on still had sufficient power, it could well be otherwise. The first John Paston instructed his bailiffs in regard to the non-paying tenants of Calcot early in Edward IV's reign that they should 'politicly put them in jeopardy of losing their farms'. Men holding unfree land may have been particularly at risk. In May 1465 Harleston, the duchy of Lancaster under-steward, told such tenants at Drayton that if they paid their dues to John Paston he would put them out of the lands they held there 'bondly' and furthermore he would distrain and trouble them until they were weary, which put them in fear.[38]

The legal device for enforcing the payment of rents, or non-fiscal manorial services for that matter, was the process of distraint.[39] Although eviction was threatened, as we have seen, it was probably as difficult in the later Middle Ages, as it had been earlier, for a lord to eject a tenant for simply not meeting his manorial obligations, provided that is, he was not two years in arrears. Distress took the form of seizure by the lord (i.e. the party claiming seisin in the manor) of some of the tenant's personal property until the latter paid the arrears or gave surety to contest the seizure in court. The distrainor, it need hardly be said, could not sell the chattels impounded in order to satisfy the debt owed him; nor, if they were animals, could he use them for purposes of cultivation. There were furthermore rules as to which chattels he could take and in what order they might be seized. Although before the thirteenth century it had been the practice for a lord to distrain for debts including rents only after securing a court judgment, by the fourteenth, to all appearances, such niceties were not observed.[40] Distraint by then may well have been taken for a prescriptive right and a weapon essential for success in the land wars, though whether financial reasons for its employment prevailed over desire to use it as proof of seisin for purposes of later litigation is not clear. There was probably an element of both. Sir John Paston wrote to his brother in October 1465 to tell him he had distrained the Hellesdon tenants in order 'to gadryd some syllvyr' but in August 1461 the first John Paston wrote to his wife Margaret to tell her to arrange for the distraint of such beasts as 'occupie the ground' at Stratton, apparently as a part of or as an adjunct to making 'cleyme and contynuans' (i.e. continual claim) to the manor. Distraint could be made to serve a third purpose in the land wars. This was the straightforward oppression of the tenants by those who had entered the manor so as to embarrass the party currently seised and cause him to lose face by his failure to protect them. In March 1469 William Yelverton and his men distrained plough animals at Guton so that the tenants were unable to till the fields at a crucial time in the agricultural year. Unless Sir John Paston could find some remedy, so he was told, he would 'lese the tenauntis hertis' and would thereby be greatly hurt, a statement which demonstrates the vital role of distraint in the disputes over land even in the later fifteenth century.[41]

As in other situations engendered by the land wars, those who sought to take a distress recognized that they must act successfully or lose face among the tenantry, among their associates, and indeed in the whole county. Thus we hear of parties at feud sending their men to distrain in substantial numbers. In May 1465, so we are informed, the duke of Suffolk's bailiff of Costessey went to distrain at Hellesdon accompanied by no fewer then 160 men. The number was large no doubt because the duke of Suffolk's household and his tenantry were large. The Pastons never seem to have used more than thirty men. To seize back a distress Elizabeth Brews requested of the third John Paston that he should lend her twelve men; they were, however, to be in harness and equipped with bows and other weapons. William Yelverton took eight 'with jakkys and trossyng doblets' when going in January 1467 to distrain in manors once the property of Sir John Fastolf. This band took with it 'bombardys and kanonys and chaferdeyns' and were reported ominously as doing 'whatsoever they will with their swords and make it law'. This suggests that the party to be distrained, usually a supporter of the distrainor's adversary, might well use force to try to prevent the occurrence.[42]

It was perhaps to be expected that when two parties claimed title to land, and each had a supporting faction there, they should be tempted to use distraint as a weapon to counter earlier distraints of their own followers by the adversary. Thus Margaret Paston, in

May 1465, told her husband that the duke of Suffolk's bailiff had said he would respond to the Pastons; supporters distraining to the value of a hen by the taking of a distress to the value of an ox, and if that was impossible then he would break into Paston's tenants' houses and take all they contained. Clearly distraint was often the use of force, if not of actual violence, to support a claim to title. The cloak of legality was an invaluable guise for what was often direct action to harrass the opposition. Furthermore, the practice of distraint might be utilized to conceal what a seised adversary feared most, namely an entry and ouster by force. For example, the third John Paston was told sometime in Henry VII's reign that Sir John Howard and Sir Gilbert Debenham were getting together a great band of men 'to take stresses of the Lady Roos'; however, additionally and under cover of this, they intended to try to seize the manor of Cotton.[43] The subterfuge, we must admit, was a neat one and certain to have been adopted many times, since it provided a rare opportunity for the gentry to ride quite legally with more men at their back than their station in life normally permitted: men, moreover, who were armed and armoured. It also put the distrainor-entrant beyond the reach of the statutes on riot, which defined that offence as three or more persons banding together for an illegal purpose, with at least one of them actually executing a deed to that purpose. As far as is known, neither king and Parliament nor the judges of the benches felt inclined to make the taking of a distress by prescriptive right into riot, although in 1531 the question was apparently put to the latter in regard to distraint which was thought to have been excessive.[44] Nor could one who claimed to be distraining on the strength of his title to the land be charged with the other criminal offence associated with the land wars, namely, forcible entry, at least not before his adversary had proven in court the superiority of his own claim to the manor in question.

The history of the last quarter of the fourteenth century and the early years of the fifteenth show the English Crown, and indeed the upper classes in general, were extremely concerned about two types of misdemeanour, the two which came to be called riot and forcible entry.[45] Both categories of crime were clearly products of quarrels amongst the upper classes over land. We may also view the several statutes of this time against illegal retaining, illicit giving of livery, and maintaining quarrels (for example, 1 Ric. II c. 4, 1 Ric. II c. 7, 13 Ric. II st. 3, 20 Ric. II c. 2, 1 Hen. IV c. 7, 7 Hen. IV c. 14, and 8 Hen. VI c. 4) in the same light, since in the land wars reasonable numbers of followers were essential if entry, ouster, and distraint were to be pursued effectively. Furthermore, it is fair to say that so great was the concern about these disturbances that new truncated methods of accusation, and even of trial, were set in place to implement the relevant laws. The laws concerned with forcible entry, which were perhaps those most central to the land wars, suggest that by Henry IV's reign there was amongst the class of substantial landholders a new sensitivity to the use of force in making the entries so vital for the successful pursuit of feuds over land.

During the middle years of the fourteenth century the judges interpreted the common law relating to ownership of land in such a way that a party with title, but not in occupation, was not jeopardized in his right of entry by sheer lapse of time unless, that is, the occupier died and his heir succeeded without the rival party exercising his right. Then, early in the reign of Richard II, came the rule that a right of entry continued to exist regardless of feoffment over. The reason for this softening of the law may well have been that many of the feoffments made by occupiers at this time were feoffments made to the use of the grantor.[46] Such feoffments were not usually known to the claimant and he would be ignorant anyway of the names of the feoffees to uses, those persons he must sue in court over title. Such frustration was likely to cause him to enter with force. In altering the law the Crown was trying to persuade would-be entrants that they would not endanger their rights by postponing their entry. To supplement this diminution of the need for entry there was promulgated in 1381 the first statute of a series designed to dissuade and punish those attempting entry by force. The Act, 5 Ric. II st. 1 c. 7, stipulated that there must be no entry except where it was allowed by law, in which case it must be in peaceable guise and not with a strong hand or a multitude of supporters. Offenders were to be punished quite severely, that is to say by imprisonment as well as fine. A later statute, 15 Ric. II c. 2, demonstrated how concerned the government was over forcible entry in its conceding to justices of the peace the power of summary conviction where entrants by force were caught in possession. A third statute, 4 Hen. IV c. 8, provided the victim of a forcible entry with the opportunity to sue out a special assize, which if successful would bring double damages from the offender.

A fourth, 8 Hen. VI c. 9, extended the provisions of the 1391 Act to those who entered in peaceable fashion but afterwards held by force, and to entrants by forcible means who were no longer in occupation when the justices of the peace arrived. In addition, it declared those enfeoffments void which had been made by entrants to a lord who had maintained them, and, furthermore, it offered treble damages to a party put out who won an action of novel disseisin or trespass.[47] This Act, although directed against the 'strong hand' of an intruder, allowed any party, who had been in possession of land for three years or more, to use force to retain it and not be liable under the earlier forcible entry statutes.

The careful extension over the next fifty years of the measures set out in the original statute dealing with forcible entry, so as to cover a variety of criminal situations and to provide more efficient methods of judicial process and effective compensation for victims, demonstrates a deliberate policy to encourage indictments in this field. Relatively few, however, have been found in the legal records. One reason for this is that since forcible entry was a trespass (misdemeanour) the offenders would usually have been tried, if tried they were, at the peace sessions. Unfortunately, very few indeed of the rolls of the justices of the peace survive for the fifteenth century and the first half of the sixteenth. Another reason is that those offending under the statute 15 Ric. II c. 2 could be dealt with in summary fashion; and indictment and a trial were not essential. After the promulgation of the Act 8 Hen. VI c. 9 forcible entry was probably handled for the most part by indictment but the scanty records of peace sessions which we possess show very few of these cases. In the earlier sixteenth century there was something of a change. The files of the Norfolk justices of the peace for a single regnal year of Henry VIII's reign, 1532–3, show nearly seventy persons indicted for their entries by force and subsequent ouster of the occupier. Many others were said to have supported them but these, no doubt, could not be indicted because their names were not known.[48]

These files contain also at least seven cases of riot, involving another sixty or so persons in what may be called typical land-war offences. Falling within the technical definition of riot were such misdeeds as the seizure of carts, the destruction of hedges and ditches, the taking of corn, the driving off of animals, the assaulting or detaining of people, and the lying in ambush to injure them: what we might call misbehaviour ancillary to the main purpose of entry and ouster.[49] There was probably no intent to steal, and certainly none to kill, merely the desire to intimidate and make difficulties for the opposing faction and its supporters. It seems not unlikely that those who incurred charges of riot had recently attempted, yet failed, to enter land and oust the party in occupation, or had been involved in distraint which had led to confrontation. The accusation of riotous behaviour would probably be brought by the occupying party when its supporters, animals, and property had suffered injury or damage, especially perhaps when the adversary had persuaded tenants on the manor to join him and his force.[50]

The statute under which most riotous behaviour was handled was 13 Hen. IV c. 7, which might well be called the Statute of Riots.[51] As with the most important statute on forcible entry, 15 Ric. II c. 2, those discovered committing a riot by two justices of the peace and the sheriff could be convicted by their record. If, by the time the law officers arrived at the scene, the rioters had dispersed, then an inquest was to be held into the circumstances and, presumably, those named by it were tried on the findings at the peace sessions. If the facts could not be discovered in this manner, then the details of the case were to be certified, no doubt by the two JPs and the sheriff, to the king's council, where the offenders would be punished if they admitted the truth of the charges. Should they deny the matter, it was to be tried in the king's bench.[52] Failure to appear on the part of the accused within three weeks of being summoned resulted in their automatic conviction. One of the many noteworthy features of this procedure was that it was all designed to be set in motion by a mere informal complaint to a justice of the peace.[53] There was, of course, another way riot could be brought before the courts: this was by the presentment of a jury or, from the early fifteenth century, by a bill of indictment given to the justices for putting to a grand jury.[54] Both these latter methods could only operate when sessions of the peace were about to be held. The value of the procedure under 13 Hen. IV c. 7, was that the victims of the riot could seek and expect immediate action on the part of the justices of the peace.

Such was the basic machinery for dealing with the most salient categories of criminal trespass produced by the land wars. The social status of those accused ranged from esquires at the top to labourers at the bottom with yeomen, husbandmen, and such unlikely ones as mercers and carpenters, in between. Even if records had survived in greater numbers we should not normally expect to find any nobleman indicted and only rarely a knight. It is, of course, quite possible that some of the rioters in the plea rolls, and even the forcible entrants, were engaged not as agents pursuing the land wars of the upper classes but as parties in their own petty feuds, since connections between those charged and their employers were never set down in the records of the criminal law unless the accused was a household servant or had illegally received livery. We might well expect that indictments of forcible entry and riot, which had been the recourse of those involved in upper-class feuds in the fifteenth century, were being utilized by men further down the scale for their disputes in the sixteenth. On the other hand, riots and forcible entries of both the late medieval and Tudor periods, which on first inspection seem to have been isolated events, turn out not infrequently to have been part of a county-wide land war. The 120-plus men indicted for forcible entry and riot for trial at Norfolk peace sessions in a single year of the earlier sixteenth century was probably not an exceptional number for the time. When, in 1580, the marquess of Berkeley was quarrelling with Sir Thomas Throckmorton over the Oldminster tithes, indictments for riot and forcible entry, says Smyth, were 'almost numberless' at the assizes and quarter sessions, and at one juncture as many as forty of the Berkeley servants were indicted and fined.[55]

Most of this concerned the combating of land-war adversaries at the regular sessions of the king's courts, usually before the justices of the peace, but it is important to notice that there was another way of dealing with the assaults, damage to property, and the taking of livestock, which made up the offences of forcible entry and trespass, and it was one which was common to the end of the fourteenth century at least. This was by means of a commission of oyer and terminer, which was a method of supplementing the operations of the permanent court system. The party entered on would seek a commission to hear and decide his complaint which, in theory at least, was supposed to be a great trespass (*enormis transgressio*, according to the statute of Westminster II c. 29). These commissions might proceed by means of hearing private suits as well as by receiving presentments and indictments from juries on the king's behalf. They often dealt with trespasses suffered by one complainant alone rather than with such offences perpetrated on the population of a particular area: thus they have been referred to as 'private' oyer and terminer commissions. The individual, usually a member of the upper classes, who sought such an enquiry into offences committed against him, would address a petition to the king and his council, Parliament, or the chancellor.[56] If he petitioned successfully, he would expect to pay between 10 and 40 shillings into the hanaper, as well perhaps as having to reward a courtier or servant of the king for interceding for him, but he was apparently entitled to choose the justices himself.[57] These were drawn from members of the gentry with a legal background, and from judges of the two benches. The plaintiff was probably expected to pay the justices' expenses.

There were three notable features to the proceedings by these justices. They were speedy, rarely taking more than a year; they were usually confined to the hearing and deciding of a private suit: and the plaintiff seems to have defeated the defendant in the vast majority of instances. The speed, and the fact that the plaintiff was usually victorious, accounted for some of the popularity of the 'private' commission, but the sizeable damages the plaintiff might be awarded, and the possibility his adversary might be sent to gaol, must also have contributed. One reason for the plaintiff's frequent success may have been that the justices selected were his friends, but another may have been the justices' practice of holding the proceedings at times and in places to suit him. The choice of locality would probably ensure that the jurors who decided the suit were drawn from an area where the plaintiff was powerful. All the defendant could do, if he heard about his adversary's petition in time, was to try to ensure it was not granted. He might, for example, contest the qualifications of the suggested justices, or argue that the offence was no enormous trespass as the law demanded, or he might seek for the case to be moved into the king's bench or before the council.[58] He could not counter by seeking an oyer and terminer commission of his own, at least not over the same issue. Thus many defendants responded initially by threats or violence: others, more sensibly, counter-sued in another court.

The seeking of private oyer and terminer commissions continued to be popular throughout the fourteenth century but in the early fifteenth the impulse, if we judge by the number allowed, declined markedly. Where they had amounted to around forty a year in the period 1373–6. they declined to an annual rate of about eight in 1391–4, about five in 1401–4, and to between two and three a year in 1442–5. In the same period there were also appointed commissions of oyer and terminer of another type, general commissions. These were intended to deal not with private suits but with one or several categories of offences seen as particularly dangerous to public order, such as murders, treasons, riots, or malfeasance of office by officials, which necessitated prosecution at the king's suit. Such commissions numbered about forty a year in 1391–4, the same in 1401–4, and about two a year in 1442–5. In the years 1472–5 there were appointed eight of these general commissions but none of the private variety, and the same pattern continued into the reign of Henry VII. Of the general oyer and terminer commissions of 1472–5, four were given competence in more than a single shire, one indeed in four shires. The indictments and trials resulting might therefore have been numbered in scores, even hundreds. At the end of the fourteenth century and at the beginning of the fifteenth a large percentage of the offences dealt with by such commissions were not connected, in a direct way at least, with bastard feudalism and the land wars, but by the 1470s the majority undoubtedly were.[59]

How contemporaries viewed the two kinds of oyer and terminer commissions, in the mid-fifteenth century at least, is revealed to us in the correspondence between the first John Paston and his London legal factotum, James Gresham. Paston wanted a private oyer and terminer commission against Lord Moleyns, who had seized his manor of Gresham and taken £200-worth of goods and chattels, but initially Moleyns was able to convince the chancellor (who at the time had the decision) that the request should be denied. The reasons which Moleyns had advanced were his own involvement at that time in suppressing an insurrection in Wiltshire, and that a private oyer and terminer would cause a rising in Norfolk. Paston's rejoinders were to the effect that he, Paston, should have the commission because Moleyns, aware of the inferiority of his own claims, had refused to allow the matter of title to be decided by two judges out of court: furthermore, the justices whom he (Paston) had nominated to sit on the commission were unbiased in their sympathies. Paston also pointed out that when Moleyns had entered with force a justice of the peace had certified the occurrence into chancery, and he argued in a more political vein that rather than be moved to hostility by the granting of a special oyer and terminer commission the country would rise up against the Gresham entrants if they were not punished.[60]

Paston's case for the granting of a special oyer and terminer was a blend of shrewd legal argument and political blackmail, but his requests did not stop at the private commission. His bill to the chancellor, which has survived, shows that he wished the oyer and terminer to deal not with a suit by him of trespass or forcible entry, perhaps involving title to Gresham (he must already have won a claim to title there in the courts since he possessed a writ of restitution), but rather with the land-war misdemeanours, namely the trespasses, extortions, riots, forcible entries, maintenances, champerties, and embraceries, which presumably had been committed by the Moleyns faction against him and his followers in the course of the quarrel. Paston was in fact seeking a private oyer and terminer to do criminal justice, justice at the king's suit, by obtaining indictments and making the accused answer to them. He requested a private oyer and terminer despite being aware that there had recently been granted a general commission of oyer and terminer for his home county (Norfolk), which in theory should do the same work.[61] In one letter Paston pointed out that the particular value of proceedings under a private oyer and terminer, as against under a general one, was that they could not be dashed by a writ of *supersedeas* and that the obtainer of the commission was able to decide the duration (and presumably the scope) of its work. He was, however, willing to have as justices for his private commission those on the general one with two exceptions.[62]

Paston was not, despite his seeking of a private oyer and terminer commission for the purpose of indicting his foes, intending to ignore the matter of Moleyns' occupation of Gresham. Yet rather than try to use the private oyer and terminer for that purpose he sought the granting of a special assize.[63] These were awarded under the statute 4 Hen. IV c. 8, which stipulated the party grieved should 'affiance' the forcible entry to the chancellor, who had the power to grant the assize himself. Attractive to the supplicant must have been the knowledge that if the defendant was convicted of the disseisin he was to be liable to a year in gaol and the payment of double damages. Either on account of the latter, or because of there being a greater chance of success for the plaintiff at the assize, the private oyer and terminer had become a relative rarity by the mid-fifteenth century. It was from not long after that time that the general commission of oyer and terminer became less used for dealing with land wars but more used for handling insurrections, overt or anticipated. Symptomatic of this change, perhaps, was the substance of a debate between the judges of the two benches in the exchequer chamber at the outset of Henry VIII's reign. They decided that under what had become its usual form the commission did not provide for the handling of indictments of forcible entry.[64] Yet if its land-war connections were weakening in the sixteenth century, there can be little doubt that the oyer and terminer commission had played an important role in regard to the feuds of the high age of bastard feudalism. Furthermore, that role remained on record because there was a rule that when the sessions ended the files of any oyer and terminer commission should be sent into the king's bench, even the undetermined indictments.[65] As a result a fair number of such records are still extant, and they probably offer more information about the land wars than any other single source.[66] They show particularly well the periods and extent of upper-class feuds, and their political aspects, although like so many other court records of the period they are by themselves of no great value in fathoming the motivation and the mentalities of the age.

Chapter Three

LITIGATION

The causes of litigation were numerous (some of them have been already noted on pp. 35–8) for lawsuits sprang from circumstances similar to those which gave rise to land wars. Most prominent, perhaps, were dashed hopes of inheritance and, in the period under review, it was often a hostile will which decided a disappointed person to turn to the law courts. By the sixteenth century, maybe earlier, men were ready to litigate in addition in order to obtain for themselves, their relatives, or their clients offices for profit. Again, however, the resort to law may have been the result of frustrated expectations.[1] A rather different reason for bringing a lawsuit was a desire to aid an ally or tenant. Thus a man might bring a suit against the enemy of a friend, or an associate of an enemy of a friend, for the purpose of harassment.[2] Motives were not necessarily altruistic. There must often have been the fear that should such legal action not be taken the plaintiff's own interests might suffer. As with the beginning of a land war, a lawsuit was started not necessarily when the wrong was perceived but rather when the party affronted believed, correctly or erroneously, that he was in a position to sue with a fair chance of success. Thus a son, who had recently succeeded his father or mother, might feel the desire to pursue claims to land which his parent, through age, bitter experience, or debility, had not dared to do in his later years. Similarly, a woman who married, or a widow who remarried, might acquire a partner who took it upon himself to pursue claims possessed by his spouse which she had not dared do anything about.[3]

It was a foolhardy and indeed a rare man of lesser standing who decided to bring a suit against a magnate who had unjustly deprived him of land. All writers of the period were agreed in allowing such a person only a slight chance of success in the courts. Unless a person had powerful sponsors, he was wise to go to law only against those whose wealth and status were equal to or less than his own, when politics, national or local, gave the intended adversary no particular assistance, and when the latter had no allies of greater standing than the plaintiff's 'good lords'. It was, however, a most fortunate plaintiff who enjoyed all of these benefits, and most members of the upper classes were ready to go to law with two, or even only one if they were sufficiently enraged. There were certain occasions when a man must sue in the courts or lose face. This was when he had been grossly and openly affronted or dispossessed, and not to act would lead to his discredit in the county community and encourage others to seek similarly to appropriate his property. His failure to sue would be taken as indicating that he had no confidence in gaining the jury's verdict, which in turn would demonstrate he was without influence. To sue and to lose, certainly to lose frequently, was also bad for a man's prestige. It was taken as proof of bad judgement and lack of good connections.[4] There was thus nearly always more at stake than simply the title to the land at issue. If a man was over-matched, if he was wronged or put out of land by a magnate or someone of much greater wealth and status than himself, he was well advised to put aside all thought of suit in the courts. He would do best to petition the king or seek out the legal counsel of the offender and ask for redress, as did Sir John Paston in 1475 in regard to the duke of Norfolk's seizure of Caister, and as his father did in 1450 in regard to Lord Moleyns' entry into the manor of Gresham. When Osbert Mundford was put out of Braydeston in 1452 by Thomas Daniel of Rising, Norfolk, probably with the backing of the duke of Somerset, he determined to write to the king and 'other my gode lordes' to seek their intercession against his adversaries before he brought actions of forcible entry, trespass, and novel disseisin.[5]

Those who were defendants in legal actions seem to have viewed forthcoming litigation very similarly to the plaintiffs, although, of course, the options available to them were fewer. To be certain that their friends and 'good lords' were ready and willing to support them in the coming suits was usually their first concern. Sir Robert Plumpton, in May 1500, was told his best protection when there was a writ of novel disseisin out against him was to 'make many friends and of the best'. He was advised further to 'make your frynds to take your part, as frynds shold doe'. When William Roubotham was cited before the court of arches by Thomas Worth in 1496 for slander, Robert Pilkington, whose tenant Roubotham was, sought straightaway the support and intervention of the earl of Derby, of his son Lord Strange, and of the chief chaplain to the court of arches (who was Pilkington's cousin and the earl's auditor), which proved eventually to achieve the desired result for the case was dismissed.[6]

Often precipitated into litigation against their wishes, defendants not infrequently faced the handicap of not knowing until the hearing of the suit was imminent who was suing them and over what matter. Thus they might have little time to inform their supporters and protectors, and there would be still less for these to intercede with their adversaries and their masters before the hearing commenced. A petition to Henry VI by the first John Paston in 1450 complained that his tenants and servants in Gresham were unable to discover who was suing them in the local hundred court. They could not get copies of the plaints against them because the court keeper was in cahoots with Lord Moleyns, an enemy of Paston's. Robert Pilkington tells us that he had only five days' notice, instead of the stipulated minimum of fifteen, of the action of novel disseisin which was to be brought against him at Derby in 1497. When he appeared in court on the day, he had not even had the opportunity to retain counsel.[7] This was not an isolated instance. The first John Paston, obviously apprehensive about this problem, was told by James Gresham in July 1450 that Caly and Yates, two legal agents, had promised that no writ should be returned against him 'but that ye shall have copies thereof at reasonable tyme to make your avantage as the law wole . . . to caste your esson [essoin, i.e. excuse] or suyche other'. To avoid this same embarrassment, Sir William Stonor in 1481 and 1482 employed men in London whose duties specifically included searching for actions newly begun against him.[8] By the sixteenth century the legal agents who kept watch in the central courts at Westminster for the commencing of actions against their employer were referred to frequently as 'solicitors'. It was accepted that one of their duties was to supervise the defence against these actions and advise the employer as to when he himself should sue. We are told that solicitors were instructing counsel, and that their general savvy and the manner in which they carried out their task were crucial to the success of any suit: 'and such as the Sollicitor is, such commonly is the successe'. John Smyth, the historian of the Berkeley family, was very ready to find the cause of the loss of certain of its suits in such things as the employment of one solicitor, who knew no Latin, and another, who was unable to find a crucial lease.[9]

If success in litigation depended much on careful instruction given to attorneys, there is evidence that the best instruction was given, if he knew a reasonable amount of law, by the party himself. In James I's reign Ferdinando, earl of Huntingdon, advised his son to keep a personal watch over his lawsuits of importance. John Smyth praised Maurice, Lord Berkeley as being an expert and successful litigant, and this success he attributed largely to Berkeley's close personal attention to his suits and the legal knowledge he had acquired 'by adversity and experience'. This made Lord Berkeley and his eldest son into 'excellent Solicitors in their own persons'.[10] Although there is no proof of it, there is every likelihood that in the mid-fifteenth century the first John Paston also acted as a 'solicitor' in his own causes and that he was a successful one. He had attended the Inns of Court and was certainly knowledgeable about the law. The manner in which he was able to satisfy Sir John Fastolf in the handling of his legal affairs, the way he was able, with a considerable degree of success, to defend his property against persons of superior status and wealth, together with the respect accorded to him in the Norfolk county community at large, speak volumes for his legal acumen, a quality he had no doubt inherited (along with good title to most of his property) from his father William, the puisne judge.[11] Even if their instructing was not up to Paston's standard, most fifteenth-century litigants, unless they were uninterested, wealthy, or notably lacking in legal knowledge, communicated directly with the attorneys who were to represent them in court. Disputes in the majority of cases, as we have seen, concerned land, and therefore it was not unusual for the litigant early on to show his legal counsel all his 'evidences' (as deeds, copies of court judgments, and chancery records were called) in regard to property and settlements, together with any relevant proof of entail, the marriage of parents, and so forth. A letter of the Plumpton family of May 1500 shows Sir Robert Plumpton, who was about to be sued in an action of novel disseisin, being requested to set down all these necessary facts 'verbatim' and on paper.[12]

The hiring of one or more attorneys to represent the plaintiff or defendant in court was clearly a step of great importance for achieving success, yet there is only a small amount of information about it to be gleaned from contemporary writings. Robert Pilkington, in his autobiographical account of his 'great cause', writes as if it would have been a major disaster had he not, when he arrived at a special assize at Derby in 1497 on only five days' notice to answer the suit of John Ainsworth, been able with 'gret labur and gret cost' to secure the services of Robert Brudenell as his counsel, although Brudenell had no prior knowledge about the case.[13] It is quite possible that Pilkington had failed to retain counsel 'owte of his cuntre' (i.e. the Manchester region), as he put it, because no attorney wished to oppose so great a man as Thomas Savage, bishop of London, who was in fact the true bringer of the assize, his nephew Ainsworth being only the technical plaintiff. The Paston correspondence provides an example of a would-be plaintiff in the 1440s being unable to obtain legal counsel in the normal manner against Agnes Paston because her late husband William had been judge and their son John was a 'man of court'. The plaintiff, a chaplain, who was intent on contesting title to the manor of Oxnead, eventually petitioned the archbishop of Canterbury asking he should order three lawyers to take his instruction.[14] The number of counsel retained depended on the wealth of the party retaining, the importance of the suit to him, and the might of the adversary. When, in May 1501, Sir Richard Plumpton was expecting the 'great man' Sir Richard Empson to sue out a writ of novel disseisin against him, his solicitor, John Pullan, retained on his behalf John Yaxley and Thomas Frowick, serjeants, as well as Gregory Edgar and John or Richard Brook. The indenture of Yaxley, a copy of which has survived, shows him undertaking to attend the next assizes at York, Nottingham, and Derby, there to be of counsel with Sir Robert in regard to such assizes and actions as the latter required. The contract was for a number of court sessions, not for the length of the suit. Should the plaintiff non-suit, the defendant decide not to contest the case, or there should be an out-of-court settlement, Yaxley was to receive a stipulated lesser sum. His expenses in regard to travel, food, lodgings were to be paid in their entirety by Plumpton.[15]

That part of the judicial process in private actions which was known as joinder of issue, including the mechanics of pleading, featured in the correspondence of contemporaries hardly at all. The design behind the pleadings was to narrow the quarrel between the two parties down to a single, or very few, issues of fact, the crucial points on which both sides were adamant.[16] If and when an issue was discovered, the jury was sworn, the record of the process and pleadings was opened, and the parties presented their 'evidences', including sometimes their family pedigrees. Robert Pilkington in his narrative seems to imply that he himself rather than his counsel showed his 'evidences', which were to the effect that eight of his ancestors before him had been seised of the disputed land in Mellor. The Ainsworth evidences were shown by James Savage, the bishop's brother, who stood at the bar with Thomas Jakes, Ainsworth's counsel. Pilkington reveals that the judges did not hesitate to let all know how they regarded the pieces of evidence: they 'said as favorable for the said Robert as they goodly myght and sytt as jugges', but Ainsworth's 'evidences' they would not allow. His 'ruggenall dede was haldon up with the jugges that all the pepull myght see and poyntyd with the jugges handes how hit was enturlynyd in so mone dyvers placys'. The judges said that they had never seen a deed so interlined and 'couth not alow that dede for gud'.[17] 'Evidences', in the eyes of John Smyth at least, were the best way of convincing the jurors; witnesses' oral evidence, might be used, but they may have had less effect. Smyth recorded quite bitterly how in the suit in king's bench between Lord Henry Berkeley and Sir Thomas Throckmorton over title to the tithes of Oldminster, once the property of St Augustine's Abbey, Bristol, the Berkeley solicitor failed to produce the abbot's lease or any of his acquittances to the Berkeleys in court although they were in fact in that family's possession. Instead he offered the 'testimony of witnesses, viva voce, which after forty-three years could not be certaine or direct' which contributed greatly to the loss of the suit. The relative lack of impact of witnesses' testimony on the jury was probably not uncommon, since the grants and successions to land which were being contested had usually occurred a good many years earlier; furthermore, some suits were extremely long-lasting. The suit over the Oldminster tithes extended from the twelfth to the twenty-second year of Elizabeth I's reign and the matter at issue was a lease of 28 Henry VII.[18] Witnesses had to be sought out by the party requiring their testimony, cosseted, then instructed as to what they should say in court. Sir John Paston, when he was embroiled with the duke of Suffolk in October 1479, rode to Dunstable himself to speak with one of his chief witnesses 'whyche promysed me to take labor' and he rewarded him with 20 shillings.[19] Jurors, being themselves subject to much pressure from the parties, were not inclined to believe that witnesses' testimony was unbiased.

Few trials of suits can have lasted more than a single day. In the action in the court of common pleas at Hilary term 1597 on a writ of partition against Lord Henry Berkeley in regard to the manors of Cam, Hinton, Slimbridge, the 'evidence at barre lasted from eight in the morning till fower in the afternoone' and nothing was 'left unurged or defended that art or learning might afford, or at Barre or Bench bee uttered'. Smyth also mentions another exhausting trial, of an action of *ejectio firmae* (ejectment), at Easter term 3 James I in the same court. This lasted six hours 'wherein to the Jury at the barre were delivered more than three hundred peeces of evidence'.[20] Trial was nearly always by means of a jury but there was one other means of finding the truth, namely wager of law, a procedure which had particularly strong connections with urban customs and local courts and with cases of debt and detinue. At one point in his great feud over Mellor Robert Pilkington was the object of a complaint made to Tideswell manor court by John Ainsworth to the effect that Pilkington had shot at his cattle with arrows and killed some. Pilkington entered a plea of not guilty in writing through his attorney and asked to be allowed to wage his law. He was told by the steward that there could be no wager of law in what was an action of trespass. In London Pilkington was given expert advice to the effect that wager of law in such a suit was uncommon but not illegal. However, he was denied his opportunity when the steward adjourned the court and later he had to accept trial by jury.[21]

At the heart of any trial before the king's court was the verdict of the jurors. A substantial amount of information about who was to serve on a jury, how they were to be picked and challenged, how their deliberations were to be conducted, and suchlike is to be garnered from the Year Books and sixteenth-century law reports, but more valuable insights are to be discovered in contemporary correspondence and personal writings, particularly the crucial matter of how the jurors might be influenced in coming to their decision. At the earliest moment possible in the suit, the plaintiff and the defendants, if they were wise, would make every effort to discover who was to be on the panel from which the jurors were to be selected. For one of the parties this was no easy task, since the maker of the panel was the sheriff, and he was likely to favour one side more than the other in his choosing, and would be in no hurry to reveal the names to the latter.[22] The names might have to be sought by an indirect approach. In his suit over title to Kinoulton, Nottinghamshire, in June 1501 Sir Robert Plumpton was able to acquire the vital information through the good offices of a relative, who in turn approached a local gentleman, who obtained it by means of a *douceur* of 11 shillings to the undersheriff.[23] So important was this panel selection by the sheriff that many men, even when the blood boiled, were reluctant to go to law if they knew the incumbent was an ally or associate of their would-be adversary. On the other hand, should a friend, servant, lord, or close legal associate become sheriff it was often taken as a signal for the fortunate party to bring suits against a number of rivals and oppressors. Ideally, if he had sufficient power and influence, the plaintiff would probably not wait for the sheriff to decide on the membership of the 24-man panel but send, or get a friend to send, to the undersheriff a list of names. In 14 Elizabeth I, in the case he instigated by means of an information into the exchequer against Lord Henry Berkeley, the earl of Leicester got his friend Lord Chandos to arrange it so that sixteen 'special freeholders' should be named to the panel and another ally, a knight, should nominate the other eight. When Leicester laid another information against Berkeley in the exchequer in 26 Elizabeth I he went still further. He had twenty-four names sent through Sir Thomas Throckmorton to his servant Richard Adams of Wotton 'And by him delivered to Mr Hall then undersheriffe to Thomas Baynham of Clowerwall Esq. as sent with them from the said High Sherriffe with a comandment in the name of the said Earle of Leicester that hee should ingrosse and returne them, mixed with the delivery of forty shillings then given to Hall, and some threats if hee did not'.[24]

The tactics of the Ainsworth-Savage faction almost a century earlier were not dissimilar to those of Leicester, but were less high-handed. Sometime after Michaelmas term 1496, when the Ainsworth faction had sued out a writ of novel disseisin against Pilkington in regard to land in Mellor, it gave 'grete rewarde' to the sheriff to make a panel containing Ainsworth-Savage nominees including Ainsworth's 'kynnysmen, lyancez and olde servandes, sybmen and lyancez of old Sir John Savage and his chyldur'. Later, at the Derby assizes in the summer of 1498, the same faction managed to secure the placement on the jury of those described as being 'boundmen to the Savages, dyvers ways syb or alyed, olde howshad [i.e. household] servandes free tenandes reteyned be fee or lyverey'; furthermore, 'sum were both gayne dwell ers to the Savages and thayre chyldur and dyvers of thayme syb to Ayne-sworth or his wife'.[25] The earl of Leicester and the Ainsworth-Savage faction probably had few doubts about the loyalties of the men they nominated to the panel, but other litigants, who were fortunate enough to be in the same powerful position, might feel it necessary to enquire carefully into the sympathies of those they had in mind as jurors. The first John Paston, when bringing action against William Hogan and William Jenny in June 1465, made investigation through his younger son and two associates and was told by one of the latter 'he knew non that wold pas up on any inquest for hym for he medylyd with no syche men'. The other associate reported 'he kowd assyne . . . none men for serteyn, not tyll he had spok with some'. He knew few men of that sort in Suffolk, but had the need been for men from Cambridgeshire he would have had no difficulty in providing them. At the same time Paston was also given the more satisfactory news that his wife Margaret had approached one Baynard of Sibton Abbey on the matter, who said that although he knew 'none that wold pase upon the mater at his desyer' he could name several men whom he thought disliked the Jenny faction and would 'pase upon it at your desyer if ye spok with hem you selve'.[26] This all suggests that a person with more than a little influence in his region like Paston was able with some searching to find jurors lacking any tie of blood, service, or landholding with him who would give the verdict required or at least promise to do so.

If either of the parties believed that some of the jurors were unsatisfactory because, for example, of a blood tie, or affinity with the adversary, he might challenge them. Theoretically his grounds for so doing were not the bias of the jurors themselves but the partiality of the sheriff in empanelling them; so Chief Justice Fineux emphasized in 1498. In practice, at least by the reign of Elizabeth I, the parties took what exceptions they wanted, such as that the juror was lacking sufficient income, or that 'he is alied, feed, or servant to his [i.e. the challenger's] adverse partie, he is his enemie etc'. Then a small number of jurors, who were unchallenged, came to a verdict on the matter in what was a trial within a trial.[27] If the exceptions and the verdict resulted in there being insufficient jurors to make up a full jury, then either the trial was put off to another occasion or additions were drawn from the bystanders. Jurors were supposed to own land to the value of 40 shillings and, where freehold was at issue, four out of the twelve must possess it in the hundred where the suit had had its origins, unless, that is, one of the parties was lord of the hundred in which case they were summoned from hundreds adjacent. A panel seems to have comprised twelve jurors from the part of the shrieval bailiwick close to where the land at issue lay and the other twelve from the other side of that territorial unit.[28]

The challenging of the panel and of individual jurors took place at the trial. Before that, as soon as the names became known to the parties they would make great efforts to bring pressure to bear. In the language of the time this was known as 'labouring', an unspecific term roughly the equivalent of the modern British phrase 'having a word with', meaning trying to make the listener appreciate the speaker's position. We find no reference to threats of violence towards jurors who failed to oblige, but there were undoubtedly menaces of other types. To seek out jurors so as to apprise them of the merits of your claim to the land in question was expected, and there is no indication anyone ran foul of the law for so doing. The argument has been made by historians that, given the trial procedure of that period, labouring was a necessity if the jurors were to be reasonably supplied with the background to the quarrel. The practice was, of course, self-sustaining. A party felt the more obliged to labour jurors because he believed his adversary was likely to do so. We read in the Paston correspondence that the prior of St Benet's, Holme, when he was engaged in a suit against Lord Scales in 1459, 'spake maysterly to the jurrorys' and told them that if they 'had dred of God and hurt of here sowlys they wold haf some instruccyon of the one party as wele as of the other'.[29]

There are several interesting contemporary descriptions of jurors being laboured and in different ways. The third John Paston as we have seen, used his principal witness for a forthcoming trial to obtain certain evidence pertaining to his title and to labour the jurors about them. When, in 1497, the bishop of London was suing in John Ainsworth's name to recover land in Mellor from Robert Pilkington, he first saw to it that the sheriff should make a panel containing his kinsmen, old servants, and allies, and then he and his protegé wrote to each to tell them to be certain to attend the sessions. If they did not, 'they schuld neyver have thayre gud hertes'. When the panel met at Derby it was apparently spoken to by the bishop's three nephews, who told its members individually that the bishop would rather lose 500 marks than have the verdict go against Ainsworth. The Savage faction must have felt sure of the jurors' support, and did not think it needed to emphasize particular facts in the case. If a party felt less certain of his influence with the jurors, and was nervous about their attitude, he might eschew a direct approach to them and try instead to change their views by labouring their social superiors. Thus, in his suit over Kinoulton in June 1501, Sir Robert Plumpton was urged by a knowledgeable adviser to contact the bailiff of the Bingham wapentake, Nottinghamshire, in which Kinoulton lay, and also that bailiff's 'master', Sir Nicholas Byron of Colwick. Both of these persons were thought to be receptive to labour by Plumpton, and thus presumably willing and able to influence the sympathies of the jurors by direct pressure of a local sort.[30] During the period between the assizes of July 1498 and its successor, when his suit was in adjournment, Robert Pilkington made 'grete labur' to the jurors. He did so actually in the places where the panel members dwelt. Twelve of those were inhabitants of Scarsdale wapentake near Nottingham, while the other twelve were drawn from the Chapel-en-le-Frith and Tideswell areas in Derbyshire over 35 miles to the north-west. Pilkington's policy on his visits, in addition to explaining his claim, seems to have been to suggest that if they did not favour his cause they should absent themselves from the assizes. Those from Scarsdale, who apparently believed they ought not to have to serve in the suit, rejoined that if they were forced to attend they 'wold take gud hede and passe with ryght wysnes'. Those from north Derbyshire affirmed a similar intention of staying away, but did not promise 'gud hede' or passing with 'ryght wysnes'.[31] In the event, all the panel members attended the assize and the verdict went against Pilkington.

Those chosen for the panel, when being laboured, might well take the opportunity to ask one or other of the parties for their 'costs'. These were the expenses they would incur in attending the forthcoming sessions. The third John Paston told his father in June 1465 that two jurors selected for their case had informed him that their costs, when they had last travelled to London in that capacity had totalled 10 shillings and that they would not go this time unless that amount was paid to them. This was not an exceptional demand. In May 1451 Sir John Fastolf was told in regard to one of his lawsuits that 'it wold drawe xx marc to labour the Jure to London'. Sometime in 1476, so it seems, the Oxfordshire esquire William Stonor was informed that a suit in which he was involved was to be moved to Exeter and that his servants would therefore have to carry certain jurors thither at his cost, a statement which implies he and his allies had arranged to pay their expenses originally.[32] Explicit references to jurors in litigation demanding actual bribes are rare. There are but two instances where the word occurs in the Paston correspondence, which suggests that to ask for such was viewed with distaste even in the hard world of the fifteenth-century land wars. One is a simple report that X had met the jurors and given them money. The other was the occasion when the third John Paston had been investigating the loyalties of the jurors chosen for his father's suit against William Jenny in 1465. He reported to his parent that two of the panel expected their expenses paid if they travelled to London for the trial, or alternatively 'they wold have had a brybe of you . . . for to have bedyn at home'. This pair, the younger Paston noted somewhat bitterly, 'have no othyr levying but brybs'. The power of the jurors is particularly well displayed here. They knew full well their value and intended to profit whatever option the party decided on. It seems from other evidence that the same men were empanelled to serve as jurors in private actions and for the king time and again. We hear of *cisours* (i.e. 'assisers') jurors, and 'questmongers' being hunted down in London and Southwark at the time of the Peasants Revolt of 1381, as if these were their chief occupations and pursued for life.[33]

When the jurors had heard the evidence they retired to consider their verdict on the issues. In this period of seclusion they were supposed to be without the comforts of food, drink, light, and heat, the idea being that such severity would hasten their arriving at the necessary unanimous verdict. Should they fail to observe these rules their verdict would probably not be accepted by the court and they would be punished. While in seclusion only the judges and their messengers might speak with the jurors. Thus in the Pilkington-Ainsworth case at the Derby assizes in 1498 the judges sent the sheriff in to the jurors to relieve them of their weapons and later on one judge paid them a visit himself, apparently so as to explain one feature of the evidence. When they were agreed the jurors returned to the court to give their verdict. On some occasions they may have returned to find the judges had risen from the bench, in which case they could only give a 'privy' verdict, the formal one to be delivered in court when it sat once more.[34] Judges were known to refuse to accept a jury verdict if it was at odds with contemporary legal convention, and this seems to have been what occurred in the Pilkington-Ainsworth suit. We are told that the inquest found that Pilkington had had, presumably in the land in question, an annuity of 40 shillings 'or they wyst not what yt was forsoth'. This apparently annoyed the judges who rebuked the jurors 'and drave thayme agayne into the counsayle howse'. The cause of the judges' disapproval is probably to be discovered in their admonition to the jurors that they 'schuld fynd authere all or non dew'. This was because according to the common law a jury must find entirely for one party or the other: it could not, as appears to have been done in the Pilkington-Ainsworth case, find the title to the land lay with Ainsworth but soften the blow for the adversary by deciding Pilkington had an annuity there.[35]

Occasionally, just before the moment when the jury announced its verdict, a plaintiff might decide to non-suit. This legal manoeuvre was in essence a default, a withdrawal from the action. The point in time when it occurred suggests that the move was somehow connected with the direction the jurors were heading in their deliberations, although it is possible it might be connected with the arranging of a late hour 'treaty' (an out-of-court settlement). There is luckily a reference to an example of non-suiting from the middle of Elizabeth's reign which shows exactly what happened in one such case. At the trial over the title to Haselbach farm between John Vernon, esquire, of Sudbury, Derbyshire, and his brother Henry in the court of common pleas in 22 Elizabeth I, as the returning jury came to the bar to announce its verdict one juror privately indicated to a servant 'by a compact underhand' that the verdict would go against Vernon. He meant, in fact, Henry Vernon since John Vernon had brought the suit in the name of one Buck. The servant, forgetful of this crucial fact, immediately told his master John Vernon, quite erroneously, that the jury was about to find against him. Therefore John Vernon non-suited without delay.[37] The reason persons, who believed they were facing defeat, so acted was in order that they might begin a new suit over the same issue at some future time; once a verdict went against them, they were barred from doing this.

If the verdict went in favour of the plaintiff, he was entitled to costs and damages. The former were to cover the payments he had made in the course of bringing the action, the latter were to compensate for the defendant's misbehaviour. Damages and costs and their awarding were of great importance to litigants, particularly when the action was brought under a statute which multiplied their amount several times over. This part of the law was closely connected with the choice of actions to acquire possession of land available to plaintiffs and the question of why they selected one rather than another in their land wars, basic aspects of litigation which we have not as yet considered. In the period under discussion, c. 1350–1600, the options of significance were four: namely, the assize of novel disseisin, and actions of trespass, forcible entry, and ejectment. Novel disseisin was first on the scene, then trespass, which was no great rival to the former before the reign of Richard II. In a novel disseisin case the plaintiff might enjoy the benefit of trial by default should the defendant not appear. On the other hand, to be victorious he had to win not one but a series of issues: specifically, was the plaintiff seised of a freehold, was the defendant tenant in the land, and did the defendant wrongly disseise the plaintiff? Suits at the assize by the sixteenth century were not as short in duration as they had been in the century following its inception, yet they were probably of no greater length than those under rival actions. The actions of trespass and forcible entry, which in the fifteenth century attracted plaintiffs away from novel disseisin, were personal actions, and by their nature he who employed them could not be frustrated by legal manoeuvring on the part of his adversary which was to conceal who was the current tenant of the freehold. Not infrequently this obfuscation was the effect of a feoffment to uses. However, while trespass and forcible entry actions provided benefit in this respect, and where the plaintiff was successful won him damages, they did not, unlike a similar action of novel disseisin, give him seisin. This disadvantage was more apparent than real, since few defeated defendants were willing to encourage a second suit and more damages; so they would usually withdraw from the land at issue. Successful plaintiffs in actions of novel disseisin sometimes encountered difficulty in getting the damages assessed, which in turn delayed their recovery of the land because this had to come after. If the successful action was one of trespass or forcible entry, the collection of damages was relatively easy because the defendant, having been found to have broken the king's peace (unlike defeated defendants in novel disseisin cases), had to go to gaol until he made a fine with the king, and this he could not do until he had paid the plaintiff his damages. There was thus great incentive for the defeated party in these actions to pay quickly, a factor which increased their popularity with plaintiffs. If the number of times they are mentioned in sixteenth-century Year Books and law reports is a reasonable yardstick, then actions of novel disseisin may have risen again in number relative to trespass and forcible entry actions during the first three-quarters of the sixteenth century, but thereafter the decline was sudden and complete.[37] The reason was probably *ejectio firmae*, originally an action intended to provide damages for the evicted leaseholder, which, it was discovered, could be converted through a lease by the claimant to a friend into a method of trying the former's right of entry.

When the trial was over, the victor, who was expected to pay for the jurors' dinner, may sometimes have demonstrated his pleasure by giving them rewards as, we are told, did the earls of Leicester and Warwick to each one of those who tried the issue in their important suit against Lord Henry Berkeley in 14 Elizabeth I. That there should be recompense for the jury was logical enough in a society where the same men might serve as jurors on many occasions and a litigant of substance wished his generosity to be remembered in the future. Yet it would be wrong to imagine jurors gave their verdict to whoever was expected to pay them better after the trial. Their vision, if self-centred, was greater than that, and they may even have borne in mind their promises to act in good conscience and heed the information the parties had given them. Yet, when they retired to consider their verdict, they may have remembered more clearly such a thing as the magnate who appeared in the court room to 'countenance' one of the parties, and they probably gave considerable thought, as did a juror mentioned in the Paston correspondence, to the question of who in the future 'schuld rewle in this schere'.[38]

When the verdict had been given, a losing and dissatisfied defendant might seek to arrest judgement by a bill of exceptions, complaining for example about misconduct on the part of the jurors, or by a motion of misjoinder of issue, but the standard method of challenging the jury's verdict was to bring an attaint. This was an action to convict the jurors of finding an untrue verdict, that is to say committing perjury. No new facts could be adduced: the 'grand' jury, which was of twenty-four men of superior station to the twelve on the first jury, simply gave its own verdict on the evidence offered earlier to its antecessor.[39] In the fifteenth century, in order to encourage the suing out of writs of attaint, statutes had been passed which awarded the successful plaintiff in that regard damages and costs and the restoration of his property (11 Hen. VI c. 4 and 11 Hen. VII c. 24). Two Acts, so that the likelihood of conviction would be increased, made the stipulation that the grand jurors, who would decide the case, should have very sizeable incomes per annum from land or in goods and chattels (15 Hen. VI c. 5 and 11 Hen. VII c. 24). The petty jurors (those on the original jury) found guilty were to be fined £5 or £20 according to the value of the property originally in dispute, pay a fine and ransom at the discretion of the justices, and never be of credence in a law court in the future. This, in fact, was a diminution of the old, traditional, punishment, which had been extremely severe, and the design may well have been to provide a more moderate penalty so that grand jurors would be less hesitant to find the first jury guilty. Half of any fine which the justices themselves imposed on the defendant was to go to the plaintiff as a form of reward for his bringing the attaint.[40] The statute 11 Hen. VII c. 24 expired in 1509 but was largely renewed by three successive Acts of Henry VIII's reign and finally made perpetual in 1571. A letter to the first John Paston concerning an action of attaint which Sir John Fastolf had in mind in November 1459 shows that it was considered even more important than in other suits to give the sheriff substantial rewards to make the jury; the letter also shows Paston seeking the good lordship of the duke of Norfolk so that this would be done quickly and so that the grand jury would find as Fastolf wanted. Often the grand jurors acquitted the first jury out of pity. Indeed, Sir Thomas Smith noted that in his time the former preferred to absent themselves from the trial 'and in the meane time they will . . . entreat the parties to come to some composition and agreement among them selves'; only if the corruption of the first jury was very evident would they convict. As well as having only a slender chance of success, the plaintiff had to face heavy legal expenses on account of the quality and quantity of the legal counsel usually employed and the extended duration of the suit. When the first John Paston brought an action of attaint in 1456 he retained as his counsel John Markham and Richard Chokke, serjeants, Thomas Littleton, king's serjeant, William Jenny, John Jenny, Richard Illingworth, and William Dyne. At the trial Markham reminded the court, we are told, of the 'longe hangyng' of the matter.[41]

Another option for a defeated party was to bring a writ of error. The error was usually detected by the party or his counsel in the procedural handling of the case just lost. Robert Pilkington tells us that he chose to sue out a writ of error, despite his counsel's suggestion of an action of attaint, because he believed his opponents, the Savage-Ainsworth family, were too powerful for him. By this he meant that they might well have superior influence with the sheriff and thus over the selection of jurors. On a writ of error there was no verdict by a jury, simply a ruling by the court. For Pilkington the first step was to obtain copies of earlier process and trial record, which he passed on to his counsel-learned, presumably so that they might search for the necessary legal error. Pilkington seems to have had to show the judges in common pleas that there was a prima-facie case of error, but the matter was then moved into king's bench. There was no decision in Pilkington's lifetime. His account of what happened in king's bench refers to Ainsworth's counsel getting delay after delay, and states that the writ of error could 'have no spede be cause at the recordes were alway changet and mendyt agaynis the said Robert'. Pilkington therefore arranged to return to the north and not visit London until his counsel-learned instructed. His expenses mounted: he paid his two counsel 40*d*. each time they appeared in court, and significant sums went to their clerks also. Eventually counsel argued the law on the matter on the morning of 11 June 1499 but this only led to another adjournment. Pilkington was then ordered by the judges to bring in precedents from the court of common pleas 'of other matters in like adjudged', which forced him to discontinue while the search was conducted. The next term (Hilary, 1500), the bishop of London, through an intermediary, approached Pilkington out of court offering to buy out his claim to the lands in Mellor. As a means of persuasion he threatened to 'sewe grete accyons of dettes and for costages of damagis' against Pilkington should he be unwilling to accept. Pilkington answered that 'for drede of his saule' he would not 'sell nor forbare his ryght and taylyd enheretanse'. However, he offered, if the bishop would renounce his claim to the Mellor lands, to allow him the marriage of his son and heir. No agreement seems to have been reached, but what exactly happened we cannot be sure because Pilkington's narrative tails off at this point. The suit appears to have continued into the early years of Henry VIII's reign when his son sought to revive it; Robert had died in September 1508.[42]

Robert Pilkington's tale of his lawsuits, with his great cause against John Ainsworth and the Savage family at centre, tells us a great deal about fifteenth-century litigation which cannot be found elsewhere, certainly not in the records of the courts. He is more instructive on this matter than even the voluminous Paston correspondence. The theme, underneath the legal detail, is how he suffered one 'great hurt and hynduryng' after another. Certainly, if his account is veracious, and although there may be some omission there seems little reason to doubt its essential honesty, Pilkington does appear to have been a thoroughly unlucky litigant, one frequently thwarted when he ought to have been having the better of his adversary. Several times he felt that he was deprived of rightful victory by delays, particularly the failure of his opponent to appear. At other times it was the malpractices of the clerks, who operated in and around the courts, which worked against him. There were also occasions when the opposing faction employed its influence to interfere with legal process and trial procedure. From our position of advantage it is not difficult to discern why Pilkington was unsuccessful. Given his situation and the way in which the law operated in the later fifteenth century, the failure was predictable. He was guilty of several errors of judgement in pursuing the suit. The worst was the very basic one of going to law against an adversary who had powerful protectors in members of the wealthy Cheshire family of Savage, of whom the most prominent was Thomas Savage, successively bishop of Rochester (1492–6), bishop of London (1496–1501), and archbishop of York (1501–7).[43] Pilkington received some support from his 'good lords' the earl of Derby and his son Lord Strange, who wrote to the justices on his behalf, but this may have been assistance pro forma only. In his capacity as a member of the king's council the bishop was able to benefit John Ainsworth directly. Although his personal interest in the matter was apparent to all, he was able to prevent Pilkington from obtaining a decision on the title to Mellor there. He got the matter remitted to the common law courts; he paid the sheriff to empanel his own nominees and did all he could to influence the jury's verdict. When Pilkington, to circumvent this, petitioned the king asking for the cause to be tried in the duchy of Lancaster chamber, his bill came to the notice of the bishop who made sure it went no further. The power of the Savage faction was probably reflected in the way the sheriff, after Ainsworth had emerged the victor at the Derby assizes in 1498, put him in possession of twenty more acres of land than had been contested in court.[44]

In his legal wars Robert Pilkington may have been handicapped by his modest wealth; and if he was better off than he appears to have been (it is impossible to do more than guess at his income), then by his parsimony. His account of his suit against Ainsworth and the Savages is punctuated by references to his expenses. Clearly the fees he had to pay to lawyers and clerks made a big impression on him. The cost of his writ of error and of the suit as far as it progressed amounted, he tells us, to £12. 9s. 4d., no small sum it is true. He calculated that from his father's death, which we know to have occurred in 1475 or 1476, to his defeat at the Derby assizes in 1498, he had spent in legal expenses £58. 8s. 0d., again not an inconsiderable amount but probably nowhere near as much as the Mellor rents for that period. In that period men were capable of becoming highly emotional about particular pieces of property which they or their families had held at one time, what we might call their old, ancestral land. It appears as if Mellor was such land to Pilkington, but so it may also have been for his adversary since Pilkington was distantly related to Ainsworth. A clear example of how the upper-class litigant was willing to spend far more than the value of the land in dispute to achieve victory in the courts is to be found in the history of the Berkeleys. In his suit from 1570 to 1581 against Sir Thomas Throckmorton over the tithes of Oldminster, Lord Henry Berkeley was reckoned to have incurred expenses and fines amounting to £1,500 and he lost the disputed lease. Throckmorton, the winner, affirmed that he had spent on the action £1,000 more than the lease was worth.[45]

The manner in which Robert Pilkington in his narrative dwells on the cost of lawyers and process is alternatively explained by his relative *naïveté* in matters relating to the law. How he differs in his writings from the Pastons is most striking. Most of that family were fully at home in the modes and by-ways of the common law, but to Pilkington the legal world was a mysterious one, full of pitfalls and intercessions from above which the litigant could not guard against. In particular, Pilkington seems to have made no arrangement with a lawyer or clerk employed around the central courts in London, nor with similar in Derbyshire, who could provide him with early warning of writs taken out against him. Thus he was frequently pressed to arrange for legal defence of his interests at short notice. Nor did he use a solicitor to instruct counsel, as some of his contemporaries were doing. In addition he does not seem to have understood the value of giving *douceurs* to judges' servants, who, so it was generally reputed, had the power to delay or speed one's suit.

The litigation between Robert Pilkington and John Ainsworth and the Savages over title to Mellor provides an interesting demonstration of what may be termed the place of litigation within the feud, and its relationship to the land-war manoeuvrings and violence which were the backdrop; for litigation was hardly ever the sole manifestation of a quarrel. The chronology of this feud, the sequence of events, may well have been typical of a substantial segment of the other long-lasting disputes among the upper classes of the period. We notice that the quarrel had its origins in descent of land from an ancestor common to both parties, and had been festering for several decades when the chief protagonists, Robert Pilkington and John Ainsworth, made their appearances. The two sides do not appear to have resorted to the courts until that time, and the reason may have been that the Ainsworths did not have the nerve or the wherewithal to challenge the Pilkington title claim until William Ainsworth, father of John, secured the maintenance of the powerful Savage family, but it is noticeable that even the Savages were hesitant to sue. What seems to have moved the quarrel into high gear was direct action, namely the kidnapping of Pilkington by his adversaries in 1478 in order to force him to accept arbitration, the provisions of which were to endure two years. The quarrel was renewed when Ainsworth's chief backer, his relative Sir John Savage, who at that point was in possession of Mellor, distrained the tenants for rents and evicted those who would not pay. Pilkington responded by securing the support of his patrons, the earl of Derby and his son Lord Strange, and then making an entry into Mellor with around 160 men 'in privy harness' at his back, with the intention of taking the rents himself and driving out non-payers.

It was only at this point that one of the parties decided to sue in court: Ainsworth brought a bill of riot before the council. This was in 1493, fifteen years after the kidnapping. Pilkington, after he had been examined there about the matter, asked that the council should try the two claims to title in Mellor, which was allowed, and both sides presented their evidences: 'whedur of us ys the ryght ayr be lyne of blode and be owr evydencez', wrote Pilkington. If we believe him, things went badly for Ainsworth but the latter succeeded in getting the council to delay the giving of judgment and in the interim both sides attempted to take rents from the Mellor tenants. Up to this point neither side had employed common law criminal process against the other but then, in November 1494, the Ainsworth faction obtained the indictment for 'felonye, ryott and trespas' of a good number of the men of 'Master Vernon', an ally of Pilkington. The only comparable incident occurred in July 1495 when associates of Ainsworth contrived, so we are told, the indictment for either felony or riot of all the Mellor tenants. Later the conciliar suit between Ainsworth and Pilkington was resumed and the latter was ordered to give her dower to the former's mother. However instead of then giving judgment on the main issue, the Mellor title, the council remitted it to the common law.

Whether it was the result of this conciliar decision or not is unclear but at Michaelmas term 1496 Pilkington brought a common law action of trespass in the name of one of his tenants against Ainsworth at relatively remote Tideswell. He did so because the latter had sued that tenant and others for trespass there, which 'myght have touched the ryght and fre holde of the said Roberts'. Pilkington's response of moving these suits by writ of *certiorari* to a higher court suggests he recognized an unfavourable verdict at Tideswell could endanger his claim to title in Mellor. The eventual outcome of Ainsworth's suits is not mentioned but they may well have precipitated the next phase of the quarrel, the decisive action of novel disseisin over Mellor which the Savages brought against Pilkington in Ainsworth's name at Derby assizes in 1497. The overall impression, therefore, which Pilkington's narrative presents of his litigation is of his own and his adversaries' reluctance to bring a suit over title, and of hesitation to seek the indictment of opponents involved in land-war activities, at least until the battle in court over title had finally been joined. The position of the tenants in the land at issue, and their potential for turning litigation into a land war through their withholding of rents, their eviction, or their own quarrels and suits, are very noticeable and suggest that litigation over land without the accompaniment of force in some form was unlikely.[46]

Chapter Four

MASTER AND CLIENT

Much of the attention devoted by historians to bastard feudalism has not been directed at land wars, litigation, or sheriffs, justices, and juries, but towards the relationship between master and client and how this affected the well-being of the late medieval English state and society within it. Nineteenth-century writers, who in their historical works touched on bastard feudalism, took a position which was generally critical. This was largely because they found it hard to believe that the civil wars and the apparent intransigence of the nobility in the fourteenth and fifteenth centuries were not in some way connected with what they took to be the impermanent nature of the relationship between the magnates and their followers.[1] They contrasted the maintenance, livery-giving, and retaining of that period unfavourably with the more durable tie based on military service in return for a fief which characterized earlier centuries. The last forty years or so of historical scholarship has, however, produced a notable revision: the denigration was unfair, the quality of government and the tone of the relationship between the upper classes and those who served them were not inferior but different. Indeed, the implication is that they might on closer inspection turn out to have been improved and beneficial.[2] Thus it was the view of K. B. McFarlane that in regard to lawlessness, which bastard feudalism was reckoned to have engendered, the later Middle Ages was no worse than the centuries preceding. He suggested that from the time of Edward I disorder took subtler forms and rivalries were resolved through the courts, perverted or not. Maintenance, the illicit support of a suitor, an accused, or even an accuser at law, which figures substantially in contemporary correspondence, complaint, and legal records, did not originate in the later Middle

Ages; its frequent mention at that time was because it was 'being measured by men with a higher conception of public order'.[3] Society had simply become more sensitive; there was a growing respect for the law and in any case maintenance was an improvement on more direct forms of self-help.[4]

The dark side of the master-client relationship, so it is generally agreed, lay in three different categories of offence but three connected with each other and two intimately connected. This trio was maintenance, the illegal giving and taking of livery, and the illegal retaining of followers or being so retained. Maintenance, probably the greatest threat of the three to public order, usually took the form of tampering with the juries of indictment and of trial or with the justices, and it was accomplished through the agency of someone of greater weight in society than the party himself.[5] Contemporaries were well aware of the great danger posed by maintenance and how the three offences were causally connected. The Act of Edward I's reign, which is reckoned to have been the origin of the crime of conspiracy in law, gave as one definition of that offence the retaining of men by robes or fee to maintain malicious enterprises.[6] The articles of enquiry for the presenting jurors who were to provide charges for the king's bench at Wigan in 1322 commanded that they should report those who retained men in their district in their livery and at their fees in order to maintain their evil undertakings, and the takers as well.[7] The statute 1 Ric. II c. 7 was directed against those of small revenue who were retaining followers by giving liveries and taking from the recipients the value of that clothing or more as assurance they would maintain each other in their quarrels. A justices' charge to jurors dating from c. 1403–4 stipulated that they should report those who gave robes, hats, or other liveries of company to maintain their misdeeds.[8]

The first two of these examples of the connection between maintenance on the one hand and livery-giving and retaining on the other come, it will be noted, from the reigns of Edward I and Edward II, well before what is taken as the high period of leglisation against the evils of bastard feudalism. Indeed, maintenance itself was first mentioned in legislation in the first Statute of Westminster (1275), where royal officials were said to be maintaining suits in return for a part of the suitor's gains, and sheriffs and stewards of magnates were forbidden to maintain suits in county courts. The government was much concerned with corrupt behaviour by officials at this time and the very term 'maintenance' may at first have implied just that. If such is the case, then its scope had widened considerably by the end of the reign. The Trailbaston Ordinance of 1305 emphasized rather that justice was being perverted by bands of hired ruffians, and one of its main aims seems to have been to order enquiry into all those supporting malefactors hired to ensure that juries in all sorts of courts would be fearful of telling the truth.[9] At the outset of Edward III's reign, the suppression of maintenance figured prominently in the plans of the government to remedy the lawlessness which had developed in the later years of Edward II. Four statutes promulgated in the opening years of that reign touched on maintenance: the lords in Parliament promised not to maintain miscreants (2 Edw. III c. 7) and they were not to maintain parties at law by means of letters to judges and juries (1 Edw. III st. 2 c. 14); sheriffs were to be allowed to arrest before indictment not only notorious malefactors but maintainers in addition (10 Edw. III st. 2 c. 3), while the power to enquire into and determine the activities of maintainers of parties at law was entrusted to the justices of assize and the general eyre (4 Edw. III c. 11). In 1347 there were further attempts to suppress maintenance. The statute 20 Edw. III c. 1 instructed justices to report to the king's council any letter sent to them seeking favour for a party suing or being sued in the courts. The Act 20 Edw. III c. 4 forbade anyone in the royal household to maintain quarrels by using threats or in return for gifts, while under 20 Edw. III c. 5 all magnates were to remove bearers and maintainers from their retinues.[10] This was the first time the word retinue/retainer/retaining had appeared in legislation since the first Statute of Westminster and its connection therein with maintenance was novel also.

Maintenance was the subject of further legislation in the reign of Richard II. The Act 1 Ric. II c. 4 was no doubt designed to institute a standard and severe penalty for those found guilty of maintaining a quarrel. Another statute of the same parliament (1 Ric. II c. 9), also concerned with deterrence, made void gifts to great men intended to persuade them to maintain the donor in his suits, while a third (1 Richard II c. 7) can be seen as connecting maintenance with the celebrated Act on retaining of 1390 for, in addition to ordering the investigation of fraternities suspected of the former offence, it forbade the giving of livery by persons of small revenue to esquires and others.[11] From this time onward the emphasis in legislation against offences directly related to bastard feudalism was to be against livery-giving and retaining. It was probably very apparent that the laws against maintenance were ineffective. Certainly it appears that indictments for maintenance and private actions against conspiracy were few and far between.[12] We may suppose the jurors who were expected to indict maintainers were themselves subjected to pressure, perhaps by the very same group, and thus no charges were forthcoming. Actions of conspiracy were probably eschewed because they were impossible to win for similar reasons. There were, it is true, a fair number of cases where the maintaining of miscreants by the powerful was the basis of complaints made in chancery in the later fourteenth century, but these seem for the most part to be instances where the so-called maintenance was colour to get the case heard in that court, and not the chief wrong.[13]

Although largely remembered because of its stipulations about livery and retaining, the next major piece of legislation against the evils of bastard feudalism, 13 Ric. II st. 3, was intended in the final instance to strike at maintainers, barrators, and embracers, who tampered with inquests (juries) giving decisions on quarrels. Having laid down that only those of the rank of banneret and above were to be allowed to give livery of company and that the recipients must be retained for life and must be of knightly or esquire status or household servants, the Act commanded the removal from upper-class households of maintainers, barrators, procurers, and embracers of juries as soon as they were discovered. Two later Ricardian statutes (16 Ric. II c. 4 and 20 Ric. II c. 2) then forbade specifically the wearing of livery by men of yeoman rank and below, although this in fact was implied in 13 Ric. II st. 3. Whether the emphasis on the wearing rather than the gift of livery was significant, the yeomen perhaps of their own volition deciding to wear a local magnate's colours to frighten their enemies in and out of courts, is unclear.[14] Certainly the fear of the lower-class follower, who by his numbers and availability would increase the size of any retinue dramatically, was very strong at this time, although we notice that guilds and fraternities in towns were allowed the privilege of livery of cloth and hats (13 Hen. IV c. 3).

In Henry IV's reign the pressure against the giving of livery was increased. In order that maintenance should be eschewed, said the statute 1 Hen. IV c. 7, no lord except the king was henceforth permitted to give livery to knights, esquires, or yeomen (unless they were menials, officers, or legal advisers), thus largely annulling the Act of 1390 (13 Ric. II st. 3). If indeed a liveried follower was technically a retainer, and in that the giving of cloth to be worn amounted to the giving of a fee and was therefore contractual, then this was a most severe move by the government for it meant the elimination of retainers below the social level of banneret except where the giver of the livery was the king, and even then his knights and esquires were not to wear it outside his presence. Nor did Henry IV and his parliaments retrace their steps. The statutes 2 Hen. IV c. 21, 7 Hen IV c. 14, and 13 Hen. IV c. 3 confirmed and clarified earlier legislation. They were intended primarily, however, to ensure the efficient execution of those Acts and to specify more exactly the penalties for their infraction. Thus, for example, by 7 Hen. IV c. 14 givers of livery incurred a penalty of 100 shillings for each offence and takers one of 40 shillings. Furthermore, the same statute introduced into the laws governing the abuses of bastard feudalism financial encouragement (in this case half of the penalties incurred) for him who would bring an action in the courts against the person or persons suspect on behalf of both himself and the king, a legal device which had developed in the later fourteenth century.[15] The main hope of the government, however, must have lain in the bringing of indictments, yet here, as usual, it was to be disappointed: offenders, so it was admitted in the Act 8 Hen. VI c. 4, could not be indicted because of great maintenance. The solution which this statute offered was procedural. Justices of assize and justices of the peace were given the power to compel the appearance of those they suspected, to examine them, and if by this examination they found them guilty then to impose the fines set out in 7 Hen. IV c. 14. Here was an excellent example of what may be called the new truncated criminal process of late medieval England, which the government had been developing as an option for dealing with those suspected of trespasses related to bastard feudalism, like riot and forcible entry, since the 1390s.[16] The aim was to avoid having to rely on grand juries reluctant to find the charge a true bill and on petty juries eager to acquit so that they would not be sought out for revenge by those they had tried.

Procedural improvement was also the main reason behind the next statute of significance which dealt with livery-giving and retaining, namely the notorious 8 Edw. IV c. 2. This Act confirmed earlier legislation, especially 1 Hen. IV c. 7, slightly altered the size of the fines to be imposed, and made void all earlier retainings. We may take it that the suits invited under 7 Hen. IV c. 14 had not been forthcoming in sufficient number because the new Act of 1468 provided that charges might be brought by information given to the justices at oyer and terminer, gaol delivery and quarter sessions, or in the common pleas or king's bench. The information was to stand in place of bill or original writ and thereby save the delator time and money. Then the justices, as under 8 Hen. VI c. 4, might examine the accused and proceed to give a verdict on his crime or, if they wished, put the matter of his guilt to a jury. Furthermore, they had the power to award costs to the informer, who in addition was to be given half of any forfeiture. The accused was allowed the benefit of no essoins or letters or protection. This amounted to taking advantage of almost every procedural device possible under the criminal law to ensure accusations were forthcoming, and also loading, although legitimately, the method of trial to make conviction much more likely than acquittal. The truncated or summary nature of the process laid down was of a greater degree than under any other statute to date, with the possible exception of 15 Ric. II c. 2 on forcible entry.[17]

In its last part the Act of 1468 contained a clause to the effect that the prohibition against livery-giving and retaining was not to extend to the giving of fees, annuities, lands, and similar in return for the giving of counsel and what was called 'loial service', even if the person providing the latter was not learned in the law. The meaning of 'loial' is not clear. It might amount to 'faithful', or 'lawful' or more probably 'pertaining to the law'. This section of the Act has been taken as implying that, although confirming earlier statutes against livery-giving, it did not totally prohibit that practice, or retaining, even to those who were not menials or learned counsel.[18] Indeed, so the argument runs, it probably allowed retaining by lords to continue. This thesis is hard to accept when in its early part the statute, admitting earlier laws were being ignored, prohibited all retaining after the forthcoming 25 June. The section of the Act which mentions 'loial service' is probably best interpreted as referring to service given by legal advisers and agents who were not qualified lawyers, as indeed a subsequent clause seems to indicate.[19] Such persons were probably the solicitors, who were beginning to be of some importance in litigation, or clerks employed in the central courts at Westminster, or plain laymen who added to their income by keeping litigants in the provinces informed about writs out against them and by checking court records.[20] If we omit the matter of judicial procedure, the overall result of promulgation of 8 Edw. IV c. 2 was probably an extension of the old rule that no one under the rank of banneret should retain and no less than esquire in status should be a retainer, and then only if retained for life (13 Ric. II st. 3). The statute 1 Hen. IV c. 7 had forbidden all lords except the king from giving livery to knights, esquires, or yeomen, but it had not specifically forbidden them from retaining the same. Those given livery were perhaps not technically retainers, and it may have been possible to be a retainer yet never receive robes, cap, or suit of livery from the lord; but whatever doubt there may have been in men's minds about the distinction must have been settled by the Act of Edward IV. From 1468 lords, like those of lesser social status, might retain only menial servants, officers, men learned in the law, and those giving 'loial service'. The nobleman or banneret could no longer under the law retain a knight or an esquire.[21]

To assess how the Act was enforced is difficult. Nobles no doubt continued to retain knights and esquires out of ignorance about the law or in the hope that it would be a dead letter or even in plain defiance. If the last was the case, they would be weighing the necessity of preserving their retinue, patronage, and territorial influence against the cost of any fine or pardon. We might expect that those who were brought before the courts for retaining in subsequent decades would have been persons of lesser social status, and the few instances which have been discovered seem to indicate that this was so.[22] Because very few of the records of the justices of the peace and of the justices of assize and gaol delivery have survived from the period 1450–1550, it is impossible even to hazard a guess as to how many informations regarding illegal livery-giving and retaining were laid before those justices as 8 Edw. IV c. 2 intended. The small number of charges found in the records of king's bench appear to be in the form of indictments and thus may not have been put forward under the procedural rules of 1468.[23]

The best proof of the ineffectiveness of earlier measures lies in the appearance of further statutes against the same problem at a later date, and especially does it lie in preambles to such Acts as to their necessity. The reign of Henry VII provided plenty of this as well as other legal indications. In 1485 the nobility were asked to take an oath that they would eschew retaining against the law, while in the subsequent year the judges of the two benches confirmed that retaining anyone but household servants and legal counsel was illegal.[24] The preamble to the statute 3 Hen. VII c. 1 blamed illegal retaining and livery-giving, and maintenance, which now appeared in the statutes again, for many more evils than had ever been the case before. Because those evils corrupted the juries, men were being deprived unfairly of their property and robberies and murders were on the increase, presumably by way of revenge. Therefore a new court was to be erected with a very distinguished panel of judges. It was to be operated by a procedure which had the chancellor (one of the judges) receive the charges in the form of a bill or information and then summon the accused, victim, and witnesses ('those by whom the truth may be known') before him and his colleagues by writ of privy seal or subpoena. They were then to try the offender in a manner which was not defined but which must have amounted to examination followed by a verdict by the bench. The punishment was to be 'as . . . if . . . convicted after the due order of the law'. Of the few cases tried in this court which have been discovered, two may have involved maintenance but none was concerned with livery or retaining.[25] Yet without other record evidence we should not be too hasty to dismiss the court as ineffective. It certainly had the most knowledgeable set of judges of any, although how such important dignitaries found the opportunity to meet is a mystery.[26]

The Act 11 Hen. VII c. 3 allotted the problems of illegal livery-giving and retaining, and maintenance (the salient offence), which were still continuing, along with those of riot, embracery, extortion, excessive wages, and inordinate apparel, in part at least to the justices of assize and the justices of the peace. They were to have power on receiving information about any instance of these offences to award process against the offender as if he were already indicted. This was similar to the power entrusted to them by 8 Hen. VI c. 4, the chief novelty of the Act of 1495 being that any false informer was to pay the accused's costs and damages in addition, these being awarded at the justices' discretion. Whether in these cases there was indictment and trial by jury in the full common law manner is unclear. Probably the latter was retained but the former dispensed with and the information allowed to stand in its place. Another statute, 11 Hen. VII c. 25, passed by the same parliament, was also concerned with maintenance, and in two ways which its fellow did not touch. When justices before the trial suspected that the empanelled jurors in a private action were being maintained so they would favour one of the parties, they were to be allowed to 'reform' (i.e. amend the composition of) the panel at their discretion. To a person who thought the verdict in either a criminal case or a private action had gone against him because of the jurors' perjury the Act gave the opportunity to make complaint to the justices, who were to certify it to the chancellor. The latter was empowered to call the complainant before a tribunal comprising himself, the treasurer, the two chief justices, and the clerk of the rolls, who would examine him and the accused and punish according to their findings. This did not, however, reverse the verdict in the original trial, which remained good until overturned by writ of attaint or error.

The last statute of Henry VII's parliaments which affected the handling of offences associated with bastard feudalism was 19 Hen. VII c. 14.[27] As in other, earlier, Acts the introduction referred to the ineffectiveness of previous legislation against illegal retaining and livery-giving, but ordered they should be executed.[28] The remedy the new Act provided was a stiffer level of fines with imprisonment on conviction at the justices' discretion, and some dramatic changes in procedure. Enquiry was to be at quarter sessions by an especially substantial jury of twenty-four, and, in order that there might a greater chance of indictment, the chief constables and bailiffs of the hundreds and the constables of the towns were to give evidence on oath, which was the first time this requisite had figured in a statute. The justices of the peace were empowered to examine suspects and certify the names of those they found had contravened the law into the king's bench, the certificate standing as a conviction. If the examination showed others to be involved as well as the suspect, it was to have the force of an indictment against them. An alternative way to discover offenders which was also provided, was for an information to be brought into the Star Chamber, king's bench, or the council with the king, whither those named would be summoned by subpoena or privy seal writ to be tried by means of examination or other method. Those convicted were to pay costs to the informer, who was also to have reasonable reward from the court. For the devisers of the statute, procedure by indictment and information, reinforced and widened as both were, was still not enough, so a third method was appended. The chancellor, the keeper of the great seal, the justices of the king's bench, and the council were each to have the power to summon before them by subpoena or privy seal writ any person they knew to have offended against the Act, even if there was no indictment, no suit brought before them, nor information laid. Then they might examine those summoned and adjudge them as if convicted according to the common law. Here was a great legal rarity, the purely governmental prosecution. What the statute amounted to in terms of criminal process was the omission of the common law necessities of indictment by grand jury and trial by petty jury; instead, procedure might be of a truncated or summary nature.[29] This was not the first time such devices had been employed, but no other statute concerned with livery-giving, retaining, or maintenance, it is fair to say, went so far in that direction. It is apparent that virtually every device known to the English criminal law at that time, which might ensure the reporting of the offences in question and increase the normal rate of conviction, was utilized in the design of this statute, and it can be regarded from one angle as a high point in the history of summary procedure and from another as the moving-up of one dangerous category of trespass for trial before the highest officers and justices in the land.[30] The common element in 3 Hen. VII c. 1, 11 Hen. VII c. 3, 11 Hen. VII c. 25, 19 Hen. VII c. 14, and 19 Hen. VII c. 13 for that matter, was the downplaying, indeed the virtual elimination of the jury, both of indictment and trial, from the process stipulated.[31]

If there was any statute which by its provisions should have gone a long way towards removing the evils of illegal livery-giving and retaining it was 19 Hen. VII c. 14. Unfortunately, partly because of the range of options provided for reporting those offences, the record evidence necessary to enable us to make a satisfactory assessment of what was achieved is lacking. The years when the Act was in operation were those when Empson and Dudley, Henry VII's notorious ministers, were reckoned to have been abusing the law, and it is possible that provision for reporting offences by means of information caused exceptional resentment. Before the oyer and terminer commissions, which were appointed between July and November 1509 to investigate grievances about the old reign, there were brought some charges against the laying of false information but whether they were particularly against the operation of the 1504 Act is not clear. The terms of the commissions made no reference to accusation by informers, unless it was concealed in the authority given to deal with trespasses and offences against what was referred to as 'the statute of Magna Carta or law and custom of England'.[32] Nevertheless we cannot doubt that there was a dislike of informers in regard to their reporting offences against the laws about livery-giving and retaining. In the first parliament of Henry VIII's reign, the Act 11 Hen. VII c. 3, which had provided that method of producing accusations, was repealed (by 1 Hen. VIII, c. 6) on the grounds that some informations had been invented for the purpose of vexation. There was no need for the repealing statute to refer to 19 Hen. VII c. 14 since that had expired with the old king's death; but rather remarkable was the fact that 8 Edw. IV c. 2 was not annulled, yet it also allowed the bringing of information against those giving livery illegally. Indeed the Act of 1468 was destined to become a favourite Tudor instrument in controlling that offence.

The first occasion in the new reign on which the government showed open concern over illegal retaining and livery-giving occurred in July 1511 when by proclamation the king ordered that no one should retain or wear cognizances except as the law allowed. By October 1514 apprehension had mounted and it was proclaimed that because these offences were not being punished murder, riot, routs, maintaining, and embracery were daily occurrences. There-fore the statutes were to be observed and any permission allowing retaining and livery beyond the law was revoked.[33] Despite the danger to public order as Henry VIII and his advisers saw it, the last Act which provided a thoroughgoing system to remedy the weakness of the criminal law in the area of retaining and livery-giving had already been passed. The reign of the second Tudor king produced no novel measures in legislation. The statute 33 Hen. VIII c. 10, and 37 Hen. VIII c. 7 which slightly amended it, gave authority to justices of the peace to enquire by jury or information concerning those who retained men or gave livery illegally, as well as about maintainers, embracers, vagabonds, and commodity speculators, and to arrest and try them.[34] Procedure was therefore not of the radical truncated or summary type, which had been stipulated not infrequently in the reigns of Henry VII and Edward IV. Rather it replaced the procedurally conservative Act 11 Hen. VII c. 3 but omitted to give the justices of assize power to administer the Act like its forbear of 1495 had done. The statute of 1542 and its amendor of 1546 give the impression of having been designed so as not to upset the upper classes unduly rather than to totally eliminate the problem. There were to be no other statutes promulgated for dealing with retaining, livery, or maintenance during the remainder of the Tudor period.[35] William Lambarde tells us that 33 Hen. VIII c. 10 and 37 Hen. VIII c. 7, together with 1 Hen. IV c. 7, 2 Hen. IV c. 21, and 8 Edw. IV c. 2, were the relevant Acts which the justices of the peace were supposed to enforce late in Elizabeth's reign.[36]

It was once thought that provisions for trying cases of maintenance, illegal retaining, and livery-giving in the common law courts were not of major importance because the conciliar courts saw those offences as their own particular preserve. C. G. Bayne and S. E. Lehmberg, however, showed that this was certainly not true of Henry VII's reign, and more recently J. A. Guy has found similarly in regard to the years when Wolsey was Henry VIII's chief minister.[37] Maintenance figured in conciliar business in a very small number of cases in both these periods, and illegal retaining and livery-giving almost not at all. In a single year at the end of Elizabeth I's reign about 5 per cent of the cases heard in the Star Chamber concerned maintenance but again retaining and livery-giving were almost entirely absent. The records of the courts of common law are similarly empty. Thus the files of the Norfolk justices of the peace for 1532–3 provide only a single case of maintenance and none of the other two crimes, and the quarter sessions records of Elizabeth's reign of other counties are equally barren. The home circuit gaol delivery records of Elizabeth I provide but a single example (Surrey, 1580) of indictments for maintenance and none of the other two crimes.[38] Besides those of gaol delivery and quarter sessions, the courts mentioned in 8 Edw. IV c. 2 as being the ones to which the informer might go were the king's bench, the common pleas, the exchequer, and those held by commissioners of oyer and terminer.[39] A few cases concerned with retaining and livery probably went, especially if great men were involved, into the king's bench or the common pleas and some must have gone before the justices of oyer and terminer, where county faction leaders and their followers traditionally fought their great battles at law, but the matter has yet to be elucidated.[40]

The continuance of illegal livery-giving and retaining into the later sixteenth century was not, however, a matter the government dared ignore. The upper classes in that period were sufficiently worried about the possibility of prosecution and large fines for them to seek licences and pardons from the Crown fairly frequently.[41] Governmental records of the non-legal variety reveal the Crown's concern about retaining and livery offences in every decade. It was thought politic to accuse Thomas Cromwell of retaining illegally at his examination in June 1540. In July 1588 the earl of Leicester reported to Sir Francis Walsingham that the number of liveries given in the last six weeks was incredible (it was, of course, a time of national crisis) but that no man feared the penalty.[42] A list of June 1596 shows that Sir John Smythe had twenty-two retainers wearing his livery who were neither of his household nor taking his wages. Most revealing, however, were the royal proclamations of 1572 and 1583. The former referred to the multitude of retainers, which was a cause of maintenance and riots, and ordered the enforcement of the relevant statutes; the latter noted that the earlier proclamation had been of no effect, the laws were not enforced and the evil, far from being removed, was increasing.[43] Illegal retaining was still recognized as a public evil under James I. Cowell's book *The Interpreter*, published in 1607, noted the problems associated with it still existed: 'Yet is it not this fault so well looked unto but that there is need of more pregnant lawes for the redresse thereof or at least better execution of those that be already made.'[44]

The aspect of bastard feudalism which had attracted the greatest attention from historians has undoubtedly been retaining and the retainer. Historians have brought out clearly the supersession of the old custom of allotting a fief to a follower in return for military service by the practice of granting a yearly fee and later of giving a promise of favour. The contract which bound lord to retainer took the form and indeed the name of an indenture, and when it first appeared (in the thirteenth century) it usually provided for the retainer to draw a specific fee from the revenues of one of the lord's manors for a period of years or, more rarely, for life. By the second half of the fifteenth century, so it has been argued, the giving of fees was becoming uncommon, being replaced presumably by favour. Some historians have been inclined to believe that agreements where the retainer secured promise of favour undermined the cohesion and durability of the retinue and therefore the stability of society. They have pointed to the fact that it was not uncommon by the fifteenth century for a retainer to have a contract with a second or even a third lord simultaneously. Recent scholarship has been at pains to emphasize the longevity of a lord's retinue and the durability of the contractual ties, arguing that the social connections engendered were such that no follower could withdraw simply as the whim took him.[45]

To try to assess which party to the contract, lord or retainer, master or client, was the more eager to enter into it may be futile, for the institution would not have persisted had not both sides been able to benefit. It is, however, worthy of notice that sanction clauses against those who defaulted on their obligations are reckoned to have disappeared from indentures about the middle of the four-teenth century, which is suggestive of a rise in the bargaining power of the retainer. From Richard II's reign retainers were to be found taking fees from more than a single lord and the proportion of gentry in a county who entered a retinue may have increased beyond the thirty-three to fifty per cent which had been the figure in the fourteenth century. This could indicate retainers were being sought by lords increasingly, or it could have been that the benefits of being in a retinue were becoming so great that no member of the gentry wished to be excluded. Rather than this being simply a social phenomenon, one view has it that politics played a role and that the coming of the Wars of the Roses forced the nobility to engage in competitive recruitment for retainers. How much of their revenues lords were willing to expend on annuities to retainers is a similarly vexed topic, but the percentage does not seem to have risen with the passing of time. What is more certain is that the majority of retainers who got fees received an amount which was only a fraction of their total annual income, and this was probably still true where a man took fees from several lords.[46]

To reach the heart of bastard feudalism it is necessary to provide an accurate assessment of how lord and retainer each benefited from the institution. Yet before this can be done the lord-retainer relationship must be placed in a wider social context, for although the retinue was central there were other important elements which impinged. One was the lord's tenantry. A tenant might be a retainer but this was not frequent.[47] Retainers were usually gentry who lived some distance from the lord's county seat and demesne, although probably close to some parcel of his lands or to where he had a claim.[48] Tenants might be of use as harassers of the foe, in and out of the local courts, in the frequent land wars, and were generally treated with respect because of the rents they provided. They were used as troops only infrequently and were not likely to travel with their masters to 'show the flag' as a retainer would.[49] Those of the gentry, or even the nobility, who were allies or associates of a retaining lord in his land wars, litigation, and every day legal transactions were often referred to as 'well willers'.[50] We hear of them sharing the costs which jurors incurred in travelling to sessions. Occasionally the term was used in reference to lesser men. The Paston family employed it to describe sympathetic tenants in a manor of divided loyalties.[51]

About the involvement of a lord's household servants we know relatively little, but a certain amount can be deduced. The laws on retaining in no way limited their number and a member of the upper classes could therefore, if he wished, employ as many persons in the running of his house and household as took his fancy. He could therefore in theory host a small army within his own walls and he ought not, it can be argued, have had to look further than to his own kitchen and stable minions for the men he might need in his land wars.[52] Yet few of the upper classes seem to have made great use of this option. They would have had to pay many men wages over an extended period and keep them busily occupied. In any case the majority of household servants were probably poor material from which to recruit for expeditions of a semi-military variety. The skills and dexterities required for the efficient and decorous performance of duties and services in the hall and chamber would be of little use in ambushes and head-breaking, although servants who were proficient riders might, if properly clothed, be used to add size to retinue. On the other hand a retainer might sometimes double as a household servant. This we are told by an Elizabethan writer who adds, somewhat mysteriously, that the upper classes found this a more attractive arrangement.[53] Comments by John Smyth support this. He tells us that among Lord Henry Berkeley's servants were gentlemen and esquires of 'remarkable families and descent'.[54] The explanation must be that the retainer-servant was valued because his social standing and graciousness gave a certain glory to the master in whose following he was, something that was doubtless thought particularly valuable at gatherings and occasions of display. A term used sometimes in contemporary correspondence for followers utilized in the land wars was simply 'men'. Thus Robert Pilkington tells us about how he went with 'iii score men to Mellur' and how Thomas Legh of Adlington, esquire, did 'sende . . . a hundreth men and moo in preve hernes', although elsewhere of another occasion he refers to Sir John Savage sending some gentlemen and his houshold servants to drive out William Roubotham.[55] The term 'men' does not seem in the Pilkington narrative or the Paston correspondence to have been entirely, or even mainly, a generic term of convenience. It might be used in a specific manner in regard to the followers of gentry who were possessed of no great wealth, or to followers assembled for the time being by magnates. Thus the suspicion arises that many of the 'men' referred to in the land wars were not retainers, servants, or even tenants, but followers recruited *ad hoc*. They might be given temporary lodging in the master's household but they were there as hired 'muscle' on a *per diem* basis. We hear of the archbishop of York, in his quarrel with the tenants of Knaresborough Forest in 1441 over tolls at Ripon fair, hiring men from the north at sixpence or one shilling a day and bouch of court (i.e. sustenance), of a household being increased so the master could expand his quarrel, and of a gentleman borrowing from an associate strong young men when embarking on a land-war expedition.[56]

For a member of the upper class to have a sizeable retinue was probably an end in itself. The lord sought the glory of having retainers at his back because it confirmed his status and local authority as well as demonstrating his open-handedness in employing and clothing them. He took his retinue with him when he went on progress round his estates, when he travelled to tournaments, parliaments, or assemblies, when he went hunting, and on martial occasions. At his seat his retainers were expected to be present when distinguished guests paid him a visit. Like feudal vassals of old, the members of the retinue probably had the opportunity to provide their master with counsel (they might even serve as his legal counsel) and he used them in administrative positions on his land. When the lord visited the locality where the retainer had his lands, it was expected that the latter would give him 'attendance' and 'wait upon him'. In the fourteenth century the retainer may have actually waited on his master at his meals, but later simply being present and offering general service was probably more important than performing domestic services. The lord would know that when the client 'waiting upon him' or 'giving attendance' said he was ready to 'do him pleasure' it might well herald a request for the lord's support or some intervention in the client's affairs.[57]

Even an outsider who hoped to gain some favour from the lord would behave in this way. The first John Paston was asked in 1450 to persuade the earl of Oxford and Sir Miles Stapleton to wait upon the duke of York 'in the most wurchepfull wyse that they kun and do hym as good attendaunce and pleasaunce as they mown'; the intention was to secure the duke's assistance against Lord Moleyns.[58]

From the retainers, associates, tenants, and servants, who collectively made up what was known as his affinity, the lord expected a variety of services. What these had in common was that all were intended to 'help him forward', that is to say increase his family's wealth and prestige.[59] His retainers and associates the lord would expect to be his witnesses to contracts, his warrantors to those who purchased from him, his feoffees to uses, and his executors after his death. The last two of these tasks, if they could be burdensome, might also be very profitable and were more likely to be sought after than avoided. Less enticing to the client but crucial in the lord's eyes was the task of labouring jurors. This was not necessarily to be done where the lord was himself involved; it could be another member of the affinity who was in need of such assistance. The first John Paston was asked by the earl of Oxford, whose tenant Nicholas Hert was being sued in an action of debt by a Norwich butcher, 'that yue wole calle the jurry before you that arn impanellid between thaym and opne thaym the mater at large at myn instance and desire thaym to do as concyens wole and to eschue perjury'.[60] To act in this way was not, strictly speaking, illegal but it was something so mighty a man as the earl could not do himself, even if he was inclined to, without losing some of his dignity. Furthermore, if he did address the jury himself, a backer of the butcher might charge him with maintenance before a higher court merely as a harassment. It was therefore left to the retainer or well-willer to perform the task and incur whatever legal risk there was. There were others as well as jurors for clients to cajole or impress on their master's behalf. When parliamentary elections were at hand clients might be of service by ensuring the freeholders voted for the candidate whom he preferred. The Willoughby family's correspondence shows that a client might also be expected to ensure the support of his kinfolk went to the preferred candidate.[61] Another task we hear of, which retainers felt obliged to undertake, was the settling of quarrels between other members of the affinity; sometimes the retainers so entrusted were acting as part of, or in conjunction with, the lord's council. Retainers had to play their part also when their master decided that he could enter a rival's land, although they were less likely to be required to assist in the taking of a distress. Rarer, but it did occur from time to time, was the occasion when the lord went with or sent his retinue to overawe a court in session and impress the jurors directly. Sometime before January 1505, Sir Richard Empson, with no fewer than 200 knights, gentlemen, and yeomen in his entourage, attended York assizes to 'countenance', as the term was, a suit against Sir Robert Plumpton. He did not leave until the assize passed against the latter.[62] Not only might a retinue be of assistance to its master in politics, it could also benefit him in a direct financial manner, for retainers and tenants and well-wishers as well were willing to offer not just their aid but actual gifts to obtain that vital support known as 'good lordship'. Such bribes might take the form of money or objects, valuable animals for example, but often the lord's support was obtained by promising him (quite illegally) a share in the profit to be made from a successful outcome to the client's current lawsuit or land war.[63]

From the viewpoint of the retainer or more distant member of a lord's affinity, the advantages of the connection were substantial. The client could count on the lord assisting him to win his suits in the courts. The lord could ensure the necessary judicial writs were forthcoming, put pressure on the sheriff, give assistance in labouring jurors, and write to the justices demanding a 'fair' trial of his client's cause at the least, although we may suspect he would be perturbed if the follower making the request did so too often or if he sought assistance in a case in which the facts were very much against him.[64] Direct intervention by the lord, however, was often unnecessary. To gain the verdict, it was sometimes sufficient simply to be known as the lord's client.[65] Wearing the lord's livery in court would probably have the same effect. The king's council in 1471 ordered Lord Grey of Codnor to discharge all those he had retained in Nottingham contrary to statute so that those inhabitants against whom there were complaints might be 'justiced', as it was put, by the king's officers.[66] If he was an active participant in the lord's land wars, the retainer or member of the affinity would take heart from the knowledge that it was reckoned an obligation for his master to recompense him for loss of property sustained therein and that should things go awry and he find himself besieged, captured, or in danger of his life the lord would seek intercession in the feud at the highest level.[67] Not to do so would ruin the lord's reputation amongst his peers. Clients also sought the favour of their 'good lord' for more direct benefits than assistance in local feuds. Frequently their desire was for an office or position in the lord's administration or for help in acquiring similar from the king. In the latter case the lord would be expected to supplicate to the king's ministers and offer the sum of money which the client was willing to pay for the office.[68] A retainer could rely on his lord's services in settling in an informal manner any disputes he had with those of roughly the same social status, other retainers in particular. When Sir Gilbert Debenham and Sir John Paston and their followers seemed likely to come to blows in a quarrel over the rents of Hellesdon, the duke of Norfolk, who was lord of both knights, intervened by summoning both men to visit him and ordering them to dismiss their men. He then placed a keeper, acceptable to the two parties, in Hellesdon Place.[69] An observant lord would hope to intervene before quarrels between his followers erupted into open strife and instruct them not to resort to direct action or the law courts before he took the matter in hand. This probably meant referring the matter to his legal advisers, his 'councell', who had the necessary knowledge of law to be able to make a fairly evenly balanced settlement, or 'direction' as it was called.[70]

To what degree were retainers and the members of an affinity involved in crime as distinct from the formal aggressiveness which characterized the gentlemen's land wars? There is some indication that followers were not always under the lord's strict control and indeed might become a menace to public order.[71] The most notorious band of errant followers about whom we have a reasonable amount of information was that headed by Charles Nowell, bailiff of Braydeston, Robert Ledham, and Roger Church, bailiff of Blofeld hundred, which operated in Norfolk and Suffolk in the years 1450–2.[72] Nowell, who seems to have been the leader, was an esquire of the duke of Norfolk, and it is likely that his associates in crime were also from the Norfolk retinue or affinity with a leavening of servants and what were called 'misgoverned people'. What made this band turn to violence and harassment is not clear, but factional dispute at the national as well as at the local level may have played a part. According to an information into the king's bench (presumably under the statute 13 Hen. IV c. 7) in 1452, they had, using Ledham's house as their fortress, issued forth to ambush, assault, grievously wound, take prisoner, seize cattle and sheep, enter land forcibly and disseise occupants, and stir up an insurrection in the countryside and accuse other of being the promoters. At first sight this seems to be a clear demonstration of chronic lawlessness, yet on consideration it is evident that, except for the last, these were all crimes which were typical of the land wars and its levels of violence. That violence was limited in its scope. Nowell's band, stated the information, had attacked the first John Paston at the door of Norwich cathedral intending to murder him. However, we notice he was fit enough soon after and the servant whom the miscreants hit over the head with a sword in the same incident was not reported as dying. One John Wylton was beaten by the band in Plumstead churchyard and said to have been in danger of his life, but he seems to have lived. John Coke of Witton was maimed and his mother hit on the head, 'which wound never healed before her death' but it was not said to have caused it. The son of one Alred of Earl Soham was killed on 1 April, stated the information; 'perhaps by the fellowship' (i.e. Nowell's gang), it added in a lame and indeterminate manner.

The land wars were in fact relatively bloodless. There were threats, assaults, ambushes, entries by force into land and buildings, some sacking, considerable shooting of bows and guns, but little serious theft or thrusting with cold steel. There was, it seems, a great deal of trespass but where were the felonies?[73] Were there no retainers, servants, or others in the affinities of the upper classes with a proclivity for real criminal activity like highway robbery and murder? Were there no latter-day Folvilles or Coterels, the notorious gentlemen-criminals of the 1320s and 1330s? Did not the phenomena of bastard feudalism, the land wars in particular, provide opportunities for crime of a more sordid and serious sort, crime which might threaten the possessions and personal safety of villagers and townsmen? The information we can elicit on this important issue from the records of the fourteenth and fifteenth centuries is minimal but from those of the sixteenth we can garner with great success. There are references which show that the felon in the households and retinues of the magnates was not an infrequent problem. Thus James Houghton, outlawed for murder, was reported in 1527 as staying in Lord Darcy's house as his servant; several murderers wearing the duke of Richmond's livery were being kept in Holt Castle in 1535; while in 1556 one Pecke, a retainer in the earl of Oxford's household who had committed highway robbery and confessed, was known to be still waiting at table. There are a good number of other similar instances and some even of the culprits being hanged. A commentator in the later years of Henry VIII's reign suggested that the committing of felonious deeds, particularly the turning to robbery on the part of retainers, was because it was not uncommon for men to be retained without wages.[74] Here again is indication that in the sixteenth century retainers might be regarded as no more than servants, but whether the incidence of serious offences committed by retainers correlated positively with their decline in social status is impossible to determine.

What we do have from the same period is a particularly instructive example of how an upper-class household could harbour felonious followers and how the master of that household, cognizant of their criminal activity, would go to lengths to protect them. It also demonstrates how maintenance in its most brazen form was still practised in the 1530s. The lord in question was Sir Giles Strangways, whose land lay in Dorset and Somerset. An information of c. 1539 stated that three or four of his servants, intimates who waited on him in his chamber, had been robbing poor men on the highway and in their houses.[75] One of these, a notorious rogue named James Ferrer who was reported to have committed highway robbery at Christmas 1528, was taken before the council where he confessed. He was sentenced to death (presumably in a common law court) but his master got him a pardon.[76] The other suspects refused to confess and continued in Strangways' service. Another of his servants named William Sampson, who was indicted five times of 'sundry felonies', Sir Giles was able to get acquitted. We are told there were 'dyvers other mo fellonies by his sarvauntes and other persons commyttyd' which showed he was a 'gret berer agaynst the kynges lawys' and the cause of 'miche perjurie . . . in that shire'. Of considerable interest is the fact that Sir Giles was concerned about how the county viewed the reputation of his servants. The information reveals that after a local robbery he enquired of an acquaintance about what rumour there was in the county concerning his servants and was told tersely 'A lewd rule and trim'. This seems to have prompted him to pay to the victim out of his own pocket a sum of money equal to the amount stolen, which suggests he had few illusions about the honesty of the members of his household. Strangways had no difficulty in getting his friends, gentlemen who were under his 'riule and commanddement', placed on grand juries so that, even when the accusers were able to point out the miscreant at the assize or quarter sessions, no indictment would be found. Nor is there reference to his dismissing any of those accused from his service. Indeed, when he himself was robbed by a servant named Brynabell he got him indicted; but at the sessions he deliberately failed to appear in order to give evidence and thus the accused was acquitted. It would probably be incorrect to suggest that Sir Giles encouraged his servants directly to indulge in felonious activity. They appear to have been eager to benefit themselves rather than their master. Very likely he was in a quandary which faced many of the upper classes in the fifteenth and sixteenth centuries: the need to have around him able-bodied men for use in the land wars but an inability to keep close control over their behaviour 'off duty'.

We have seen elsewhere that the land wars, which sprang from bastard feudalism, resulted in the perpetration of very few serious crimes (that is to say felonies) by the participants. Yet might it not have been, we may ask, that the land wars, with the riotous and menacing behaviour on the part of the retainers and other participants, were so damaging to public order through the harassment of those whose duty it was to maintain it that offences of the truly criminal sort, for example homicide and serious larceny, perpetrated by the population at large, increased? The answer seems to be that the incidence of felony rather than rising in the fifteenth century was in general and substantial decline. In Yorkshire between 1300 and 1348 there was an average of about 114 persons arraigned before the king's justices of gaol delivery for felony each year, whereas between 1439 and 1460 the average was no more than about twenty-eight. In Norfolk between 1300 and the Black Death those similarly charged with felony averaged about seventy-eight per year but in the 1430s the number was around thirty-four. There is no reason for thinking that the machinery for producing accusations was failing in the fifteenth century, nor that the definitions of what was felony were altering.[77] Of course the several visitations of plague in the eighty years subsequent to 1348 caused a great decline in population, but not one of such a magnitude that it would explain the tremendous fall in felony charges. The proper explanation could well be that the decline was caused by the notable improvement in the fifteenth century in the lot of the lower classes, which reduced the need to thieve and rob merely in order to exist. What then ought we to make of felons like James Ferrer who were to be found in the retinues and households of the upper classes? The answer must surely be that they were there to handle what are euphemistically called 'heavy' duties. They probably served as their masters' 'enforcers', whose threatening presence was called for when stubborn tenants had to be brought into line, when debts had to be collected, and when hostile witnesses and jurors had to be spoken to. No gentleman would want to employ many such men since they might additionally commit crimes to profit themselves alone, misdeeds unconnected with their master's feuds which could be very embarrassing. Thus, on the grounds of their small numbers we may conclude that they were not likely to have affected the incidence of felony to any marked degree.

Chapter Five

THE SEARCH FOR ROYAL FAVOUR

For the member of the upper classes, who in the land wars was unable to take or keep what he took to be rightfully his on account of the power his opponent wielded in that part of the country, it was an attractive strategy to seek to outflank him by gaining support at the highest level, that is to say from the king, the ultimate source of good lordship. Those who might roar like lions in their own locality were not necessarily influential at Court as everyone knew. Furthermore, royal favour shifted periodically and the king, if approached in the right manner, might be ready to do a powerful man a bad turn and the supplicant a good one. Magnatial rank did not necessarily ensure royal sympathy against an adversary of meaner status.

To supplicate to the king usually meant to go to Court. In essence, the Court was the social side of the activities of the king's (and the queen's) household in which the high-ranking members of those households were joined by the king's ministers (when present) and by those of the upper classes currently staying in that milieu. The king's household, which in the later fifteenth century probably numbered 500 or 600 persons holding positions, provided for the daily necessities of the king and the Court in the form of sustenance and valeting. Periodically the English kings issued ordinances to regulate their households, as for example in 1318, 1445, 1471–2, 1526, and 1604.[1] The intention was to define the duties of all those who held posts there, to set a total establishment in order to eliminate the tendency for numbers continually to increase, and to ensure all departments accounted with the countinghouse. Although we might hope to find in the ordinances information which would throw light on the functioning of the Court in the period under review, in fact they provide relatively few insights because they deal primarily with household affairs 'below stairs' and not with upper-class life in and around the royal chamber. By the early fourteenth century, the chamber was where the king withdrew to dine and thus where he spent most of his time. The prime importance of the chamber in the Court life of the fifteenth century is demonstrated by reference in the Black Book of Edward IV's reign to the 'inner' and the 'utter' chamber, the former being, no doubt, what was commonly called the privy chamber under the Tudors.[2]

Those who held appointments in the inner or privy chamber were of major importance in the functioning of the Court. Technically they were members of the household, which had in addition another role of importance. Persons of the upper classes who came to Court and stayed for any length of time sought not infrequently to obtain for their servants room and rations there beyond what was allowed, an abuse which was indeed one of the causes of the formulation of the household ordinances. These were full of references to *bouche au court*, as it was known, the lodging allowance of bread, wine, clothing, and fuel.[3] Those at Court who held important offices, the king's ministers, used the household in another way. William de la Pole, duke of Suffolk, when dominant at the Court of Henry VI in the later 1440s, found household posts of the superior type for many of his own retinue. Thomas Cromwell in the 1530s staffed the privy chamber with men he chose himself. Robert Dudley, earl of Leicester, when a leading favourite of Elizabeth I, so a contemporary if hostile commentator tells us, was careful to ensure that all those with positions in the privy chamber were his own creatures. Furthermore, doubtless in order to give additional strength to his influence with the queen, he interfered in appointments and promotions at lower levels in the royal household. Into vacant 'roumes', as positions were called, he thrust 'any person whatsoever so he like his inclination or feele his rewarde', even if the appointee was unfit for the post and had not held what was regarded as a suitable preparatory appointment in that milieu.[4] Favourites and ministers were not alone in searching for posts in the upper levels of the royal household. By the late sixteenth century, and probably much earlier, there was considerable competition among sections of the upper classes to secure positions for their sons as clerks to the officers of the Green-cloth. The aim of these young men, so we are told, was then 'to rise in preferment in being sworne our Clerkes in Household'.[5]

In addition to the royal family, members of the household, favourites, and certain of those who held great offices of the kingdom, there were present at Court a good number of other persons whom history knows simply as 'courtiers'. These were members of the upper classes, but whether they came to Court as they thought fit or needed some form of invitation or approval is unclear.[6] We do know that on occasion they might be told their attendance was no longer required. Perhaps it is best to regard them as suppliants, who visited Court in order to offer the king their services, a polite way of indicating they wanted him to grant them favour, usually a financial one. Since it was the right of every person in England to petition the king if the opportunity presented itself, and the obvious inconvenience this would cause at Court if large numbers of the lower classes came for that purpose, there must have been a screening process to keep out undesirable suitors. Indeed in 1594 a system of licensing by masters of requests was proposed, incorporating a stipulation that suitors should leave the Court as soon as they received an answer.[7] Those of the upper classes who visited the Court to supplicate the king claimed in their correspondence to be 'waiting on' or 'attending on' him. What we cannot tell is if those who undertook this exercise had any prior intimation, either from the king himself or more probably from a third party, that the time was propitious for the would-be suppliant to come to Court. Perhaps it was hinted to him that his offence might soon be forgiven him, or his known quest for payment or property acceded to. Such a change in fortune for the interested party would probably be caused by a shift, perhaps only slight, in the political scene occasioned, for example, by the rise of a patron in Court circles or by a relative achieving a household office.[8]

Whatever brought the suppliant of gentle blood to Court he was rarely going to gain success in his quest overnight. After the verdict had gone against them in their case in the court of the exchequer in 14 Elizabeth I, Lord Henry Berkeley and his wife 'all the year after . . . kept London and the Court as petitioners for pardon' of part of what had been adjudged against them. In 1539 or 1540 Henry Willoughby, son and heir of Sir John Willoughby, mentioned in a letter that he had 'gyffen attendaunce at the courte this terme for the space of vii weekes. And I do truste too opteyne sume thyng of the kyngis grace this next terme of Candylmes'. There were times when the king was on the move, but this did not stop the giving of attendance by an eager supplicant. In October 1475 Sir John Paston, who hoped to obtain a letter in his favour from Edward IV, was advised by his brother 'to awayte on the Kyng all the wey . . .' to Walsingham.[9] What 'attendance on' and 'waiting on' amounted to in the Court environment is never indicated. Maybe the supplicant assisted the king's personal servants in dressing him, bringing him food and drink, carrying his messages around the Court and so forth, but this supposes the supplicant was allowed into the recesses of the chamber which would require high rank. Perhaps it was sufficient simply to be one of the throng always about the monarch, thereby, as was the belief of the times, adding to the royal glory.[10]

Frequently the seeker of a favour at Court must have found the path of supplication was a difficult one. To achieve a meeting face to face with the monarch was fraught with difficulty, as the second John Paston discovered on his first visit to the Court of Edward IV.[11] This was because access to the king was not there for the asking but under fairly strict control. Although those who could provide such access might seem on the face of it to have been the gentlemen who served the king in his chamber, the decision must not infrequently have been made by a chief minister or leading favourite, whose clients the chamber gentlemen sometimes were. It was they who were in a position to monopolize the king's giving of favour. At the Court of Elizabeth I, so we are told, Robert Dudley, earl of Leicester, maintained a 'reign' that was absolute in the privy chamber and in other parts of the Court. No bill, supplication, or complaint could even go to the queen without his approval; it was said 'no sute can prevaile . . . except he first be made acquainted therwith and receive not onlie the thankes but also be admitted unto a great part of the gaine and commoditie therof'. Leicester made the excuse that the queen was parsimonious and 'very difficile to graunt anie sute were it not onlie upon his incessant solicitation', but few got the opportunity of testing this statement by making their own approach to the queen. Although Leicester was perhaps not quite the typical ascendant adviser to a monarch of this period, the situation where a powerful minister or courtier, or a small allied group of the same, had fairly good control of access to the monarch must have been a common one. The occasions when the king had in his chamber personal servants loyal to himself exclusively must have been rare, for few monarchs possessed the necessary stamina, skill in ruling, and dominant personality to be able to do without close advisers; and these, in order to preserve their position, would try to see to it early in their period of ascendancy that the servants in close proximity to the king were, or became, their own clients.

Many supplicants for royal favour must have recognized the difficulty of getting to meet the monarch face to face and planned their tactics accordingly. They seem to have decided that intermediaries were the solution. A connection through a blood relationship with anyone in the upper levels of the king's household was probably seen as being a particularly promising route. In August 1461 the second John Paston on his arrival at Court contacted John Wykes, a cousin of his father's, who was usher of the king's chamber. Wykes apparently promised Paston he could and would take him to meet the king, but he never fulfilled his promise. In November 1479 the third John Paston planned to supplicate to the king through the good offices of Sir George Brown, his uncle, whose job it was to 'wayte most upon the Kyng, and lye nyghtly in hys chamber'. In 1450 John Payn, servant of Sir John Fastolf, was saved from execution by the intercession of his cousins who were yeomen of the Crown and obtained a pardon from the king himself for him.[13] If lacking well-placed relatives, the supplicant must find other intermediaries to speak with the king, persons either high in social status or having a post which provided the holder with everyday proximity to him. The second John Paston in the summer of 1461 tried to get the earl of Essex, the treasurer of England, to speak on his behalf to King Edward. He told his father that everyday he had laboured the earl to move the king concerning the manor of Dedham, over which the Pastons were embroiled with the duke of Suffolk. On the other hand Godfrey Greene, servant of Sir William Plumpton, mentions in a letter of c. 1475 how he was instructed by his master to labour to Sir John Pilkington, a knight of the body, so he might in turn approach the duke of Gloucester or the king himself over the keepership of Knaresborough castle.[14] In general the Pastons appear to have preferred to seek the intercession of persons high on the social scale, particularly if they had a close connection, familial or by the nature of an office held, with the monarch. In June 1469 the third John Paston reported to his brother Sir John that he had been busy labouring three members of the queen's family, Earl

Rivers, Lord Scales, and Sir John Woodville, and also Thomas Wingfield 'and othyr abowt the Kyng'. Rivers had promised that he would move the king to speak to the dukes of Norfolk and Suffolk and tell them not to claim title to land which had been Sir John Fastolf's. In November 1479 the third John Paston informed his mother he was planning to use the lord chamberlain to enlist the support of Bishop Morton of Ely with the intent of their getting the king 'to take my servyse and my quarrell to gedyrs'.[15]

How did one approach an intermediary who was to assist in getting the desired favour? Probably it was very much in the same way as when the approach was directly to the putative benefactor himself. The supplicant with or without his servants 'waited upon' the intermediary showing a willingness to do him service. If the intermediary promised assistance there might still have to be a series of reminders. When the second John Paston was labouring the earl of Essex to speak to Edward IV about Dedham manor and the duke of Suffolk, he spoke to him every day before the earl went to the king, 'and often tymys inqueryd of hym and he had mevyd the Kyng in these matyers'. Essex always answered that he had not but Paston 'lawberyd to hym contynually' and prayed Barronners hys man to remembyr hym of it'. Barronners told Paston that his father, the first John, 'must nedys do sum wate for my Lord and hys' and suggested that it might take the form of paying back the sum of money he owed to 'a jantylman of Estsexe called Dyrward, seyying that ther is a myche be wern [between] my seyd Lord and the seyd jantylman of the wyche mony he desieryth your part'. The mention by the second John Paston of his making use of Essex's 'man', Barronners, is probably of considerable significance. Sir William Stonor, in April 1481, was told as though it were a matter of some importance, that the Marquess of Dorset's servants reported him to be, when he had been attending on their master, the most courteous knight they had ever known. Richard Germyn, Stonor's correspondent, made another important comment about Sir William's relationship with Dorset. It was not simply his attendance which made him 'the grettist man with my lord, and in his consaite'. It was also because of a gift he had made: 'because of your hors geven'.[16]

The making of gifts to intermediaries by parties seeking favours was probably a common occurrence. Little could be accomplished around the Court without free spending, as the second John Paston

must have discovered in 1461. His father was told in August of that
year that although his son was 'well in acqueyntaunce and be lovyd
with jentilmen aboute the Kyng' he might be handicapped by his
father's failure to provide him with sufficient money. Without it he
could not 'reasonably spende among hem' and as a result they
would not sit by him.[17] This was a form of hospitality, a necessary
business expense as we say nowadays. The practice of giving direct
reward of a calculated value to those who would further one's search
for favour and profit from the king must also have been prevalent.
The extant correspondence of Sir John Gates provides some very
clear examples of this from the years 1542–6. Gates, a page of the
wardrobe of robes from 1537 and from 1542 a groom of the privy
chamber, received requests for assistance in the procuring of a wide
range of material benefits. Among the things he was asked to obtain
by intercession with the king were offices such as the customership
of Bridgewater and the deanery of Peterborough, the farmership of
a benefice, licences such as for the export of cheese wey, the
purchase of lead and of religious land, as well as the success of mere
'honest suits' whose nature the beseecher would define after Gates
had agreed to the size of the payment for his services.[18] In almost
every instance the requester offered a reward which was substantial.
A tun of Gascon wine, a dozen of kersy cloth, were promised by
two suitors. 'Your friendship herein I will consider with 100 marks
sterling', said another. This sum was matched in a similar instance,
while on another occasion Gates was promised 20 marks a year.
Gates may have had a weakness for horses since one correspondent
offered him £20 'to buy a nag' while another had apparently sent
a similar amount at the time he made his request: 'I trust the horse
you had of me proves good,' he wrote. Only one correspondent
whose letter survives failed to offer Gates a substantial *douceur* and
that was his own sister, who sent a bracelet of silk saying she was
sorry it was not of gold.[19]

In most of the cases mentioned Gates was expected to 'move the
king', as it was put, by speaking with him. One of the supplicants,
we notice, admitted to having already tried to gain the favour
required from the king by a direct approach on his own part. He
had failed despite one of his attempts having had the backing of
the chancellor. Two supplicants sent bills on behalf of third parties
for which Gates was asked to obtain the king's signature. Another
supplicant assumed that Gates's position as a gentleman of the

privy chamber was so important that he could personally bring about the desired end simply by speaking with the party in question himself and therefore that there was no need to bring the king into it at all.[20] How Gates was expected to broach these requests to the monarch, how he was actually to phrase the supplication, we are not usually told, but in two instances the correspondents themselves suggested tactics which they felt would assist in obtaining royal approval. The supplicant who wished to purchase land from the Crown made it clear that he was willing to pay as much as 100 marks (much more than the normal entry fine) to ensure that the king viewed his request with favour. He suggested to Gates, doubtless as information to be passed on to the king, that the lands in question were 'mean things, incapable of improvement, and . . . were it not that they lie intermingled with my own lands I would never require them'. There was another letter to Gates in a similar vein. It shows how those who knew Henry VIII reckoned it was wise to ask for nothing as a gift pure and simple but to offer hard cash; also, if seeking land near one's own, to explain that it was desired because of proximity which provided convenience in administration or because it rounded off the supplicant's estates.[21] There is no reference in Gates's correspondence to him being offered a percentage of the value of the grant or office he was to request from the king but the practice certainly existed in the sixteenth century. It may have derived from the device of earlier centuries whereby one party enfeoffed a great man of part of the land at issue prior to the commencement of a land war.[22]

A good number of those who sought Gates's intercession must have been courtiers, persons who spent extended periods in proximity to the king, although they probably did not hold an office which compelled them to do so. They were hardly there for good company or simply to encourage the king in his rule. Often they were at Court as part of an extended campaign to profit themselves or their clients by acquiring offices or grants of other sorts, developing connections with the powerful, or marrying off their children. In essence a courtier was one who was waging a war of supplication and for this there was a manner of behaviour, which, if adopted, would make success the more likely. It might be imagined that a smooth tongue, the ability to flatter, was the talent which was all important. At the Court of Elizabeth I it was indeed reckoned a profitable practice to commend everything the queen did, yet in most reigns flattery does not seem to have been regarded as an absolute essential. Modesty in a courtier's speech was of little value, as was skill in rhetoric. On the other hand boldness of conversation and suppleness and quickness of mind, 'ingenuity' as it was called, were reckoned great assets.[23] These qualities, if they were combined with a handsomeness of person, would go a long way towards producing the arrogance of attitude which was of great value amongst other courtiers and no handicap when in the presence of the king himself. Few courtiers can have been persons of humble mien and without the facility of making astringent responses. Also held in high esteem at Court was bearing, physical deportment of a particular sort. Generally admired was the ability to be neat and nimble when providing services, like attending on the king in his chamber; so too were fine manners, which were taken as proof of being brought up in a magnate's household. No yeoman's son, it was reckoned, because he would lack the bearing and the courtesy, was suited to be a servant in a nobleman's household.[24] Athletic ability was also highly regarded. Skill at dancing drew appreciative comments from Elizabeth I. Robert Dudley, Earl of Leicester, was proud of his expertise at 'stoball', and Henry VIII clearly admired those who were good archers.[25] The most prestigious skill, however, was horsemanship and its application to the hunt and warfare, particularly the latter. Until the later sixteenth century there were opportunities to demonstrate one's mastery of the dexterities of war (upper-class warfare of course) by participation in tournaments and performance in the tilt yard, where horsemanship, strength, technique with weapons, and sheer nerve could be evaluated by knowledgeable onlookers. The risk of injury, serious injury, was always high and thus the degree of glory for the successful participant the greater. Willingness to go on military expeditions was usually greatly valued by the monarch and any success in that milieu a fairly sure way of gaining royal favour, at least for a time.[26]

By the sixteenth century theatrical, musical, and writing skills were recognized as being beneficial in gaining attention and winning prestige at Court, even as they were at the lesser level of the nobleman's household. The esquires of the king's household were expected in afternoons and evenings, for the purpose of occupying the Court and entertaining strangers, 'to draw to lords' chambers within the court, there to keep honest company after their cunning in talking of chronicles of kings and other policies or in piping, or harping, singing . . .'.[27] Castiglione's *Il Cortegiano*, translated by Sir Thomas Hoby in 1561, advised courtiers to study famous poets and write verse themselves. If in fact the royal household was similar in this respect to those of prominent noblemen, and surely it was, then a good number of those who served the monarch must have possessed skills in music. A list dating from 1538 of the marquess of Exeter's servants, including his gentlemen, gentlewomen, yeomen and grooms, shows that it was thought meritorious (and worthy of recording) in that household to play well on musical instruments such as the viol, lute, harp, or virginals, to 'sing properly in three-man songs', or to teach music.[28]

One way to be certain of gaining the king's attention, and indeed his confidence, was to be in a position to provide gratification for his sexual whims. This might be done by bringing to the king's notice an attractive woman belonging to the courtier's own family and encouraging his interest in her and hers in him. It was a rare woman, whatever her marital status, who refused the king's advances and a rarer man who took offence at the sexual liaison between the king and his wife or daughter. A courtier might bring to the king's attention an attractive woman who had no familial connection with him, and he might become engaged in arranging times and places when she could meet with the king. Such a role, what medieval Englishmen identified as that of the 'common bawde', may have been what Sir Thomas More had in mind when he noted that Elizabeth Woodville, Edward IV's queen, disliked William, Lord Hastings because he was 'secretly familiar with the king in wanton company'. Dominic Mancini tells us further that Hastings and the queen's own sons by her earlier marriage, the marquess of Dorset and Sir Richard Grey, together with her brother Sir Edward Woodville, were the leading 'promoters and companions' of Edward IV's vices.[29]

Traditionally the king sought the company of his nobility to hear their counsel, although in any period few who came to provide counsel can have received tangible reward or gained favour for so doing. He also affected to believe that having members of the upper classes around him kept him in touch with what was happening in the shires, but again providing such information would bring little profit for the attenders. The times when the king had the greatest need of the upper classes were when he was threatened by invasion or rebellion, or was about to undertake a campaign on foreign soil, and required military assistance; yet neither could he do without them on ceremonial occasions. These were when he felt the need to impress foreign dignitaries by giving demonstration of the wealth of his subjects of gentle blood as well as of their loyalty. Such events were costly for the attenders. Lord Henry Berkeley and his wife were commanded by Queen Elizabeth in 1581 to be present at Court for the visit of the duke of Alençon. Their attendance lasted thirteen weeks and cost them the very substantial sum of £2,500; it brought them no material advantage or favour.[30] This must have been a fairly common experience. To bring a campaign of supplication for a favour of any size to a successful conclusion it was of only marginal use to prove one's loyalty, to provide the king with the support that others of similar rank did, or even to have superior manners and social accomplishments. It was foolish for a male courtier to hope to become the king's personal friend, for those he acquired in his youth or early manhood, but there was sometimes the chance of marriage with a female relative of the king or queen.[31] Given the right circumstances a supplicant might be able to move the king by claiming the public weal demanded he intercede to prevent feud or the collapse of public order in a locality. There was a much greater chance of success, however, if the supplicant, either through an intermediary or in his own person, could interest the monarch in a scheme which, while gaining the supplicant the assent he required, also profited the king financially, provided him with a political advantage or alternative policy, or, at the very least, improved his image and prestige. Such private deals with the king, for such in fact is what they amounted to, were by far the best route to success in the search of favour.

As an example of what prompted men of the upper classes to go to Court in their search to gain advantage over local rivals, and the pitfalls, expenses, and profits this avenue led them to, the career of Sir John Paston (1442–79) is worthy of close study. He is perhaps the only person of the period whose Court experiences can be reconstructed in any detail. The founder of the Paston family's fortunes was William Paston (1378–1444), a judge of common pleas, but advancement beyond the social level of the squirarchy was the result of services undertaken on behalf of Sir John Fastolf in his declining years by William's eldest son, the first John Paston. John, whose wife Margaret was a cousin of Fastolf, was rewarded by being made chief beneficiary in the knight's last will and chief executor of the same in addition.[32] Given the relatively turbulent times and the first John Paston's hitherto modest social position, it was obviously going to be difficult for him to hold on to the property he had acquired so fortunately but he set about the task with dexterity and determination. He seems to have decided to present a higher profile, perhaps prompted by a belief that predators would be more hesitant about attacking a person with more than a local reputation. Paston refused knighthood but sat as a knight of the shire in the Parliaments which met in October 1460 and November 1461.[33] Between these two sessions, early June 1461, the duke of Norfolk occupied Caister castle, the most desirable property Paston had inherited from Fastolf, and almost at the same time the former appeared at Court, two events which cannot have been without a connection, although we are not told if Paston made supplication to the king or his council for remedy. Despite what must have been a disastrous blow to his pride and pocket, he sought friendly relations with the dispossessor by placing his second son (the third John) in the duke's service.[34] The third John served with Norfolk in the campaign in the northern counties of 1462–4, and was mentioned as a servant of his household in October 1465. He remained a servant of the duke for most of the time until the latter's death, despite the Pastons being engaged in a feud with the duke over Caister.[35]

On 27 July 1461 the first John Paston and his co-executor Thomas Howes were granted a payment of 1,200 marks in return for handing over to Edward IV jewels pledged by his father, the duke of York, to Fastolf. There can have been no option for Paston here but the completion of this piece of intimate business would have brought him to the king's notice for certain. By late August of the same year Paston had sent to Court his eldest son, the second John Paston (later to be Sir John Paston), intending perhaps he might obtain a position in the king's household.[36] There he could maintain a watch over his father's interests, seek out a suitable patron amongst those highly placed, and supplicate to the king through his intercession. The second John sought assiduously to get the earl of Essex, treasurer of England, to speak with the king on his father's behalf but Essex was not to become his patron. John's uncle reported that his nephew was unable to find success at Court because he was not bold enough. It was also suggested that he might meet with more success if his father were to allow him more money. How long the eldest Paston son stayed at this time in the environment of the king's household cannot be determined with any accuracy. All we can glean is that, despite warnings by those who knew the Court that to bring him home might be taken as an insult by the king or alternatively give the appearance that he was no longer *persona grata* at Court, he was back home by January 1463.[37]

Despite this, the second John Paston had found life in the king's entourage to his liking and intended to go back. In May 1464 he joined King Edward on his expedition to the north-east, and after his father's death (May 1466) he was at Court frequently. There he became a friend of Anthony Woodville, Lord Scales, the brother-in-law of the king, which must have been the key to the acceptance in royal circles for which he had been searching. He was invited in April 1467 to a tournament at Eltham where he fought on the same side as Scales and the king, a signal honour and testimony to his skill at arms. In 1469 Paston consolidated the connection with Scales by becoming engaged to his cousin, Anne Hawte. He was soon grateful for Scales' support, for John and his brother the third John, rather surprisingly, fought on the Lancastrian side at Barnet in April 1471; Scales it was who interceded to obtain pardons for them.[38] The explanation of their desertion of the Yorkist cause is probably to be found in their continuing struggle with the duke of Norfolk to hold on to Caister castle. The duke had seized it once more from the Pastons in September 1469, and by October 1470 the second John had become a client of the earl of Oxford, a staunch supporter of the house of Lancaster, who was believed to have a hold over Norfolk. Furthermore, Oxford promised the second John (who had been Sir John from 1463) the constableship of Norwich castle.[39]

What we know of Sir John's career to this point suggests that, in contrast with his father, he had the open-handedness and the assurance of the truly privileged, the noble class. He possessed the skills and graces which that group admired and in good measure. He was accomplished in the use of arms and the handling of horses; he was at his ease on military expeditions and when travelling abroad. He was very much at his ease in female company and, judging by his badinage with the duchess of Norfolk, able to jest with social superiors of the opposite sex without giving offence. He seems to have been athletically handsome, and a friend said that he was the best chooser of a gentlewoman he ever knew, which suggests that he was, in nineteenth-century jargon, a 'womanizer'. Sir John also possessed a considerable library and had a book containing chivalric treatises compiled for him. He appears to have had the type of literary interests which would be a definite asset in the Court environment.[40] These were qualities and interests which would have drawn him towards the Court of Edward IV even if his father had not sent him there. Persons with the personality traits which Sir John possessed often incline towards extraversion and seek a life of style and individual prominence. To them external appearances matter a great deal, while the pettifogging detail and matters of small moment, which clutter everyday existence, are often thought by them unworthy of persistent and serious attention.

Yet despite what appear from the Paston correspondence to be weaknesses of character, Sir John's career was no disaster to the fortunes of his family, as the last seven or eight years of his life were to prove. Historians have tended to ascribe any improvement in his family's circumstances to sheer luck, yet the case can be made that Sir John's strategy was by no means unsound and that his execution of it was commendable. The year which saw Edward IV's triumphant return from exile found Sir John and his brother the third John fighting on the losing side at the battle of Barnet, and thus being forced to purchase a pardon for their palpable treason. Although the pardons themselves may not have cost a great deal, regaining possession of one's lands, technically forfeit through opposing the king in battle, could be expensive. In the years which followed, Margaret Paston, Sir John's penny-conscious mother, complained bitterly about the family's shortage of cash for paying off its debts and her eldest son's plans to remedy the situation, but he was seemingly not moved.[41] From 1472 Sir John appears to have been a client of William, Lord Hastings, whose prestige at Court was rising steadily. Hastings was lieutenant of Calais and may have been responsible for the employment of Paston on a mission to the Court of Burgundy at Ghent early in 1473. In January 1475 Sir John took steps to enlarge his retinue, bought himself a new horse and harness, and visited the Burgundian army then besieging Neuss in the archbishopric of Cologne, though in what capacity is unclear. As part of the forces stationed at Calais he and his younger brothers may have served in Edward IV's expedition into France in the summer of 1475, and Sir John travelled with Hastings to Calais in March 1476.[42]

While engaged in the military life in this period Sir John Paston found time to supplicate, either in person or through others, to the duke and duchess of Norfolk, the duke's council, and even to members of the Norfolk household, to remind them of his grievance over Caister.[43] According to the third John Paston, the council of the duke accepted the validity of his brother's claim to Caister, but knowing it could not get its master to see reason its members hinted that the Pastons ought to get some great man to put pressure on him. Sir John's attempt to enter Parliament in 1472 may have been an effort to achieve such an alliance, or at least to provide a *point d'appui* to petition the king or his council. At about the same time the two Paston brothers comforted themselves with the belief that they had secured the support of the duchess of Norfolk in their quest. The younger of the pair visited her at Framlingham, and the duchess, who was pregnant, expressed the hope that Margaret Paston would be with at her forthcoming confinement. Sir John made a further major effort at supplication but in another direction. Either by the impressive nature of his military service, or by means of astute lobbying, he was able to remind the king of his grievance over Caister even during the campaign in France in 1475. As King Edward returned from the expedition he spoke with the duke of Norfolk, who had accompanied him, telling him to take the advice of his legal counsel over Caister 'and to be sywer that hys tytle be goode', for if he did not do the right thing by Paston he would lose royal favour.[44]

There was no satisfactory result from this royal intervention and therefore in October 1475 the third John Paston told his elder brother that he ought to get letters from the king to each of the members of Norfolk's council telling them how the king had brought up the matter of Caister with the duke when they were overseas that summer, and how the latter had promised to discuss it with them. They must see to it that such discussion occurred and then certify the result to the king. The younger Paston also advised his brother to 'awayte on the Kyng all the wey' on his forthcoming journey to Walsingham. Towards the end of the month the Pastons were beginning to force the issue and the third John told the duchess bluntly that he would do the duke no more service, although he was apparently ready soon after to suggest to his mother she should be attendant on the duchess at the forthcoming birth. As it turned out, the need to put pressure on the duke came to an end at the beginning of 1476 when he died. Sir John, on receiving news of Norfolk's demise, immediately made a technical entry into Caister regretting only that he had not heard of the duke's expected death before the event. If he had, he might have entered earlier and avoided the danger of *descent cast* jeopardizing his claim. In the event it did not matter since the question of title to Caister was settled before the king's council. There, late in May 1476, wrote Sir John, 'alle the Lordes, Juges, and Serjauntes . . . affermyd my title goode'. 'Item, blissed be God, I have Castre at my will. God holde it better than it doone her to foore', so reads a letter he sent to his brother at the end of June.[45]

Had the struggle been worth it? The most frequently expressed view has been that a feckless Sir John had beggared himself to hold on to a property which was too magnificent for a man of his station. A better interpretation is that he could not do otherwise. To surrender Caister without a fight would be the signal for all those with remote, even fraudulent, claims to the erstwhile Fastolf lands to try to seize them. Others might be encouraged to seek to recover other Paston property. Overmatched, Sir John conducted his campaign against the duke of Norfolk not in the county but at Court. It was the only sensible option open to him, because there was no uncommitted nobleman with sufficient influence in East Anglia to whom he could turn for effective assistance. The earl of Oxford may have provided a little indirectly on occasions but he never intervened in the Norfolk land wars to any effect. The duke of Suffolk laid claim to the ex-Fastolf manors of Hellesdon and Drayton in April 1465 and was thus a second major foe for the Pastons to face. Fortunately the two ducal families never made an alliance against them.[46]

When a member of the upper classes was subjected to claims on his lands by a dangerous and more powerful rival, or if he needed the support of such a party to further his own territorial ambitions, the proper tactic was for him to buy support by enfeoffing such parties in part of the property in dispute. Although there is no letter in the Paston correspondence which actually comments on the matter, Sir John appears to have been trying to buy off the duke of Norfolk in October 1467 when he granted him the manor of Henmales in Cotton, but unfortunately for Paston the duke wanted something more substantial.[47] Despite their relatively meagre holdings of land in Norfolk and Suffolk, Sir John appears to have been angling for the support of Queen Elizabeth and others of the Woodville family when in March 1469 he gave the free chapel at Caister to her chaplain Master John Yotton. By this time Paston was an associate and probably even a friend of Anthony Woodville, Lord Scales, and by April 1469 at the latest he was engaged to his relative, Anne Hawte. No marriage resulted however, and there must be some suspicion that Sir John used the arrangement to get assistance from Scales against the duke of Norfolk. The Pastons' adherence to the Lancastrian cause in 1470–1 may have prevented the marriage, but the alliance with the Woodvilles was restored in July 1471 and probably continued until Sir John's death in 1479, for it was rumoured in May 1478 that he 'shuld mary rygth nygth of the Qwenys blood'. The success of Sir John Paston's alliances with the nobility and the social stature he had acquired are attested to in the same letter for his mother noted that it was reported that the eldest son might 'do as meche with the Kyng, as any knygth that is longyng to the corte'. This rise in Sir John's influence and weight in political circles seems to be reflected in his litigation against the duke of Suffolk over title to the manors of Hellesdon and Drayton at this time. Sir John showed no trepidation about the outcome of the suit; indeed he was confident. Suffolk, on the other hand, appears to have been rather desperate. He offered to meet Paston in individual combat and declared that he would have to be killed before the latter would get the two manors. Margaret Paston, a persistent pessimist where her eldest son's land wars were concerned, was confident that he would win the suit even though his adversary was a duke.[48] All the signs are, then, that had not Sir John died at the age of thirty-seven or thereabouts in November 1479 he might well have risen to greater heights of favour and acquired royal offices which would have recompensed him for his financial outlay in the years preceding. We may conclude, therefore, that the Court-based strategy of Sir John met with a good measure of success.

The king's role at this time as the receiver of supplications is full of interest, yet historians have told us very little about it.[49] Virtually everywhere the king went in the fourteenth century he must have been exposed to those who wanted to request a favour of him either by word of mouth or by pressing a written petition in his hand. His withdrawal for part of the day to the recesses of the inner chamber in the fifteenth century must have been prompted, at least in part, by the desire to avoid much of such supplication. Another way of placing some sort of control on petitioning in the Court environment was to limit it to a particular hour of the day and to a particular location. Stow, the Elizabethan chronicler, tells us that Henry V, like his father Henry IV, after dinner on days 'when no state was kept', had a cushion put on a cupboard where he placed himself for an hour or more 'to receive bils and heare complaints of whomsoever would come'. Whether the need for such control ceased when the king made his withdrawal into the inner chamber later in the century is not clear. There is some evidence that supplicants expected that the vital access to the king would necessitate careful planning and considerable waiting. Thus the monks of Christ Church, Canterbury, had an intermediary at Court whose job it was to lie in wait to catch the king in his leisure moments in order to get his signature on a grant. There may well have been a relatively greater number of opportunities to seek favour of the king when he was travelling about the kingdom on business. William Paston, uncle of Sir John, seems to have found the opportunity to speak to Edward IV in June 1469 concerning his nephew's quarrel with the duke of Norfolk when the king was at a sessions of oyer and terminer.[50]

The opportunity to supplicate to the king, infrequent as it must have been for all except ministers, favourites, and the gentlemen who served the monarch in his privy chamber, was sometimes of no great benefit to the petitioner if the king was not in an amenable mood, something all those with experience around the Court were well aware of. The seeker of favour or his intermediary, if he knew his business, was careful therefore to make his move only when he had sure information that the king was currently of a giving or forgiving disposition. To lighten the burden for the king, it was wise for the supplicant to have his request in written form, and preferably already counter-signed by officials who might be affected should it be granted. The second John Paston, in August 1461, when supplicating over the manor of Dedham, presented a bill into which his father had incorporated a copy of a section of the court roll of that manor, no doubt to show that the Paston family or its servants had held the sessions there.[51] Petitions delivered in person to the monarch in the later Middle Ages seem to have been shaped much as were parliamentary petitions, that is to say phrased so that when approved they provided the relief or advancement required without

further process. If we judge by what is written in the Paston correspondence, a king was capable of taking a great deal of interest in
what the petitioner said and proffered to him. Edward IV is a
prime example. He seems to have enjoyed contact with his people
more than most monarchs, as his personal appearances in the king's
bench and other courts testify. He had, furthermore, a good memory
for names, where land was, and to whom it belonged. Because he
was interested in a suit, he visited the scene of a destructive riot
three and a half years after the event.[52] Like Henry V, Edward took
it as one of his chief duties to try to compose feuds among the upper
classes, which was what in essence a large number of petitions were
about. Not infrequently the king must have found it politic to do
nothing about the petition he had received. There is a reference to
Edward IV actually agreeing to a request by a supplicant for the
repayment of 400 marks owed him by the Crown but no further
satisfaction being given; it must always have been difficult to extract
hard cash from the king. The monarch in the fifteenth century, as
in the sixteenth, was more likely to agree to, and act on, a supplication where he could see some benefit accruing to himself or where
there was at least the certainty that it would not put him out of
pocket, a fact which was recognized by supplicants. For example,
when in 1479 the third John Paston asked Sir John to obtain from
the king for their younger brother Edmund the wardship of John
Clippesby, he suggested that their intermediary Sir George Brown
might point out to the king that the grant would cost him very little
in income, since the child could not have the land during the lifetime
of his mother who was still young.[53]

Should the king receive a petition from someone of relatively
modest rank against the misbehaviour of a magnate he would not
ignore it out of favour to the nobility, nor yet, if we judge by Edward
IV, go to the other extreme of immediately disciplining the great
man. Early in 1475 Sir John Paston used John Morton, master of
the rolls, and Sir Thomas Montgomery, knight of the body, as
intermediaries in his suit to King Edward to get the duke of Norfolk
to restore Caister to him. The account of the third John Paston as
to what then happened is revealing. The king, he says, himself
asked Norfolk what he was going to do about Caister, but the duke
would not answer. Edward then asked Sir William Brandon, one
of Norfolk's affinity, who was present, what his lord was intending,
reminding him that he had asked him to bring the matter to the

duke's attention on an earlier occasion. Brandon answered that he had indeed done so; and when Edward pressed him as to what the duke had answered he was told that he had said, 'the Kyng shold as soone have hys lyff as that place'. When Edward asked him if this was true the duke admitted it was. Edward, we are told, 'seyd not a woord ayen but tornyd hys bak, and went hys wey'. However, added Paston, the duchess of Norfolk had told him that had the king spoken to her husband about the matter again the duke 'wold not have seyd hym nay'.[54] That the king was unable to have his way in this confrontation with one of his nobles is at first sight surprising but much less so on further consideration. The crucial feature of this case was that it concerned title to land and everyone knew the king could not deprive a man of his land unless he had been convicted of felony or treason. When kings were petitioned over title to land they would often suggest a treaty, or that the matter should go to the courts or the council. What seems to have happened in the Caister case was that Edward IV had become personally convinced of the rightfulness of Sir John Paston's cause and therefore took it upon himself to hint to Norfolk he should listen to good legal advice, which would inevitably be that his claim was legally indefensible. When rebuffed, the king could only let the duke understand that his future requests for favour would be unsuccessful, which by itself would have been sufficient to bring most magnates to heel since those members of the upper classes known to be out of royal favour were likely to begin to lose more than their fair share of cases in the courts.

To manoeuvre in search of the king's favour as did Sir John Paston in the 1460s and 1470s cannot have been uncommon in fifteenth-century England, although comparable examples are denied us by the failure of contemporary correspondence to survive. Very likely the same scheming was practised extensively in the fourteenth century also, and even earlier. The royal household in the fourteenth century, although less sophisticated, appears to have operated according to the same principles as prevailed later on, and local politics with their factions, feuds, and land-hungry upper classes were essentially of the same substance as in the sixteenth century, the period from which most examples of supplicatory manoeuvring have usually been drawn by historians. As to their outcome, what we are reminded of by Sir John Paston's machinations is that the king, when his interest and favour were won, would dare to interfere in the processes of the common law only very rarely. All he might do, and all the supplicant probably expected him to do, was either to reproach the magnate or faction which was said to be the cause of mischief, or to entertain and settle the issues before his council where decisions might be arrived at through consideration of political as well as legal factors.

Chapter Six

THE END OF BASTARD FEUDALISM

If we judge by the number of times the offences which were part of bastard feudalism appear in court records it seems incontestable that that type of society continued to flourish well into the Stuart period. Illegal retaining, as we have seen, was a not uncommon occurrence in the later years of Elizabeth I. Star Chamber records of the first year of the queen's reign suggest that some 7 per cent of the cases which came before that court involved riot and as many as 38 per cent forcible entry. In the regnal year 1601–2 riot cases made up about 14 per cent of business, forcible entry cases 12 per cent, and those concerned with maintenance over 4 per cent.[1] In the Star Chamber of James I one quarter of offences charged were of the conspiratorial-maintenance-embracery-subornation variety and 37 per cent involved riot, unlawful assembly, or forcible entry. Only in the 1620s and 1630s may this high proportion of bastard feudalism cases have shown a marked decline.[2] The records of common law courts might easily be regarded as confirming this picture of longevity. Quarter sessions files of the last part of the sixteenth century show indictments of forcible entry and riot virtually every time the courts met, and sometimes in substantial numbers. Between 1575 and 1589 the Wiltshire justices of the peace had before them over 150 persons charged with one offence or the other.[3]

Despite the number of cases, we must doubt whether forcible entry, for example, in the late sixteenth century was as dangerous to society as it had been fifty years earlier. Those persons indicted at the Wiltshire quarter sessions were largely husbandmen, artisans, or yeomen; there were few gentlemen. They do not look like those who practised the same crime in the fifteenth century or even in

Henry VIII's time, although it is by no means impossible that the entrants were sometimes acting on the instructions of a local person of importance, as seems to have occurred on several occasions in Elizabethan Essex. The trivial nature of the threat which these entries posed for public order is shown by the small size of the fines imposed, mostly of no more than a few shillings. The nature of the forcible entries and riots which figure in later Elizabethan and in Jacobean Star Chamber records may well have been similar. In 1626, Bishop Williams, the lord keeper, commented how in ancient times the diet of that court was all 'battayles and ryottes soe outragious whereas now wee here not of one in our age'. This implies that large numbers of participants, extensive damage and taking of chattels, and actual fighting were virtually unknown by that time.[4]

Even in the reign of Elizabeth I the most notorious examples of riot and forcible entry showed much hesitancy and restraint. At the 'very great' riot at Drayton Bassett, Staffordshire, in October 1578, in which as many as 7,000 men were reported to have been involved, there was only a single death, which seems quite remarkable considering the entrants into the manor were only driven out by cannon fire after five days in possession. Another notable riot of the Elizabethan period, one which was 'such as has not been heard of in the Queen's time', was caused by Lord Dudley distraining 300 sheep, his adversary Littleton replevying them, and Dudley then rescuing them with 400 of his tenants and allies. This was not an event which could have caused comment a century earlier. Even the most violently inclined among the upper classes of the later sixteenth century were hesitant in using force to further their land feuds. Such hotheads as Henry Clinton, earl of Lincoln, and Sir Edward Dymoke never progressed as far as a physical confrontation, despite the former constructing a watch-hut and manning it with a garrison in order to interfere with agriculture on Dymoke's estates, and despite the structure being destroyed by the Dymoke faction. Later the earl sought to provoke bloodshed by insulting Dymoke at Horncastle fair and he planned to destroy the latter's house in the same town, even, so it was noted, if it meant a fine in the Star Chamber.[5] Here is revealed to us the sheer pusillanimity of the land 'war' at the end of Elizabeth's reign. Only in the extreme north of England does it seem that there occurred situations which resembled the late-medieval land war reasonably closely.

The limited nature of the later sixteenth century land war's violence was probably the result of several developments. There was, for example, a much greater likelihood of conviction in the courts for a criminal offence than ever before. Furthermore, the law of homicide was in a state of flux and the periphery of murder was extending. It was quite possible that where death resulted from a riot an inadvertent party might be charged with murder, or if all of one faction in a riot resolved to slay the opposition and one rioter did commit a killing, then all might be tried for murder.[6] In the middle years of the sixteenth century noblemen responsible for the deaths of others, but who had not done the killing themselves, were found guilty of murder and executed.[7] The rise towards the end of the century of duelling suggests that followers were becoming reluctant to do the dirty work and assault the upper-class adversaries of their master; he must now fend for himself.[8] The effect of these changes can only have been to make men more circumspect and less hearty in quarrels over land.

A vital if undramatic constituent element in bastard feudalism had always been maintenance, the support of a suit in which the supporter had no technical share. This was usually done, as we have seen, by bringing pressure to bear on the juries or the officials involved in the doing of justice. There was also a variety of subtler moves: witnesses might be detained, records of preliminary proceedings or verdicts stolen, 'evidences' forged, and sheriffs' bailiffs or undersheriffs bribed. The elimination of maintenance appears to have taken considerably longer to achieve than the violence associated with upper-class riot and forcible entry. If we judge by Star Chamber business, the campaign was still being waged hotly in the 1620s and 1630s. Indeed at that time the volume of maintenance cases was increasing, which is further indication of the decline of the more violent approach to quarrels over land and a rise in legal manoeuvre and chicanery. Bishop Williams noted that in his day the Star Chamber spent most of its time dealing with 'conspiracy and barratry', the first of which usually amounted to plotting to affect the outcome of a case and the second to persistent maintenance.[9] Despite the longevity of maintenance, and to a lesser degree of retaining, we cannot doubt that most of the danger to good government and public order associated with bastard feudalism had been dissipated by the end of the sixteenth century.

There is on the other hand evidence that bastard feudalism was still in vigorous health in several parts of England in the reign of

Henry VIII and that the forcible entries and riots then committed were in their nature very much the boisterous crimes of the upper classes which had plagued the fifteenth century. Thus, in Yorkshire in around 1530, Sir William Gascoign was accused of inciting his followers to kill one who had brought an action against him, which they nearly achieved, and at a later date, when the latter tried to complain to the justices of the peace, Sir William rode to the sessions with 100 retainers to frighten the adversary away. We are told that Sir William was 'of suche power and strengthe in those parties and hathe the moste parte of the comen jurors in those parties an othere meytenours and oppressours of your subjects in his retinue, bache, lyvery and unlawfull confederacy and is hymeself at every Sessions of the peace and there causith all such as displeysith hyme, be it ryht or wronge, to be inditted'. In 1525 Sir Richard Sacheverell's feud with Thomas Grey, marquess of Dorset, disturbed the Leicestershire assizes and quarter sessions. It was declared that Sacheverell's attendance there was disruptive of business and court order: he came with a company of 100 or more so that 'he ruleth the whole court'.[10] These instances of interference with the doing of justice in a direct manner, that is to say by threat of force or actual use therefore, to say nothing of the employment of criminal prosecution against one's private enemies, are very reminiscent of land-war episodes of the mid-fourteenth century and indeed of those celebrated in late medieval history. For the moment we are in the world of *Gamelyn*. The large size of the retinues, the men well-armed and armoured and on horseback, with the magnate in person at their head, were all features of the high age of bastard feudalism.

In seeking to understand the decline of bastard feudalism it is necessary to pay particular attention to the reign of Henry VII. This monarch and his advisers, we cannot doubt, made a great and continuous effort to control the evils attendant on that system, although whether the king himself was the master-mind behind the campaign, or whether a particular officer like, for example, James Hobart, was, is not clear.[11] The goverment's drive against bastard feudalism took the form of a series of attacks on several fronts. What these had in common was the utilization of legal procedures which were not in accord with the traditional methods of the criminal side of the common law, although there was little that was entirely novel. Thus the statute 11 Hen. VII c. 3 allowed charges against rioters, those retaining or giving livery illegally, embracers, and maintainers to be brought in the form of informations, that is to say accusations verbal or written and not necessarily by the party injured, which did not necessitate an appearance in court and which might in some circumstances provide the delator of the successful information with a share of any property forfeited. The employment of an informer as an instrument in the enforcement of the criminal law was not at all uncommon in the later Middle Ages, although it was rarely stipulated or permitted in regard to offences of the bastard feudalism variety. The Act 8 Edw. IV c. 2, however, had allowed information to be laid against those breaking the laws against illegal livery-giving and retaining, and before a wide variety of justices. There had also been three statutes (28 Edw. I c. 11, 7 Hen. IV c. 14, 8 Hen. VI c. 16) permitting penal law procedure (which was frequently, but by no means always, associated with informing) against livery-giving and corrupt jurors, and another (8 Hen. VII c. 9) permitting it against entry into land and the forcible holding thereof. [12]

The provisions of the statute 11 Hen. VII c. 3 in the area of illegal liveries and retaining were extended by 19 Hen. VII c. 14. Instead of the laying of information and the trial being before justices of the peace or of assize, the delator, under the Act of 1504, was offered the more grandiose prospect of going before the chancellor and the keeper of the seal in the Star Chamber, or before the king's bench, or council. Those he accused were to be summoned by subpoena and tried either by examination or by normal common law practice. The informer might be allowed costs, a reward, and half of any forfeiture, which was not an unattractive proposition. This was an Act, furthermore, which in regard to proceedings before trial at least, circumvented all the normal common law apparatus. In section five the statute empowered justices of the peace to examine those suspected of retaining illegally or being so retained, and allowed the certificate of their findings, if condemnatory, to amount in law to a conviction in the case of the person retained or as an indictment in the case of the person retaining. In this way it was like its companion statute 19 Hen. VII c. 13, which provided that where a jury could not find forcible entry of maintenance or embracery a sheriff's certificate to that effect would provide an instant conviction. These procedures were not a total novelty in the field. Trial by examination had been permitted by the Act 8 Hen. VI c. 4 for those suspected of giving livery illegally. Even earlier the statute 13 Hen. IV c. 7 had allowed justices of the peace to convict those whom they personally observed in riot by mere record, while in other circumstances their certificate describing events was to serve as an indictment. The statute 19 Hen. VII c. 14 stipulated the use of another reinforcement of criminal procedure. This was that chief constables and bailiffs of hundreds should give evidence on oath to the grand jurors in support of charges laid. It was the first time such a requirement appeared in a statute.[13]

Another device intended to make criminal procedure in regard to one of the offences characteristic of bastard feudalism more summary was introduced by the statute 11 Hen. VII c. 7. It was stipulated that those against whom there had been complaint of riot should be told by proclamation by justices of the peace to appear to answer at the next general sessions or stand convicted. There was to be no need for an indictment and a trial. Possibly the Act derived from 13 Hen. IV c. 7 which had decreed that failure to appear within a certain time before the council or in the king's bench would result in automatic conviction; or from 2 Hen. V st. 1 c. 9, which in regard to both felonies and riots allowed the chancellor to issue writs of proclamation for appearance on pain of conviction; or from 8 Hen. VI c. 14, which made failure to appear in king's bench on a set day carry automatic conviction. A radical development in criminal law of another kind was introduced in a statute of the first parliament of Henry VII's reign. This Act, 1 Hen. VII c. 7, was intended to discourage an activity frequently associated with land wars, namely destructive or provocative hunting on an adversary's land and specifically when the hunter operated in disguise.[14] Accusation was to be by information to justices of the peace or to the council, who were to order arrest and then examine the suspects. If the latter admitted guilt the crime was to be rated as a misdemeanour, as indeed it normally was, but should the accused deny it and refuse to name associates then the offence was to be classed as a felony. This was a remarkable statute. There had been nothing quite like it in the criminal law of England, although there had been petitions in Parliament in the Lancastrian period seeking the classification of particular instances of murder and other felonies as treason, and since Edward I's time rape had been divided into two types, the trespass variety and the felony.[15] Perhaps the drafters had in mind the great riot Act of 1411, which provided that when rioters refused to admit their guilt before the council they were to be tried in the king's bench. The novelties in procedure under the criminal law and the way experimental devices embodied in earlier legislation were refurbished and developed, many of them having the closest connection with bastard feudalism, made Henry VII's reign nothing short of revolutionary and it is quite remarkable that this has gone unnoticed.[16]

The most notorious of the alterations made to the criminal law by Henry VII and his advisers, although not deservedly so, was probably the establishing by an Act of 1487 (3 Hen. VII c. 1) of a court comprising two judges, two or three principal officers of state, and a bishop and a lord of council, who were to hear bills and informations on a wide range of offences relating to bastard feudalism, that is to say concerned with retaining, livery, mainten-ance, embracery, riot, and corrupt behaviour by sheriffs in regard to empanelling jurors. The intention behind the setting up of this conciliar court, tribunal, or committee may well have been to avoid having to use the council proper because of the long-standing oppo-sition to the practice of entertaining there accusations which were not indictments or presentments nor private actions begun by orig-inal writ.[17] The design must also have been, where specifics of procedure were involved, to make special use of the relatively new form of accusation, the information, and to ensure the appearance of those reported by a method disliked but doubtless effective, the writs of privy seal and subpoena. Normal common law process was to be eschewed since all too frequently it was subject to the inter-ference of feuding parties. After 1495 some cases which might earlier have gone before this court were probably heard by the justices of assize and of the peace under the statute 11 Hen. VII c. 3, whose concern with the same categories of crime and similar reliance on information we have noticed above. After 1504, under the Act 19 Hen. VII c. 14, those cases relating to livery and retaining probably went to the king's bench, council, or before the chancellor and the keeper of the seal.

By a statute promulgated in the parliament of 1495, 11 Hen. VII c. 25, another court to be served by distinguished judges was established to deal with an area of crime closely connected with bastard feudalism which the 1487 Act omitted, namely the juror or official who behaved corruptly through his perjury, as it was put. This court also, being in the conciliar mould, was to employ trial by means of examination. The very few records of cases which survive suggest that as with the court established in 1487 the preferred method of accusation was by information, the delator being the attorney-general. When it was that these two courts ceased to operate is unclear although 11 Hen. VII c. 25 was intended to be in operation only until the next parliament. Bayne, in his study of the council, argued that the last case for which we have record evidence came before the 1487 court in 1504, but that the wording of the statute 21 Hen. VIII c. 20, which in its opening section rehearsed and affirmed 3 Hen. VII c. 1, could be taken to indicate that the court still functioned in 1529. Another view is that the court had not operated from some point in Henry VII's reign and that the legislation of 1529 was merely an attempt to resuscitate it.[18]

The use of procedures alien to the common law, or at least not a traditional part of it, appears to have aroused considerable criticism and hostility by the end of the reign of Henry VII, as we have noticed in an earlier chapter. This was true whether the offences investigated were connected with bastard feudalism or not, for there were by this time a good number of statutes which allowed the bringing of information in regard to other categories of offences. The outcry in 1509–10 was probably directed in the main against the laying of information, the form of charge the upper classes had the least chance of stifling, but the Act 19 Hen. VII c. 14 may have also been disliked because it permitted suspects to be summoned by subpoena before the chancellor, the council, or the justices, without even information or suit. This statute expired automatically in 1509 and was not renewed; 11 Hen. VII c. 3 was annulled by statute in Henry VIII's first parliament (1 Hen. VIII c. 6). The fact that the court established by 3 Hen. VII c. 1 was intended to proceed against persons accused by information as well as by bill lends support to the theory that it did not function in Henry VIII's reign. These statutes, or at least the machinery they introduced, were centrepieces of the new criminal law edifice which Henry VII had erected. When they were gone, the Crown had to change its methods.

In the years immediately subsequent to Henry VIII's accession, the procedural options of the criminal law by which the complex of offences related to bastard feudalism could be attacked were limited. Still in operation were medieval statutes like 15 Ric. II c. 2, 2 Hen. IV c. 21, and 13 Hen. IV c. 7, which provided conviction by record for forcible entry, riot, and illegal livery but only so long as justices of the peace reached the scene of the crime while the offenders were still misbehaving. There was also 8 Edw. IV c. 2, which provided for information about livery and retaining offences (and even allowed conviction by examination) but into the common law courts.[19] Otherwise the Crown had to rely on juries of indictment to provide charges in the traditional way. Whether these could produce the results which reward-induced informations to the chancellor or to the king's council (and the ex-officio summoning of suspects) had done must have seemed doubtful. The government of Henry VIII decided, apparently, to place much of its reliance on the council, but not however the council operating as a court of criminal justice. The council was not to concern itself directly with offences of maintenance, embracery, illegal livery-giving or retaining. It could not do so because the government was now very hesitant about using the information method of obtaining charges there. Instead, it resorted to the encouragement of party suits, and these in fact totally dominated conciliar business. Extant records provide reference to only nine cases which were not party suits for the whole period when Wolsey was chancellor and presiding judge.[20] Of course the party suing might complain of maintenance, embracery, perjury, riot, or forcible entry, but each was a private complaint and danger to the king or commonwealth was no part of it. The inducement for the party to sue was his own self-interest, whereas the informer, in theory at least, was acting to benefit the king as well as himself. What was lacking from the Crown's viewpoint from the last years of Henry VII was what might be called a 'rex side' conciliar court along the lines of that established by 3 Hen. VII c. 1. This strange deficiency in the English judicial system seems only to have been noticed, or at least commented on, by Coke, who at the end of the sixteenth century argued that all private suits in the Star Chamber ought to be regarded as informations for the queen.[21]

The cases which came before Wolsey's Star Chamber concerned mainly assault, the carrying-off of goods and persons, ouster from land, and forcible entry. Claim to land was the underlying cause in the vast majority and indeed they are best categorized as land-war crimes. There were also a small number of cases where the suer's complaint was about corrupt courts or officials. It was a common practice for the complainant to aver the offence had been committed 'riotously'. This was the traditional way of bringing the case within the council's jurisdiction but most of the misdeeds were committed in circumstances which made them technically riots as well as being assaults, forcible entries, abductions and the like. Riot, it will be remembered, was where more than two people came together intending to do something against the law and then at least one must have actually executed a deed to that purpose. It was essentially a misdemeanour committed by a band of persons, and it was no accident the word 'riot' should have begun to appear in statutes at the same time as the combination of the use with the will became popular and land wars became recognized as a major problem.[22] Regardless of whatever mischiefs complainants alleged had befallen them, the cases which the Star Chamber handled in the earlier sixteenth century appear to divide into two main categories. There were those where the essence of the suit was title to land and there were the others. In Wolsey's time as chancellor apparently about 40 per cent of the cases heard fell into the 'title' category, and when Sir Thomas More was chancellor about 44 per cent.[23] In a bill about title the complainant would explain his claim to a particular piece of property before he alleged the offence; in a non-title suit the complainant identified his status and habitation but then plunged straight into a description of the misdemeanour. The non-title suits were most frequently about assault but abduction, asportation, and corrupt behaviour by those with official responsibility in administering the law also figured. Why this type of complainant brought his suit into the Star Chamber we can only speculate.[24] It may well have been because he had a better chance of obtaining satisfaction both in the gaining of the verdict and the execution of the judgment;[25] furthermore, as the sixteenth century progressed the Star Chamber showed itself increasingly willing to award damages.

The suit in Star Chamber concerning title was not frequent throughout the whole sixteenth century. Its high period was the years before the reign of Elizabeth. From the early 1550s the government seems to have sought to exclude it although without total success.[26] The term 'title' may be something of a misnomer. Those who brought these suits do not seem to have believed that a decree by the Star Chamber could necessarily provide them with seisin and an unimpeachable title. Their expectations were smaller. They wanted quickly to be put back into possession of the land from which they had been ousted so that they could draw the profits from the agriculture or rents from their tenants. It may well have been like bringing an action of novel disseisin at the end of the twelfth century: if successful there would have been restoration, but a final decision on title must depend on an action of right, or in the sixteenth century a suit in the common law courts. Most suitors no doubt hoped a favourable judgment in Star Chamber would give them possession of the land claimed for an extended period, but they probably expected to be involved in an action over the same land in a court of common law in the future if they were not already. In such a suit they hoped that the decree in the Star Chamber validating their claim would be of some value towards winning. We should notice, however, in regard to Star Chamber decrees that, like awards by arbitrators, they might embody decisions on a number of matters on which the parties differed and not necessarily all in favour of the same party. In this way they were quite distinct from judgments given in common law suits which followed jury verdict on a single point of law, the issue, and which made one party a total winner and the other an absolute loser.

The importance of the role of the Star Chamber in reducing the land wars of the early sixteenth century can be demonstrated not only by recognizing its ability to decide title in an efficient manner but also by studying the complainants in this category of suits and their legal relationship to the land which was involved. It was perhaps only about a third of those suing over possession of land who claimed seisin. The remainder were *cestui que usent* (5 to 10 per cent of complainants over title), lessees (about 40 per cent), and a small number of copyholders and tenants in tail.[27] What these holders of land, apart from the last, had in common was tenure that was relatively insecure. The *cestui que use*, often a person of superior social status, was in a particularly vulnerable position. In order to devise land as he thought fit, to avoid feudal obligations, execution of debts, and possible forfeiture to the crown for great offences, the feoffor as *cestui* had to divest himself of seisin. But thereby he also deprived himself of much of the protection of the common law. He could not, for example, if an adversary entered the land of which he now enjoyed the use, have resort to an action of trespass, forcible entry, or novel disseisin, the methods normally used against intruders, because title had been vested in the feoffees to uses. It is not unlikely that the phenomenon of the land war, so prominent in the English social scene from the late fourteenth century onwards, was fuelled to no inconsiderable degree by the restricted legal options available to the *cestui que use* to defend the property of which he was the user. Such limitations must have encouraged the adversary to enter on the *cestui*. So indeed did the very nature of a use. The fact that a *cestui*'s land was held by shadowy feoffees, whose identity his adversary could not discover (which was necessary if the latter wished to bring a suit at common law), might well provoke him out of sheer frustration to enter and expel.[28] Thus the *cestui que use*, and his enemy also on occasion, was very ready to seek remedy outside the courts of common law; he did so primarily by means of a suit in the Star Chamber. When it was exactly the council began to entertain the complaints of the *cestui que use* may never been ascertained, but the practice was flourishing in Henry VII's reign.

Of the other recognizable categories of complainants besides *cestui que usent* in Star Chamber cases which hinged on title, copyholders were relative newcomers to the land wars. They were involved in a modest 3 or 4 per cent. Although by the late fifteenth century they may have been manipulated or used by the parties at feud, they were not a basic element in bastard feudalism and therefore they are omitted from the argument here. On the other hand lessees, or termors as the law called them, who had become numerous by the early fifteenth century, were involved in a large proportion of Star Chamber business. Like the *cestui que use* the lessee was unable to employ the legal actions to protect his tenure which a person with seisin could. If he was entered on, all he could do under the common law was to sue on the covenant in the lease or, in the late fifteenth century, bring an action of ejectment. The fifteenth-century action of ejectment, however, had very distinct limitations: it could not recover the ousted lessee's term for him, and it was designed for use against the lessor. Only from about 1530 could it be employed with success against a stranger, but it gave no security against an entrant who was a freeholder with good title.[29] The lessee therefore of the late fifteenth or early sixteenth century who was entered on was very much attracted to the Star Chamber in order to regain possession of his land. Since a good percentage of lessees were persons of considerable wealth, we can see that the Star Chamber of Henry VII and Henry VIII, in providing them with legal remedy, was making a notable contribution towards the elimination of land wars and the evils of bastard feudalism.

Among the suits involving uses which came before the council in the Star Chamber in the reigns of Henry VII and Henry VIII were a number where the plaintiff described himself as the establisher of what may be called an entailed use or use in tail. This meant X would enfeoff Y to his (X's) use and that of his heirs, although there were instances where X enfeoffed Y and his heirs to the use of X and his heirs, a perpetuity only likely to fail through lack of heirs or the dishonesty of Y or his line. The result was a *cestui que use* who was a tenant in tail, or a tenant in tail who was a *cestui* and protected from the financial burden of feudal obligations. The Crown cannot have failed to recognize the use in tail could deprive it of the feudal perquisites attendant on succession not just for one turn but forever. Such a device must have contributed in no small measure to the government's rising hostility in the 1520s to the employment of uses in general. St German held that uses were responsible for 'unquietness and trouble' in society but particularly so were uses in tail.[30] Whether this was primarily because of the entail element (next heirs were frequently tempted to enter in retaliation for what they took to be alienation of entailed property on the part of the tenant), or the use element (uses, as we have seen, made for a relatively impotent *cestui* at common law when entry occurred), or the combination of the two is not evident.

Governmental hostility to uses manifested itself first in the statute 4 Hen. VII c. 17, 'an act against fraudulent feoffments tending to defraud the king of his wards', which affirmed the Statute of Marlborough (1267) and stipulated that a *cestui que use* must declare a will if he was to save his under-age heir from the feudal incidents occasioned by his death. Government policy in the 1520s, so it seems, was to assert through its lawyers that the use had never been part of the common law.[31] This was a difficult position to maintain in light of the Acts 1 Ric. III c. 1 and 4 Hen. VII c. 17, and it meant a reversal of the Crown's earlier attitude, although it appears to have tried to disguise the fact by referring to the collusion and conspiratorial nature of many enfeoffments to uses.[32] When eventually a suitable case arose where the Crown's lawyers could argue to that effect in court, the escaetorial inquest into the lands of Lord Dacre of the South in January 1534, the jury was persuaded to find covin and collusion to defraud the king of the wardship and marriage of the heir. When Dacre's feoffees traversed the finding in chancery, and then later when the matter was debated by the judges of the two benches in the exchequer chamber, the Crown lawyers shifted their attack and argued rather that a *cestui que use* could not make a will of his lands unless there was a local custom to that effect.[33] This was only accepted by the judges after direct intervention by Thomas Cromwell, and a miscount of opinions by Chancellor Audley.[34] The potential effect of the volte-face, for such it was, was startling. It imperilled all the many instances where the use-will combination had been employed to devise land in the past. The possession of such a potent weapon, it might be argued, must have led Thomas Cromwell to believe that he could press on with his plan to alter the law on uses by means of statute without any fear of violent opposition.

Yet it seems quite likely that Cromwell and the Crown's legal advisers were already confident that they could count on support at large for such a revolutionary move, for there survive several indications of hostility to features of the land law among contemporaries. Christopher St German argued that feoffments to uses defrauded lords of wardships, reliefs, and heriots, and were employed to avoid execution of debts, to put wives out of their dower and widowers out of their tenancy by the curtesy, and to cheat the right heirs. Furthermore, some of them were intended to secure maintenance by the powerful.[35] At the time of the parliamentary session of 1529 a group of nobles agreed to make a concession to the government over wardship and the payment of feudal incidents in regard to land held in their use. Thereby they hoped to obtain for themselves the power to bring actions of right (i.e. of title) against those who took the profits from the land, a very valuable privilege when, because of a use, the title-holder of land to which they laid claim was unknown to them. There was another scheme concocted on behalf of the nobility in 1533 or 1534. It criticized secret entails and uses as great evils because of the difficulties they created for purchasers. It sought the end of entails, except in regard to the property of the nobility, and stipulated all uses should be recorded. It asked that alienation by collusive recovery or fine by tenants in tail should be held to have turned the land involved into fee simple. These two schemes reflected the interests of the upper classes but particularly so those of the most senior members, the heads of families, men eager to see the inheritance descend according to their own design.[36]

Such proposals, which demonstrate how the government was assured of sympathy from a very important section of the national community, provide some explanation as to why Cromwell bullied his way through the Dacre case and then introduced legislation on uses into Parliament. Under the Act 27 Hen VIII c. 10, the beneficiary of the issues from the land held to uses, the *'cestui que use*, was to be deemed to be in lawful seisin. He could thus no longer avoid the feudal obligations of the land owner. No longer could the use-will combination be employed for devising land. In practice the statute abolished the will although it did not forbid the use. Complaint about this last step must have been substantial for in 1540 the government felt obliged to retrace its steps a little. By the statute 32 Hen. VIII c. 1 permission was given for land in socage to be wholly disposed of by written will, and land held by knight service up to the amount of two-thirds, the king to enjoy primer seisin and wardship in regard to the remaining third. There was one other statute from this period which must have greatly affected the land-holding classes. This Act 27 Hen. VIII c. 16 decreed that sales of land were to be enrolled in a king's court of record. Thereby the names of purchasers and sellers would be discoverable and the hostility engendered by the frustration of not knowing whom to sue could be avoided.

Such lessening of the tensions caused by claims to land and the holding of land was very likely the effect of these Henrician statutes overall. For example, when the *cestui que use*, through the so-called execution of the use, was given seisin, he was enabled to bring suits of trespass and forcible entry in the courts of common law and being so protected must have been less attractive as victim in the eyes of the would-be entrant. Purchasers, from 1535, were not likely to discover to their dismay that title to the land they had bought was vested in feoffees. They were less likely, therefore, to become bellicose. Creditors, who could not seek redress against *cestui que usent* under the Act 19 Hen. VII c. 15, must have comfort in the knowledge that execution on judgment of debt and damage could no longer be defeated by a use.[37] Those, who in earlier times had entered into the land occupied by a *cestui* simply because, since he had no title to the land, they could not sue him except under the statutes relating to 'pernors of profit', could now bring an action relating to that land in the courts of common law. Giving that *cestui que use* seisin ended the deceitful practice of secretly enfeoffing to uses in order that adversaries would bring real actions against the wrong person, or have to refrain from bringing them at all; both eventualities had caused much bad blood. It also meant the end of certain aggravations which resulted from the *cestui*, because of his status at law, being unable to take measures necessary for the good economy of the land. Thus he might not seize beasts which someone had put illegally on his ground, nor bring an action of waste when lessees were negligent, or one of account against delinquent bailiffs or farmers; he could not even cut down trees on the land he used. Inability, because of his legal status, to take these necessary steps had not, of course, commonly caused the *cestui* to remain inert. He had driven the beasts of others from the land he used, or impounded them, and had employed direct action such as seizing property against delinquent lessees and bailiffs, but this had given rise to quarrels and even local wars.

The gentry and nobility, who had reason to be upset when they were deprived by the statute 27 Hen VIII c. 10 of the opportunity to provide for their younger children and widows by means of the use and will, were put in better humour in 1540 when they were given the right to dispose of the great part of their land by will alone. The upper classes benefited additionally from the fact that there was nothing against entails in the statutes of uses, wills and enrolments, a means of devising they had traditionally favoured. Furthermore, by another Act passed in the parliamentary session of 1540, 32 Hen. VIII c. 31, covinous and collusive recoveries of land in tail, as distinct from recoveries founded on good title and former right and where the assent of the remaindermen and reversioners had been secured, were to be void. This was a moderate restraint on the alienation of land held in tail, and a reasonable compromise between the wishes of the establisher of the fee tail and those of his successors. Alienation had to be consultative and the assent of parties with a legal interest secured, a position taken also by another statute of the same parliament, 32 Hen. VIII c. 36.[38]

What all the ameliorations to the land law, which were introduced in the period 1535–40, had in common was a potential to lower tensions amongst those who held or had claim to land. They must have reduced the level of frustration and thereby a good deal of the aggression which had been characteristic of problems of property in land during the later Middle Ages. They did so by removing some of the more notorious imbalances and particularly those connected with the enfeoffments to uses, a major cause of much of the entering into land and ousting of opponents which had caused the land wars of the fourteenth and fifteenth centuries. That is not to say that new imbalances in the land law did not appear fairly soon afterwards. Certain types of uses were untouched by the statute of 1535 and the *cestui*'s status was unchanged. There was the use for a period of years, for example, or of copyhold, or of chattels, and the fertile minds of lawyers developed new species, notably the springing use (which came into existence on the occurrence of a particular event) and the shifting use (which shifted from one person to another after a specified occurrence). Both of these last two types gave rise to complaint. Another controversial development in the eyes of many members of the upper classes was the rise of the perpetuity, the theoretical unbreakable settlement of land. This was accomplished by such instruments as the use in tail, which we have already met, or, for example, by establishing an entail with a stipulated penalty for the tenant in tail who would put away the land from the next heir. Both methods were in operation from the outset of the sixteenth century if not earlier but only became widespread after the reign of Henry VIII. They seem to have increased in number during the second half of the sixteenth century and they were not seriously challenged at law before the 1590s when, as in the 1530s, the Crown became concerned about the feudal profits it was losing. In the last years of the century perpetuities were said to be defrauding purchasers and causing factions among kinsfolk.[39]

Yet by that time behavioural patterns in upper-class quarrels over land had altered. Men preferred to make entry into disputed property when they believed it was unoccupied; physical confrontation between followers was avoided. The land wars had become exercises in manoeuvre. Endeavour was directed not towards ouster, assault, and asportation, but towards constructing a sound strategical plan for future litigation. Emphasis was on the deployment of resources within the courts rather than both there and outside. If alteration to the land law in the later years of the reign of Henry VIII was substantially responsible for this change, so also must have been certain measures taken to improve efficiency in the trial of private suits. Of particular importance in this respect was legislation against perjury by witnesses. Witnesses had been employed when the suits of individuals were tried for centuries, but because jurors were reckoned to possess personal knowledge of the circumstances behind the action the rules governing the participation and the legal status of the private giver of testimony remain obscure. Since there is clear reference to sworn witnesses from the early years of Edward IV's reign we may take it that the giving of evidence on oath was not uncommon by the early sixteenth century.[40] However, the important step of establishing penalties for those who suborned sworn witnesses in pleas of land was only taken in 1540, the time of the important changes in the land law. The statute responsible was 32 Hen. VIII c. 9 and it showed in its content that the Crown lawyers thought that suborning witnesses was the most dangerous aspect of unlawful maintenance, the crime which had always been at the very heart of bastard feudalism. Then, by the Act 5 Elizabeth I c. 9 punishment was instituted for the convicted witness-perjuror and even for the witness who, having been paid his travelling expenses, failed to appear in court. Because the Elizabethan statute (which also increased penalties on suborners) was designed to encourage complaint in virtually every legal form, and because every complainant whose charge was successful got half the stipulated fine, the government may have been successful in bringing about the prosecution of a good number of suborners and perjured witnesses. Many of the cases and convictions appear to have been in the Star Chamber. Whereas at the outset of the reign of Elizabethan subornation and perjury cases amounted to under 6 per cent of business in that court, they had arisen to around 17 per cent in the queen's last complete regnal year.[41]

Dealing with the fraudulent deeds, charters, court rolls, and wills, all of which could decisively affect the outcome of a suit over title to land, seems also to have fallen primarily to the Star Chamber.[42] This was another important step in reducing the disruptiveness of quarrels over land taken in the mid-sixteenth century. Under the statute 5 Eliz. I c. 14 complaints of such offences could be made in chancery, king's bench, the exchequer, or the Star Chamber, by suit, bill or information, and the party grieved, if the charge was successful, was to have double costs and damages.[43] At the beginning of Elizabeth's reign such forgery cases had made up about 3 per cent of the Star Chamber calendar, but by the end they comprised 11 per cent and forgery was the fourth most common offence after riot, perjury, and forcible entry.[44] The forgery statute, like 5 Eliz. I c. 9 on subornation and perjury, no doubt gained additional effectiveness through condemning those convicted to the distinctive physical punishment of the pillory and deliberate disfigurement, the severity of which was to vary according to the status of the land at issue. Quite clearly disputed title to land still provoked the strongest of emotions although the open violence of the land war had largely been removed.

We must now shift our focus and set the findings of this enquiry about the end of bastard feudalism into a wider and more political landscape. A central feature of bastard feudalism was dispute over land, and what made that feature a socially disruptive one in the medieval period was the use of juries to settle those disputes in the courts and indeed their use on the criminal side to accuse and convict those involved in the physical conflicts which accompanied the disputes. The phenomena which accompanied the quarrels over land, the forcible entries, the riots, the giving of livery, the taking-on of retainers, were designed in the final instance to affect the verdicts of juries whether these were deciding title to land or the guilt or innocence of persons accused of committing land-war crimes.[45] The aim was to manipulate the law to benefit oneself and damage one's enemies. Thus the evil side of bastard feudalism sprang from the many attempts to control jurors. It was the susceptibility of the jury system to outside interference which was substantially responsible for giving latter-day feudalism a bad name.[46] To combat these disturbing practices the government put its faith, from about the end of the fourteenth century, in statutes which truncated the criminal process against those suspected of riot, forcible entry, illegal retaining and livery-giving by removing the need for indictment in some cases and by permitting summary conviction by magistrates in others. This, of course, raised the likelihood of conviction. In the later fifteenth century this tendency was reinforced by allowing and encouraging accusations about misdemeanours of the bastard feudalism type by means of information laid, a device which was soon strongly associated with the financial benefits of what came to be known as penal law practice.

It was in Henry VII's reign that the greatest efforts were made to control the verdicts of the juries which decided offences in the bastard feudalism category. The Act 11 Hen. VII c. 7 (riots and unlawful assemblies) provided for conviction by mere proclamation of non-appearers; 19 Hen. VII c. 13 (forcible entry) allowed, where a jury failed to convict because of maintenance or embracery, a guilty verdict to be returned simply on the strength of a sheriff's certificate to that effect. A notable feature of this reign was the

establishment, under the statutes 3 Hen. VII c. 1, 11 Hen. VII c.
25, and 19 Hen. VII c. 14, of courts where the judges were to be
men who held high, although not necessarily legal, office. Again
one intention, clearly the major one in one statute but probably so
in the others, was to circumvent the jury and the susceptibility of
the jurors to outside pressure. These courts employed neither jury
of indictment nor petty jury. Trial under 11 Hen. VII c. 25, which
was directed against jurors and officials who behaved corruptly,
was to be before a panel of distinguished office-holders and by
means of examination. The statute 3 Hen. VII c. 1, whose
competence encompassed the whole range of offences of the bastard
feudalism type, was intended to establish a court which did not
employ juries. Charges were to be made by bill or information and
the verdicts or decrees decided on were the conclusions of the
judges.[45] The courts to be employed to enforce 19 Hen. VII c. 14
an Act which was directed against illegal livery and retaining, were
the council, king's bench, or a tribunal comprising the chancellor
and the keeper of the great seal. Before these the defendant accused
was to be examined on oath and might be convicted on the examination as if condemned according to the common law. One of the
courts named, the king's bench, was of course the most senior of
all common law courts and such procedure was quite alien to it. It
can be argued that this establishing of procedure which avoided the
use of juries was not peculiar to offences relating to bastard
feudalism since the labour laws and the statutes against vagabonds
of the late fourteenth and early fifteenth centuries provided somewhat similar machinery. However, the statutes dealing with the
misdemeanours connected with bastard feudalism provided the
most extensive and sophisticated use of truncated procedure, and
indeed that procedure first found full expression in those statutes.
We should remember, furthermore, that they were intended for
application against those who were of considerable social standing
rather than members of the lower and lowest classes.

All this was on the criminal side of the law. Suits over land
throughout the medieval period were settled, unless it was by arbitration, in great part before the courts of the common law and by
decision of jurors. Under Henry VII, maybe even from the time of
Edward IV, it became governmental policy to entertain private
suits more as a matter of course than hitherto before the council.
Most of these concerned land and title to it and were of the essence

of bastard feudalism. Verdicts were given by the judges of the court. When a substantial part of the summary or truncated procedure apparatus had to be abandoned on the death of Henry VII the government was left with only the council, or at least the conciliar courts, where verdict by jurors was not a necessity. Furthermore, because of the outcry against the use of 'information' which occurred in 1509–10, it did not dare to use that method of accusation except in a very small number of cases. The Crown was compelled, as we have noticed elsewhere, to resort to the encouragement of party suits into Star Chamber as support for the relatively ineffective system of indictment and jury trial at the quarter sessions and before oyer and terminer commissions. Yet there were substantial compensations in this. Corrupt behaviour by local officials was less likely because they were less involved than in common law process. The spreading of disorder and the continuation of feuding through any one case was less, because the opportunities for out-of-court settlements and arbitrations were the greater and, as we have seen, the decrees made by the judges were not likely to be entirely in favour of one party.

There must also have been another side to justice in the conciliar courts. It may well have had a political component. Of those who sat in judgment in the council and in Star Chamber under the earlier Tudors, common lawyers were probably a minority. Even those councillors who did not come within that category must, like those who sat with them, have been aware that any two litigants of anything like substantial means who contested a suit before council the government in the form of the king, or if he was not interested then the group which at that time enjoyed his favour, was inclined to favour one rather than the other. Decrees, we may suspect, were quite likely to be more beneficial to the party which had the better connection with those of influence with the king. From the viewpoint of the government, provided this did not bring it into total disrepute, the arrangement was particularly advantageous. Through the justice dispensed in the Star Chamber it could reward the members of one county faction at the expense of its rivals. If this was the scheme of events, and we cannot be certain until Tudor county factions have been identified and their success rates in Star Chamber suits analysed, then those who were determined to sue profitably must have taken careful note of the politics of the Court to see where the royal favour lay. For a suitor to have a powerful 'good lord' within the county who could put pressure on jurors, sheriffs, and bailiffs was, where conciliar suits were concerned, of little value to him unless that magnate was a councillor of the king who held high administrative office. Perhaps this is why historians have been able to detect a rise in the popularity of attendance at Court under the Tudors. The greater volume of conciliar justice in the sixteenth century can thus be considered to have enhanced governmental authority, although not quite in the way an earlier generation of historians imagined.

NOTES

Abbreviated bibliographical references are given in full in the bibliography

INTRODUCTION

1   For example T. F. Tout's *Chapters in Administrative History* (Manchester, 1920–33) and *The English Government at Work, 1327–1336*, ed. J. F. Willard, W. A. Morris, J. F. Strayer, and W. H. Dunham Jr (Cambridge, Mass., 1940–50).

2   The pioneering study here was J. S. Roskell's *The Knights of the Shire for the County Palatine of Lancaster (1377–1460)*, Chetham Society, New Series, 96 (1937).

3   I am drawing here on my own recollections of McFarlane. There is a perceptive appreciation of him by K. J. Leyser in 'K. B. McFarlane', *Proceedings of the British Academy* LXII (1976), 485–506, and critical assessments of his scholarship and its development by J. P. Cooper and G. L. Harriss in their edition of McFarlane's *The Nobility of Later Medieval England* (Oxford, 1973), vi–xxxvii, and by Harriss in McFarlane's *England in the Fifteenth Century* (London, 1981), ix-xxvii.

4   K. B. McFarlane, 'Bastard feudalism', *Bulletin of the Institute of Historical Research*, 20 (1943–5), 161-2; J. P. Cooper, *Lane, Men and Beliefs*, ed. G. E. Aylmer and J. S. Morrill (London, 1983), 248.

5   The impact of the McFarlane school was made the greater by the expansion of university history departments in the later 1950s and early 1960s when it became *de rigueur* to have a late-medieval English historian on the staff.

6   There is one caveat I would enter, however. Whereas the constitutional historians, doubtless as a result of their analytical approach, emphasized the disparate groups in English medieval society, albeit their co-operation within limits, the practitioners of social history in recent years, especially those whose field has been the English nobility, have tended to adopt an organic or 'seamless robe' interpretation of the nation in which division is played down

and law, in the statutory sense at least, viewed as irrelevant to social development. The truth surely lies somewhere between these two attitudes.

7   McFarlane, *The Nobility of Later Medieval England*, 115; *The Collected Papers of Frederic William Maitland*, ed. H. A. L. Fisher (Cambridge, 1911), I, 443.

8   R. C. Palmer, *The Whilton Dispute, 1264–1380: A Social-Legal Study of Dispute Settlement in Medieval England* (Princeton, 1984), 11–13.

9   The author was Robert Pilkington, *c.* 1447–1508, lord of Rivington (Lancs).

10 *The Collected Papers of Frederic William Maitland*, I, 410, 419, 434.

11 D. W. Sutherland, *The Assize of Novel Disseisin* (Oxford, 1973), 121–3, 148–69.

12 This book is a development of the arguments which I advanced in a lecture on 'The gentlemen's wars' delivered on the invitation of Professor James Sweeney in April 1978 at the Pennsylvania State University, University Park, Pennsylvania. The lecture was financially supported by a grant from the Institute for the Arts and Humanities of that university.

CHAPTER ONE SHERIFFS, JUSTICES, AND JURIES

1   Fortescue, 55. By the *Articuli super Cartas* (1300) sheriffs were to be elected by the people of the county. The statute of sheriffs of 1316 changed this to the practice referred to by Fortescue.

2   *Paston*, no. 298; HMC, *Shrewsbury and Talbot*, I, 18; C. E. Long, 'Wild Darell of Littlecote', *Wiltshire Archaeological and Natural History Society Magazine* IV (1857), 219. It has been pointed out recently that England was ill-served by her medieval chroniclers in the matter of internal pressures at the late fourteenth century Court for 'There is an almost unbroken wall of silence': see C. Given Wilson, *The Royal Household and the King's Affinity* (New Haven, Conn., 1986), 260–2.

3   HMC, *Salisbury* VII, 536–7; VIII, 437; XII, 495–7. *Cal. of State Papers*, 579. HMC, *Shrewsbury and Talbot*, II, 101. The *Articuli super Cartas* c. 13, the first piece of legislation on sheriffs' qualifications, stipulated they should not be poor nor disinclined to reside for a time in one place, nor be a cleric.

4   Fitzherbert, fos. 36v.–37.

5   See 2 Edw. III c. 3 and 11 Edw. III c. 14.

6   R. B. Pugh, *Imprisonment in Medieval England* (Cambridge, 1970), 148–9.

7   3 Hen. VII c. 3; 25 Edw. III st. 5 c. 14; 1 Ric III c. 3.

8   Brinklow, HMC, *Various Colls*, II, 33.

9   *Historia . . . Gloucestriae*, III, 289–90. The first law to limit sheriffs in their selection of jurors was the *Articuli super Cartas* c. 9.

10 See HMC, *Various Colls*, II, 51–5; *Plumpton*, 150.

11 See HMC, *Various Colls*, II, 39; *Letters . . . Henry VIII, Addenda, 1509–37*, no. 783; *Plumpton*, 161; Smyth, I, 305.

12 I am referring here to misdemeanours committed by the upper classes and their minions.

13 See J. G. Bellamy, *Criminal Law and Society in Late Medieval and Tudor England* (Gloucester and New York, 1984), ch. 2.

14 23 Edw. III cc. 1–7; 7 Ric. II c. 5.

15 These officials were known as keepers of the peace before 1361. In 1390 the Commons of Parliament were able to secure the nomination of the justices of the peace for one turn: *Rotuli Parl*, III, 279.

16 *Paston*, nos xxxvi, 503; *Gawdy*, 96.

17 Requests by the Commons of Parliament for members of the peace commission to be resident in the country for which they were appointed date from at least 1348: *Rotuli Parl.*, II, 174; *Les Reportes . . . Hawarde*, 21.

18 See *Letters . . . Henry VIII*, X, no. 245; PRO SP 12/17/47.

19 *Cal. of Patent Rolls* and *Letters . . . Henry VIII, passim*; R. L. Storey, 'Lincolnshire and the Wars of the Roses', *Nottingham Mediaeval Studies* XIV (1970), 80.

20 The statute of 1394 was 17 Ric. II c. 10. Sometimes one or two of the peers on the peace commission were regular attenders: see R. B. Goheen, 'Social ideals and social structure: rural Gloucestershire, 1450–1550', *Histoire Sociale/Social History* 24 (1979), 267. By the late sixteenth century there seems to have been little attention paid to legal training in selecting justices of the peace. For a recent discussion on the authority of the justices of the peace in the fourteenth century see E. Powell, 'The administration of criminal justice in late-medieval England. Peace sessions and assizes', in *The Political Context of Law*, ed. R. Eales and D. Sullivan (London, 1987), 49–59.

21 B. H. Putnam, *Early Treatises on the Practice of the Justices of the Peace in the Fifteenth and Sixteenth Centuries* (Oxford, 1924), 328; Lambarde, 87–91. The records of the Wiltshire quarter sessions for Epiphany 1603 show forty-eight recognizances taken out of sessions and seventy taken actually at the sessions: R. W. Merriman, 'Extracts from the Records of the Wiltshire Quarter Sessions', *Wilts. Arch. and Nat. Hist. Soc. Mag.* XXI (1883), 100.

22 Lambarde, 93, 102, 109, 113, 118.

23 *Rotuli Parl.*, III, 84. The wording of the statute 20 Ric. II c. 2 may imply that procedure was to be entirely by examination. The investigation of offences of maintenance, on the other hand, was withheld from the justices of the peace and left to the justices of assize as 4 Edw. III c. 11 and 20 Edw. III c. 6 show. This may have been because maintenance emerged as a dangerous offence in Edward I's reign, before the keepers of the peace were well established.

24 At first 13 Hen. IV c. 7 was not utilized properly (as the wording of 2 Hen. V st.1 c. 8 demonstrates) but plea rolls from later in the century show it in operation.

25 Should the accused admit his guilt he would be punished by council; should he traverse the certificate he was to be tried in king's bench.

26 Lambarde tells us that Chief Justice Huse intended to 'load' the justices of the peace with the operating of the statutes on forcible entry, livery, maintenance, and embracery: Lambarde, 38.

27 It is of course very hard to gauge the incidence of cases where the justices operated in a summary manner. Because of their nature no summary convictions found their way into the plea rolls.

28 The former allowed JPs to receive presentments and informations under the neglected statutes on retainers, liveries, and maintainance. The latter was 3 & 4 Edw. VI c. 5 which dealt with park raiding.

29 B. H. Putnam, *Proceedings before the Justices of the Peace in the Fourteenth and Fifteenth Centuries* (London, 1938), 237–69. The statute 5 Ric. II st. 1 c. 7 was designed in essence to deal with peasants assembling for the purposes of insurrection. It was being misused in 1475.

30 NRO, 24 Hen. VIII; ERO, 15–18. Two of the forcible entry cases in the Norfolk records was specifically under 8 Hen. VI c. 9. The Essex total of fifty-four indictments omits presentments in regard to upkeep of bridges and unlicensed ale sellers.

31 The records of the Staffordshire quarter sessions of Epiphany 1591 show true bills in regard to six cases of forcible entry and one of riot; the Staffordshire Michaelmas sessions of 1586 provide four of forcible entry and one of riot: 'Staffordshire quarter sessions rolls, 1581–97', ed. S. A. H. Burne, *Williams Salt Soc.*, 3rd Series, 1927 (1929), 156–181; ibid. 1930 (1932), 91–9.

32 The statute 11 Hen. VII c. 3, which was only in operation until 1509, allowed the crimes mentioned above that sprang from bastard feudalism to be prosecuted alternatively by means of information with the justices of the peace 'hearing and determining them under penal laws at discretion', that is to say allowing a share of the forfeitures to the informant if successful.

33 Such summary justice, for that is what it amounted to, has for some reason gone unnoticed by historians for the period before Elizabeth I. I have made an initial exploration of the phenomenon, particularly its origins, in my *Criminal Law*, ch. 2.

34 There was 8 Hen. VI c. 9 (defaults of sheriffs in cases involving the forcible holding of land), 8 Edw. IV c. 2 (illegal giving of livery and retaining), 11 Hen. VII c. 3 (riots, illegal retaining, and embracery), 19 Hen. VII c. 14 (illegal livery-giving and retaining), 33 Hen. VIII c. 10 (maintenance and illegal livery-giving), 5 Eliz. c. 9 (perjury), 31 Eliz. c. 9 (forcible entry), 43 Eliz. c. 13 (defaults of sheriffs and clerks of the peace).

35 Probably from 1512. 3 Henry VIII c. 12 stipulated that since substantial persons were being wrongfully indicted by perjured grand jurors all panels of jurors were to be submitted to justices of gaol delivery and justices of the peace at open sessions who might remove those they wished and substitute others. See also Lambarde, 307.

36 Fortescue, 60; Lambarde, 307–8; Hughes and Larkin, II, 351, 495–7; PRO KB 9/262–270A; *William Lambarde and Local Government*, ed. C. Read (Ithaca, NY, 1962), 59.

37 See *Plumpton* cx, 171; HMC, *Salisbury*, V, 288; *Letters . . . Henry VIII*, IV, pt I, no. 681; ibid., *Addenda, 1509–37*, nos 45, 783.

38 Fortescue, 69; More, 993. More, alone of the legal commentators, noticed the connection between crimes related to bastard feudalism and truncated or summary procedure of the type we have referred to. He observed, quite correctly, that it must have been because of the difficulties of indictment that 'the statute' on riot (he probably meant 13 Hen. IV c. 7 but it would also be true of its reinforcers II Hen. VII c. 3 and 19 Hen. VII c. 13) avoided that method of procedure: More, 993. By the sixteenth century grand juries might hear both evidence and witnesses before deciding to pass the bill.

39 *William Lambarde and Local Government*, 120. So did Wilbraham: *Wilbraham*, 20.

40 Putnam, *Early Treatises*, 384; Lambarde, 385; More, 987.

41 *Cal. of Patent Rolls 1416–22*, 266; Lambarde, 405.

42 A. Harding, 'The origins of the crime of conspiracy', *Transactions of the Royal Historical Society*, 5th Series, 33 (1983), 95–7; *Select Cases in the Court of King'sBench*, VII, ed. G. O. Sayles, Selden Society, 88 (1971), 191.

43 13 Edw. I c. 38.

44 See 34 Edw. III c. 8 and 38 Edw. III st. 1 c. 12. Parties might themselves sue jurors taking bribes from adversaries; so might also any other person. Should the latter succeed in his suit he got half of any fine. The party who sued successfully was able to obtain damages. The juror so convicted was put in gaol for a year (34 Edw. III c. 8). 38 Edw. III st. 1 c. 12 made the penalty for the errant juror ten times the amount of the bribe and extended his punishment to the embracer, who was not mentioned in the earlier Act. If either could not pay he was to suffer a year's imprisonment.

45 HMC, *Various Colls*, II, 39; *Paston*, no. 840.

46 Hudson, II, 92–3.

47 35 Hen. VIII c. 6.

48 *Plumpton*, 161; Smyth, I, 321.

49 See HMV, *Various Colls*, II, 39, 42; *Plumpton*, 134; Smith, ed. Alston, 79.

50 Smith, ed. Alston, 111. Robert Pilkington states that he had no chance of securing the attaint of what he believed was a corrupt jury because of the disparity in rank between himself and his opponents: HMC, *Various Colls*, II, 51.

51 Bayne found seven accusations in the extant conciliar records which were brought under 11 Hen. VII c. 25 and four accusations (all instituted by the attorney-general) under 3 Hen. VII c. 1: see Bayne and Dunham, cxvii–cxviii.

52 J. A. Guy, *The Cardinal's Court* (Hassocks, 1977), 53.

53 More, 999; Smith, ed. Alston, 109–10; Hudson, 72.

54 Putnam, *Proceedings*, 73–8.

55 *Britton*, I, 86–95; *Historia Gloucestriae*, III, 289–90.

56 B. H. Putnam, *The Place in Legal History of Sir William Shareshull* (Cambridge, 1950) 52–4, 69–70.

57 The terms of a few commissions of oyer and terminer included such offences as oppressions, extortions, conspiracies, and misprisions: see, for example *Cal. of Patent Rolls, 1452–61*, 388 and *Cal. of Patent Rolls, 1461–7*, 301.

58 J. D. Maddicott, 'Law and lordship: royal justices as retainers in thirteenth and fourteenth-century England', *Past and Present*, Supplement 4 (1978) 40–2, 81.

59 Dudley, 35.

60 *Paston*, nos 513–518.

61 *Political Songs*, 35–6.

62 E. W. Ives, *The Common Lawyers of Pre-Reformation England* (Cambridge, 1983), 310. The reference is to Magdalen College, Oxford, Fastolf MS 42. There is a reference in Fastolf MS 71 m. 3 to Sir John's executors having to pay a court clerk 20d to get him to enter a release in the records: ibid.

63 HMC, *Various Colls*, II, 52.

64 K. B. McFarlane, 'William Worcester, a preliminary survey', *Studies presented to Sir Hilary Jenkinson* (London, 1957), 214; *Paston*, no. 19.

65 *Paston*, nos 159, 513.

66 The letter in *The Paston Letters* which comes closest to referring to overbearing and partial attitudes on the part of judges is no. 158. It tells how at an oyer and terminer session Prisot, chief justice of common pleas, refused to allow any lawyer to speak for the plaintiffs.

CHAPTER TWO THE LAND WARS

1 Smyth, I, 310; *Paston*, no. 395. Between 1413 and 1419 over half the gentry in Warwickshire were involved in litigation: C. Carpenter, 'The Beauchamp affinity: a study of bastard feudalism at work', *English Historical Review*, XCV (1980), 524. Of the eighteen gentry who served as knights of the shire for Staffordshire in Richard II's reign only one (John Delves), a lawyer, did not sue at sometime in his life at the assizes or in the common pleas or the king' bench.

2 L. Stone, *The Crisis of the Aristocracy*, (Oxford), 1965), 241.

3 *Willoughby*, 84; Smyth, I, 115, 336.

4 Thus the assault and the slight were symptoms of hostility already festering if not overt.

5 For example, the duke of Suffolk in the summer of 1465 sought to have Drayton from the first John Paston as the heir of a family, also named de la Pole, who had held it years before: *Paston*, no. 514; Smyth, I, 159. Lord Moleyns, despite what the Pastons had to say, had a genuine claim to Gresham: see PRO C 47/70/79.

6 *Paston*, no. xi. Should documents which might help the cause of your

future opponent in the courts come into your possession, you might well order them to be burned: see Smyth, I, 314.

7   N. E. Saul, *Knights and Esquires: the Gloucestershire Gentry in the Fourteenth Century* (Oxford, 1981), 194–6.

8   B. Coward, *The Stanleys, Lords Stanley, and Earls of Derby, 1385–1672*, Chetham Society, 3rd Series, 30 (1983), 44.

9   On the early history of the use see J. M. W. Bean, *The Decline of English Feudalism, 1215–1540* (Manchester, 1968), 142–74.

10   Thus Margaret Paston referred in her will to 'such londes as I have putte in feffement to accomplish my wille': *Paston*, no. 861.

11   P. Jefferies, 'The medieval use as family law and custom: the Berkshire gentry in the fourteenth and fifteenth centuries', *Southern History*, I (1979), 58, 65.

12   Bean, *The Decline of English Feudalism*, 142.

13   ibid., 172: Bean suggests the chancellor was ready to protect the interests of a dead *cestui que use* by no later than 1420. ibid., 166: it seems that in 1380 the employment of a use was still hazardous for the *cestui que use* since there was 'no general acceptance' his will must be accepted.

14   K. B. McFarlane, *The Nobility of Later Medieval England*, ed. J. P. Cooper and G. L. Harriss (Oxford, 1973), 76.

15   *Paston*, no. xxix.

16   Lesser men were usually loath to sue a nobleman in the courts of common law or even to put a bill into parliament against one, however brazen his wronging of them. They would petition to the lord's legal counsel, or seek to put pressure on the aggressor through the interference of a third party, usually another nobleman: see *Paston*, nos. 255, 766. Men of the fifteenth century felt certain that the litigant who received fees from a magnate was sure to win his suit against an adversary of roughly equal status who did not: ibid., no. 28.

17   Smyth, I, 318; HMC, *Various Colls*, II, 44. Pilkington did not act totally out of loyalty or from sheer good-heartedness. He was also afraid these suits might touch his own rights and freehold.

18   Smyth, I, 313; *Paston*, no. xxx.

19   D. W. Sutherland, *The Assize of Novel Disseisin* (Oxford, 1973), 162–5. In a case of 1407, Hugh Huls, justice of the king's bench, argued that 'when a man lays a claim (to land) it is valueless unless he makes it anew each year': *Year Books*, Mich. 9 Hen. IV pl. 18.

20   On the use of force in thirteenth century entry see Sutherland, *The Assize of Novel Disseisin*, 118–20. The estimates of plaintiffs as victors are my own impressions from examining scattered samples. They exclude instances where the plaintiff defaulted since these suggest a treaty was made.

21   Pulton, 34.

22   *Paston*, nos 514, 1003.

23   *Paston*, no. 108. A good example of an ouster by a superior party who scorned other than direct action is the famous seizure of Caister

castle from the second John Paston by the duke of Norfolk in September 1469: ibid., nos 616, 620, 626.

24 *Year Books*, Hil. 10, Hen. VII pl. 2 shows that by the end of the fifteenth century at least it was an offence for a party trying to enter to be accompanied by a band of supporters greater than the number who would customarily attend on him. From 1381 entry was supposed to be by peaceable means only.

25 In June 1470 Sir John Paston was told by his legal advisers that he might justify his defence of Caister in a military manner by 'the pesybyll possessyon that ye have had in it mor than iii yeer': *Paston*, no. 641. Since a person's goods were usually to be found in his house or his closes the party entered on probably had the right in the circumstances mentioned to defend these as well: *Les Reportes . . . Hawarde*, 140–1.

26 Smyth, I, 109–11; *Paston*, nos 636, 641–2, 666, 676–7, 688–9.

27 See particularly *Paston*, nos 67, 620.

28 *Year Books*, 22 Liber Assisarum no. 57; *Year Books of Edward II, The Eyre of London, 14 Edward II, A.D. 1321*, ed. H. Cam, Selden Society, 85 (1968), 237.

29 *Paston*, nos 518, 533–5, 592. When animals in substantial number were seized by a party entering disputed land, the subsequent indictment only rarely claimed the deed was felony, normally making the charge one of mere trespass. See for example PRO KB 9/266/75; KB 9/267/5, 7, 10, 31, 34; KB 9/270A/28, 65; KB 9/271/43. The value of the property taken was over £10 in several of these indictments.

30 See R. C. Palmer, *The Whilton Dispute, 1264–1380: a Social-Legal Study of Dispute Settlement in Medieval England* (Princeton, 1984), 31.

31 *Paston*, nos 419, 468, 529, 823.

32 ibid., no. 504; *Stonor*, no. 131.

33 *Paston*, no. 631; *Willoughby*, 45–6; *Plumpton*, 156.

34 *Paston*, nos 414, 418. To help him regain the manor of Mellor in 1477 Alexander Pilkington offered the tenants a reduction in rent: HMC, *Various Colls*, II, 29.

35 *Paston*, nos 419, lxi.

36 *Plumpton*, 156; *Paston*, no. 65.

37 *Paston*, nos 688, 693.

38 ibid., nos 504, 504.

39 Distraint was also used to enforce appearance in the king's courts in private actions especially for debt and trespass.

40 F. Pollock and F. W. Maitland, *The History of English Law before the Time of Edward I* (Cambridge, 1911), I, 352–3.

41 *Paston*, nos 408, 531, lxxx. The taking of a distress might lead to the eviction and flight from the locality of the party distrained: see HMC, *Various Colls*, II, 31, 38.

42 *Paston*, nos 418, 502, 896, lxx.

43 ibid., nos 502, 900.

44　J. G. Bellamy, *Criminal Law and Society in Late Medieval and Tudor England* (Gloucester and New York, 1984), 57–8; *Spelman*, I, 207.

45　The relevant statutes on riot were I Ric. II c. 6; 2 Ric. II st. 1 c. 6; 5 Ric. II st. 1 c. 6; 17 Ric. II c. 8; 4 Hen. IV c. 8 and 13 Hen. IV c. 7. On forcible entry they were 5 Ric. II st. 1 c. 7; 15 Ric. II c. 2; 4 Hen. IV c. 7; 4 Hen. IV c. 8; and 2 Hen. V st. 1 cc. 8–9.

46　See Sutherland, *The Assize of Novel Disseisin*, 152–66.

47　8 Hen. VI c. 9. A curious feature of the statute, but one which must have been responsible for attracting a good many bills of indictment from those put out by forcible entry, was the stipulation that if the person indicted was found guilty then the complainant was to be put back in possession, an interesting amalgam of criminal and private law. This seems to have been the forcible entry statute most later indictments were based on: see, for example, B. H. Putnam, *Proceedings before the Justices of the Peace in the Fourteenth and Fifteenth Centuries* (London, 1938), 239–41, and Nottingham City Library, CA 30 D/5.

48　NRO, 24 Hen. VIII.

49　For example ibid., 50i, 63b, 69f, 78a.

50　This last may be the reason why we meet references to insurrection in riot charges occasionally. The practice was really an abuse of 5 Ric. II st. 1 c. 2.

51　By the mid-fifteenth century the term 'riot' carried with it the idea of victims being put in fear. By the sixteenth century there was also the idea of an interest common to all the miscreants: see Bellamy, *Criminal Law*, 58.

52　See, for example, *Paston*, no. 420. A good example of such a certificate is PRO KB 9/262/46. It is a certificate by the earl of Oxford in his capacity as a JP of his observation of the riotous expulsion of John Paston's feoffees from Gresham on 29 January 1449.

53　As Margaret Paston did in August 1465 against the men of the duke of Suffolk: *Paston*, no. 518.

54　Riot was among the crimes which presenting jurors must report by 1403–4 at the latest: Putnam, *Proceedings*, 12.

55　Smyth, 310.

56　See R. W, Kaeuper, 'Law and order in fourteenth-century England: the evidence of special commissions of oyer and terminer', *Speculum*, LIV (1979) 758.

57　See, for example, the special commissions in *Cal. of Patent Rolls, 1391–6*. The minimum payment into the hanaper in the fifteenth century declined to half a mark: *Cal. of Patent Rolls, 1401–5*, 506, and *Cal. of Patent Rolls, 1441–6*, 422.

58　Kaeuper, *Speculum*, LIV (1979), 754, 757–9, 762 764, 766–7.

59　See the volumes of *Cal. of Patent Rolls* for 1391–6, 1401–5, 1441–6, 1467–77, and 1485–94, *passim*.

60　*Paston*, nos 103, 107, 108.

61　The commission's records are in PRO KB 9/267.

62　*Paston*, no. 108. The two exceptions were Lord Scales and Sir John

Fastolf. The former was related to Moleyns' wife, while Fastolf Paston hoped to recruit as his co-plaintiff.

63 The statute 2 Edw. III c. 7 made it quite clear that oyer and terminer commissions were for determining the suits of private parties as well as those of the king. Paston seems to have hoped his obtaining of a private oyer and terminer would persuade Moleyns to withdraw from Gresham without the need for actual proceedings: *Paston*, no. 103. Paston sought the special assize on behalf of his feoffees; technically he was only the *cestui que use* in Gresham.

64 Eng. Reports, Keilway, 159.

65 Eng. Reports, Brooks New Cases, 864, 868.

66 These are the so-called 'Ancient indictments' (PRO KB 9). The first extensive use of this type of evidence relating to late-medieval feuding was by R. L. Storey in his *The End of the House of Lancaster*, (London, 1966).

CHAPTER THREE LITIGATION

1 *Copie of a Leter*, 89; *Willoughby*, 37–8.

2 The first John Paston sued several actions in the names of his associates as did Robert Pilkington: see *Paston*, nos 77 and 502, and HMC, *Various Colls*, II, 38.

3 Smyth, I, 106–7; 'Chronicle of John Harestaffe', 107.

4 *Paston*, nos 235, 255, 388, 766. A large number of suits seem to have been undertaken merely to harass an enemy. The records indicate that in certain courts, notably the common pleas, very few suits ever progressed to jury verdict, which suggests that they were often tactical ploys intended perhaps to force the opponent into arbitration or to reduce his options in regard to counter suits and courts.

5 ibid., nos 77, 766, xix.

6 *Plumpton*, HMC, *Various Colls*, II, 49.

7 *Paston*, no. 77; HMC, *Various Colls*, II, 39.

8 *Paston*, no. xvii; *Stonor*, nos 291, 311, 313.

9 Smyth, I, 165, 311.

10 HMC, Hastings, IV, 335; Smyth, I, 165.

11 *Paston*, nos 211, 293. Sir John Paston retained an attorney in the king's bench, whose job it was to take heed of all indictments and other matters hanging there which might affect his employer: ibid., no. lxxi.

12 *Plumpton*, 149–51.

13 HMC, *Various Colls*, II, 39.

14 *Paston*, no. 47.

15 *Plumpton*, 150–3.

16 However there were three issues in novel disseisin actions: see pp. 70–1.

17 HMC, *Various Colls*, II, 39, 42.

18 Smyth, I, 310–13.

19 *Paston*, no. 840.

20 Smyth, I, 316, 325–6.
21 HMC, *Various Colls*, II, 45; *Paston*, no. 298.
22 On the behaviour of sheriffs see chapter 2. Sir Robert Plumpton was told in no uncertain terms by his solicitor in February 1499 that since he was to be sued at the next assizes he must secure a copy of the panel: *Plumpton*, 134. In 1500 when Plumpton was involved in litigation with Sir Richard Empson the latter ordered the Derbyshire sheriff to empanel a jury which would favour him (PRO KB 9/453/87).
23 ibid., 159–61.
24 Smyth, I, 294, 306.
25 HMC, *Various Colls*, II, 39, 42.
26 *Paston*, no. lx.
27 *Year Books*, Mich. 14 Hen. VII pl. 5; Smith, ed. Dewar, p. 99. On consanguinity as grounds for challenge to the array see *Spelman*, II, 105.
28 HMC, *Various Colls*, II, 41.
29 *Paston*, no. 341.
30 ibid., no. 840; HMC, *Various Colls*, II, 39; *Plumpton*, 159.
31 HMC, *Various Colls*, II, 41–2. Sir Robert Plumpton also seems to have sought the non-attendance of jurors in one of his suits: see *Plumpton*, 161.
32 *Paston*, no. 158, lx; *Stonor*, no. 174. Some of the examples of jurors being bribed in K. B. McFarlane (*The Nobility of Later Medieval England*, ed. J. P. Cooper and G. L. Harris (Oxford, 1973), 117) are more likely to have been the covering of their expenses, or other legitimate payments.
33 *Paston*, nos xxi, lx; *Anonimalle Chron*, 142.
34 HMC, *Various Colls*, II, 42; *Spelman*, II, 114.
35 HMC, *Various Colls*, II, 43.·
36 'Chronicle of John Harestaffe', 85.
37 For a thorough examination of the rivalry in the fifteenth and sixteenth centuries between the various actions of trespass to land and tenements, forcible entry, entry in the nature of an assize, ejectment, and novel disseisin see D. W. Sutherland, *The Assize of Novel Disseisin* (Oxford, 1973), especially 169–94.
38 Smith, ed. Dewar, 100; Smyth, I, 290, 324–5; *Paston*, no. 53.
39 According to Smith the judges should be those who heard the earlier case; if the second jury found as had the first the party bringing the attaint paid a fine to the king and damages to the adversary: Smith, ed. Dewar, 122.
40 The statute 15 Hen. VI c. 5 was also intended to stop the delays caused by each of the original trial jurors being allowed to answer 'in whatever county him pleaseth'. In providing 'reward' for the bringing of an action of attaint fifteenth-century legislators were following the fairly recently established fashion of encouraging parties, who had suffered, to sue those suspected of corruption, negligence, or malpractice, in operating the law. See J. G. Bellamy,

Criminal Law and Society in Late Medieval and Tudor England (Gloucester and New York, 1984), 90–112.

41 Smith, ed. Dewar, 122; *Paston*, nos 151, 224, 281.

42 HMC, *Various Colls*, II, 51–6; J. Pilkington, *The History of the Lancashire Family of Pilkington and its Branches, 1066–1600* (Liverpool, 1894), 41.

43 Proceedings on Pilkington's writ of error were delayed four terms when Thomas Savage was promoted to the archbishopric of York: HMC, *Various Colls*, II, 55. Pilkington's great-grandfather Ralph had married Katherine Ainsworth, and their son Alexander was for 'mone yeres' peaceably seised in Mellor (which his mother had brought to the Pilkingtons) until driven out by William Ainsworth, bastard son of Alexander (Katherine's brother) with the assistance of John Savage, the grandfather, and Sir John Savage, the father of Bishop Savage. The claim of the Ainsworths to Mellor was based on what Robert Pilkington said was a forged deed: it purported to be a confirmation of a feoffment of the Mellor lands by John Ainsworth the elder (*floruit c.* 1390) to William Hyndley, vicar of Glossop. John Ainsworth the younger, principal opponent of Robert Pilkington, was son of William Ainsworth the bastard. He is referred to in Pilkington's narrative as 'negh kynnysman and houshalde servand' of the Savages, who were, in the phrase of the time, his maintainers: see especially ibid., II, 28–9, 32.

44 ibid., II, 36–7, 39–40, 51.

45 ibid., II, 44, 56; Smyth, I, 311–12.

46 HMC, *Various Colls*, II, 28–51.

CHAPTER FOUR MASTER AND CLIENT

1 See for example C. Plummer's edition of J. Fortescue, *The Governance of England* (Oxford, 1885), 14–45, W. Stubbs, *The Constitutional History of England* (Oxford 1898), III, 548–61 and K. B. McFarlane, 'England: the Lancastrian kings, 1399–1461', in *Cambridge Medieval History*, ed. C. W. Previté-Orton and Z. N. Brooke (Cambridge, 1911–36), VIII 382–3.

2 It has recently been pointed out that the 'bastard feudal tie' is now 'less often seen as a cover for crime and a resort of criminals, but rather as an honourable tie sought by respectable gentry everywhere': M. A. Hicks, 'Restraint, mediation and private justice: George, duke of Clarence as "Good Lord" ', *Journal of Legal History* 4 (1983), 56.

3 K. B. McFarlane, *The Nobilitiy of Later Medieval England*, ed. J. P. Cooper and G. L. Harriss (Oxford, 1973), 115; K. B. McFarlane, 'Bastard feudalism', *Bulletin of the Institute of Historical Research* 20 (1943–5), 180. McFarlane seems to have changed his opinions somewhat between 1936 and 1945.

4 C. Carpenter, 'Law, justice and landowners in late medieval England', *Law and History Review* I (1983), 215.

5 *Sayles vii*, 176–7. It was maintenance even to hire an attorney for a

colleague or friend, or to offer in court to give evidence for a party, or to pay fees to a party's counsel: *Spelman*, I, 163, ii, 342–3.

6   *Rotuli Parl.*, I, 96.

7   *Sayles iv*, p. 134.

8   B. H. Putnam, *Proceedings Before the Justices of the Peace in the Fourteenth and Fifteenth Centuries* (London, 1938) 12.

9   *Chronicle of Guisborough* 361–2; A. Harding, 'The origins of the crime of conspiracy', *Transactions of the Royal Historical Society*, 5th Series 33 (1983), 97–8. See also *Britton*, I, 89, 94–5.

10   Council was to examine offenders and make them abandon such practices: 20 Edward III c. 5. This was the beginning of conciliar interest in this group of offences.

11   The act concerned with retaining was 13 Rich. II st. 3. Anyone disseised as a result of the malpractices mentioned in 1 Rich. II c. 9, if he sued successfully under that statue, was to have recovery and damages in addition.

12   There are virtually none in the extant records of the justices of the peace and justices of gaol delivery and they are rare in the fifteenth-century files of the justices of oyer and terminer. Where maintenance does occur in the latter it is really assistance given by accessories or is a general charge (colour) the specific offences alongside being usually extortions. See for example PRO KB 9/267/18, 25.

13   About 10 per cent of the cases included in Baildon were such.

14   This was apparently happening early in Henry VI's reign as 8 Hen. VI c. 4 indicates.

15   See J. G. Bellamy, *Criminal Law*, pp. 93–4. For an example of a suit (1410) under 7 Hen. IV c. 14 see *Sayles, vii*, pp. 192–4.

16   See Bellamy, *Criminal Law and Society in Late Medieval and Tudor England* (Gloucester and New York, 1984) especially chs. 2 and 4.

17   ibid., 10–11, 15.

18   See W. H. Dunham, Jr, *Lord Hastings' Indentured Retainers, 1461–1483* (Hamden, Conn., 1970), 74.

19   The Act was not to extend to persons 'for their council given or to be given and their lawful (*loiall*) service done or to be done . . . although the person or persons to whom such gift, grant or confirmation is or shall be made be not learned in one law or the other': *Statutes of the Realm* II, 428.

20   See ch. 3.

21   cf. Dunham, *Lord Hastings' Retainers*, 73–6.

22   See ibid., 82–4 and Putnam, *Proceedings*, 249–50.

23   It is unlikely they originated in the king's bench. In most cases they would have been moved there by writ of *certiorari*.

24   *Rotuli Parl.*, VI 287–8.

25   Bayne and Dunham, liv–ix. Ten have been found. One was a case or riot, one concerned corrupt conduct on the part of a sheriff, and eight were where juries were prosecuted for perjury (false verdicts).

26   Those who were to judge were the chancellor, the treasurer, the

keeper of the privy seal (or two of these three), plus a bishop and a temporal lord of the king's council and the two chief justices.

27 19 Hen. VII c. 14 in one section shows men used livery without the lord's consent. They apparently were the keener to become a lord's servant because it allowed them to wear livery. This presumably gave them prestige in the community and was influential if they had to appear in court.

28 Recent investigators have tended to regard the statute as finally making the retaining of anyone other than household servants and lawyers illegal, but, as has been pointed out above, this had been done in practice by 1401 and technically in 1468.

29 On the general theme of truncated and summary procedure see Bellamy, *Criminal Law*, ch. 2.

30 The only legal device of a summary nature lacking was conviction by record.

31 In addition under three of these acts offenders appeared before high officers of state. 19 Hen. VII c. 13 concerned cases where juries of indictment would not find riot because of maintenance and embracery. The Act therefore provided justices of the peace and sheriffs might testify the names of the maintainers and this would serve as an indictment.

32 J. P. Cooper, 'Henry VII's last years reconsidered', *Historical Journal* 2 (1959), 117–20; G. R. Elton, 'Henry VII: a restatement', ibid., 4 (1961), 26. One complaint to the justices cited the Act 42 Edw. III c. 3, which was taken as necessitating a presentment, judicial record, or original writ, before a man was put to answer. This was true, but only if life, limb, or land was at stake. Of course information could not be used to accuse men of felony.

33 *Hughes and Larkin* I, nos 62, 77.

34 The alteration which 37 Hen. VIII c. 7 made was to award to the informer half of any forfeiture.

35 Although 35 Hen. VIII c. 6 provided for more substantial jurors in private suits so as to defeat maintenance.

36 Lambarde, 383.

37 Bayne found but four cases in which maintenance was alleged (out of 194 apparent cases), and one of illegal retaining, in Henry VII's reign: Bayne and Dunham, xic-cxiv. S. E. Lehmberg counted four of maintenance or embracery: 'Star Chamber, 1485–1509', *Huntington Library Quarterly* 24 (1960–1), 207. J. A. Guy reckoned that out of 473 in Wolsey's Star Chamber documented sufficiently to enable us to discover 'the principal "real" matter' six involved maintenance, champerty, embracery, perjury, or subornation, but there were apparently none where the essence was illegal retaining or livery giving: *The Cardinal's Court* (Hassocks, 1977), 52–3.

38 NRO 24 Hen. VIII; *West Riding Sessions Rolls 1597/8–1602*, ed. J. Lister, Yorkshire Archaeological Society Record Series 3 (1888); ERO, 1565–6; *Cal. of Assize Records, Surrey Indictments, Elizabeth I* 193. Guy found only a single case of maintenance in Star Chamber

records of the first regnal year of Elizabeth I and none of illegal
livery or retaining. However the regnal year 1601–2 provided thirty-
five cases of maintenance, but only two of illegal livery giving: J. A.
Guy, *The Court of Star Chamber and Its Records to the Reign of Elizabeth I*
(London, 1985), 57–60.

39 On king's bench and exchequer prosecutions see S. B. Chrimes, *Henry
VII* (London, 1972), 191.

40 On oyer and terminer commissions see ch. 2.

41 See for example *Letters . . . Henry VIII*, XVIII (I), no. 623/80; ibid.,
XIX (I), nos 80/51, 610/72; ibid., XX (I), nos 846/92, 910/51;
ibid., XXI (I), 302/38; ibid., XXI (II), nos 200/2, 476/29; *Cal. of
Patent Rolls, 1547–8*, 249; ibid., *1555–7*, 280–1.

42 *Letters . . . Henry VIII*, XV, no. 776. Cromwell denied he retained
anyone other than household servants 'but it was against his will';
Cal. of State Papers, 1581–90, 511.

43 ibid., *1595–7*, 242; *Hughes and Larkin*, *II* 350, 495–7. The solution
proposed by the proclamation of 1583 was for justices of assize and
gaol delivery to make sure no retainer sat on a jury, a stipulation
originally made by the statutes 8 Edw. IV c. 1 and 3 Hen. VII c.
12.

44 See J. Cowell, *The Interpreter* (Cambridge, 1607), under 'retainer'.
According to 'I. M.', the author of *A Health to the Gentlemanly
Profession of Servingmen*, who wrote in the reign of Elizabeth I (1598),
the reason why the laws were not enforced was that offences were
not reported by constables or bors-holders (Sig. I3, J3).

45 See McFarlane, 'Bastard feudalism', 167; Dunham, *Lord Hastings'
Retainers*, 9, 65; C. Carpenter, 'The Beauchamp affinity: a study of
bastard feudalism at work', *English Historical Review* XCV (1980),
524; McFarlane, *Nobility of Later Medieval England*, p. 109. On the
thirteenth-century origins of contractual retaining see S. L. Waugh,
'Tenure to contract: lordship and clientage in thirteenth-century
England', *English Historical Review* CI (1986), 811–39. The contract
seems to have been intended to prevent annuities becoming
hereditary.

46 McFarlane, 'Bastard feudalism', 166–7, 173; N. E. Saul, *Knights and
Esquires: The Gloucestershire Gentry in the Fourteenth Century* (Oxford,
1981), 94, 97, 101; Carpenter, 'Law, justice and landowners', 206,
226; Carpenter, 'Beauchamp affinity', 514–15, 519.

47 McFarlane, 'Bastard feudalism', 167.

48 A major reason why a lord found a retainer at that distance so useful
was no doubt the latter's influence with the jurors drawn from the
hundred where he dwelt.

49 The duke of Norfolk sent for his tenants to help him at the siege of
Caister castle in September 1469: *Paston*, no. 620.

50 Robert Pilkington, referring to the early period of his quarrel with
the Savages, tells us that 'divers gentlemen of worship' offered him
aid: HMC, *Various Coll*, II, 31. These, in the parlance of the time,
would have been 'well willers'.

51 *Paston*, no. lxi.
52 *ibid.*, no. 502.
53 The author of the *Profession of Servingmen*, who says this, states that servants were incapable of performing manual labour (Sig. I3, J3).
54 Smyth, I, 286.
55 HMC *Various Coll*, II, 32, 46; see also *Paston*, no. 601.
56 *Plumpton*, liv-lv; *Letters . . . Henry VIII*, XV, no. 72; *Stonor* no. 190.
57 *Willoughby*, 35–6, 57–8; *Stonor* nos 285, 309; *Paston*, nos 42, 534. Additional pressure could be brought to bear by having one's wife 'wait on' the lord's wife: *Paston*, no. 765.
58 *Paston*, no. 116.
59 ibid., no. 1003.
60 ibid., no. 373. On another occasion Paston was asked by Oxford to put in a good word with a Norfolk lady on behalf of a close servant, her wooer: ibid., no. 97.
61 *Willoughby*, 63.
62 *Plumpton*, cvii.
63 *Stonor*, no. 285. A correspondent informed John Paston I in October 1450 that Sir Borle Young and one other were offering Sir William Oldhall £1000 on behalf of John Heydon and Sir Thomas Tudenham for his good lordship: Paston, no. 113. There is an instance of the seizing of a manor (Winchesters in Mendelsham, Suffolk) in January 1443 where, after the occupants had been expelled, the entrants in order to have their maintenance immediately enfeoffed no less a duo than Humphrey, duke of Gloucester and William de la Pole, earl of Suffolk: PRO KB 9/266/18.
64 HMC *Various Coll*, II, 35, 40, 44. In Elizabeth I's reign the earl of Leicester expressed surprise to hear that writing to jurors on a client's behalf was maintenance: Hudson, 72. In 1594 the earl of Essex wrote boldly to Lord Chief Justice Popham concerning a case before him involving the interests of his kinsman Sir Thomas Knyvett and ultimately himself: J. E. Jackson, 'Longleat Papers, No. 4', *Wiltshire Archaeological and Natural History Society Magazine*, XVIII (1879), 270.
65 See *Paston*, no. 28.
66 *Nolttingham*, II, 384–7.
67 On this aspect of the 'gentlemen's wars' see *Paston*, nos 620, 626.
68 *Willoughby*, 21–2, 37–9.
69 *Stonor*, no. 309; *Paston*, no. 531.
70 *Plumpton*, 33, 45–6, 72–3, 76. Thus the earl of Northumberland referred disputes among his clients to Sir Robert Plumpton, one of his officers and a member of his 'counsell'. The evenly balanced settlement was of course the essence of arbitration; neither party was usually total winner or total loser as would be the situation after trial in a court of common law. There was, however, no rule that a 'treaty' or 'direction' (as contemporaries often referred to to arbitration) must of necessity share out the benefits.

71 Even in regard to collecting rents by threat of distress: *Paston*, no. 502.

72 ibid., nos 175, 176, 178, 179, 180, 181, 201. See also PRO KB 9/271/44 (an indictment of Nowell; all the alleged offences are trespasses).

73 In the fifteenth-century oyer and terminer files the taking of goods of twelve pence or over in value was often rated as trespass rather than, as it should have been, felony. Whether this underrating was the decision of the indicting jurors or of the victim who brought the charge is not clear. Good examples of the diminishing of what appears to have been obvious felony are to be found in PRO KB 9/266/75; PRO KB 9/267/3, 5, 7, 13, 31; PRO KB 9/270A/28, 65.

74 See *Letters . . . Henry VIII*, III no. 2132; ibid., IV (II) no. 3033; ibid., IX, 510; ibid., XIV (II), no. 384; ibid., *Addenda*, I (I), no. 151; *Acts of the Privy Council*, V, 223; *Lancs. and Cheshire Cases* 120–1; Brinklow, 44–5. In 1451 seven of Lord Scales 'housold meny' were indicted for felony as 'strong thefes': *Paston*, no. xxvi. I am inclined to view the land wars of the later fourteenth and the fifteenth centuries as being dangerous to the crown in that they might lead to extensive factional dispute high up the social scale but not as being substantial generators of crimes of the type to which the lower classes were generally inclined.

75 HMC, *Middleton*, 142–6.

76 *Letters . . . Henry VIII*, IV (III), nos 6683, 6708.

77 The figures for the early fourteenth century have been calculated from B. A. Hanawalt, *Crime and Conflict in English Communities, 1300–1348* (Cambridge, Mass., 1979), 67. Those for the fifteenth century I have drawn from PRO JUST 3/209, 211, 213. Similar fifteenth-century evidence for other counties points in the same direction. It seems unlikely that the decline in felonies tried before the justices of gaol delivery was caused by new competition from the justices of the peace or oyer and terminer commissions.

CHAPTER FIVE THE SEARCH FOR ROYAL FAVOUR

1 *Collection . . . Royal Household, passim.*

2 A. R. Myers, *The Household of Edward IV* (Manchester, 1959), 106, 201. The Black Book of *c.* 1471–2 refers to 'the grete chambre' and 'the kinges chambre' (ibid., 90), the former being a presence chamber.

3 Presumably *bouche au court* was originally the right to dine in the king's hall. If we judge by the Eltham ordinances (c. 30) this was not very attractive to the upper classes, probably because the king dined there only rarely from the fourteenth century. By the sixteenth century the chief officers of the chamber and household sometimes offered open table in their lodgings to which visitors to court were invited: A. P. Newton, 'Tudor reforms in the Royal Household', in *Tudor Studies*, ed. R. W. Seton Watson (London, 1924), p. 250.

4   C. F. Richmond, *John Hopton. A Fifteenth Century Suffolk Gentleman* (Cambridge, 1981), 106; G. R. Elton, 'Tudor government: the point of contact, III. The Court', *Transactions of the Royal Historical Society* 5th Ser. 26 (1976), 217; *Copie of a Leter*, 48, 51.

5   J. Nichols, *The Progresses of James I* (London, 1828), III, 445.

6   The Black Book refers simply to 'when lords of great estate resort to court', as though they might do so at their whim: Myers, 101.

7   *Cal of State Papers 1591–4* 432–3.

8   The experiences of the second John Paston at the court of Edward IV suggests this pattern. See below, p. 113–15. Given-Wilson has argued that in the fourteenth century nobles and gentry went to court largely to supplicate for payment of annuities and war wages: C. Given-Wilson, *The English Nobility in the Late Middle Ages* (London, 1987), 176.

9   Smyth, I, 291; *Willoughby*, no. 37; *Paston*, no. 763.

10 There is little indication in England men could achieve favour by performing for the king acts of political skullduggery as may have been the case on the continent. See S. Anglo, *The Courts of Europe* (London, 1977), 33, on the writings and advice for courtiers of Louis Guyon.

11 *Paston*, no. 411.

12 *Copie of a Leter*, 48–50.

13 *Paston*, nos 99, 411, 841, 846.

14 ibid., no. 410; *Plumpton*, pp. 31–2.

15 *Paston*, nos 612, 846.

16 ibid., no. 410; *Stoner*, no. 285.

17 *Paston*, no. 409. The necessity, if they valued their fellows' good opinions, for those at court to spend freely must always have been present. The compiler of the *Gest of Robyn Hode*, a late-fourteenth-century piece, had his hero, a 'vadlet' of the king's chamber, spend £100 in fifteen months 'for knyghtes and for squyres / to get hym grete renown': see R. B. Dobson and J. Taylor, *Rymes of Robin Hood* (London, 1976), 110.

18 *Letters . . . Henry VIII*, XVII, no. 1076; ibid., XVIII (I), no. 837; ibid., XVIII (II), appendix, nos 2, 3; ibid., *Addenda*, pt II, nos 1553, 1573, 1802. According to regulations made in 1526 those who served the king in the privy chamber were not supposed to seek their own advancement or press the king over suits: *Collection . . . Royal Household*, 157.

19 *Letters . . . Henry VIII*, XVII, nos 416, 1076; ibid., XVIII (I), no. 837; ibid., *Addenda*, pt II, nos 1553, 1625, 1802. In November 1472 Sir John Paston 'for as moche as men may not lure none hawkes with empty handys' offered the duchess of Norfolk £20 'for an horse and sadell' so she might be an intermediary for him with the duke: *Paston* no. 706.

20 *Letters . . . Henry VIII, Addenda*, pt II, nos 1546, 1716, 1802, appendix. no. 3.

21 ibid., *Addenda*, pt II, nos 1625, 1784. A royal servant was thought to have a particularly good opportunity to petition the king if the

latter should visit a house of which he was the keeper: ibid., no. 1625.

22 This was champerty, which classified as a crime from the time of Edward I. In 1595 Sir Robert Cecil was offered £150 by John Daniel out of grants Daniel hoped Cecil would obtain for him from Elizabeth I: G. Chesters, 'John Daniel of Daresbury, 1544–1610', *Transactions of the Historic Society of Lancashire and Cheshire*, CXVIII (1966), 8–9.

23 R. M Sargent, *At the Court of Queen Elizabeth* (Oxford, 1935), 12–25. See also *Paston*, no. 411.

24 The qualities which the upper classes hoped to find in their servants are well described in *Profession of Servingmen*, Sig. B2-I3. They would also be those the monarch hoped to find in his courtiers. Antoine de la Sale in his *Jehan de Saintré* written in the 1450s, but purporting to describe the French court of a century earlier, emphasized that success at court went to the handsome and well-mannered. He laid particular stress on the manner in which fine clothing might gain the king's attention for the wearer and even his patronage and financial support: Sale, 49–53.

25 G. von Bulow, 'Journey through England and Scotland made by Lupold von Wedel in the years 1584 and 1585', *Transactions of the Royal Historical Society*, IX (1895), 265; Smyth, I, 291; J. Bellamy, *Robin Hood: an Historical Enquiry* (London, 1985), 81–2.

26 See G. W. Bernard, 'The rise of Sir William Compton, early Tudor courtier', *English Historical Review* XCVI (1981), 757–8 and H. Miller, *Henry VIII and the English Nobility* (Oxford, 1986), 14–15.

27 Myers, 129.

28 *Letters . . . Henry VIII*, XIII (II), no. 755.

29 T. More, *The History of Richard III*, ed. R.S. Sylvester (New Haven, 1963), 10–11; D. Mancini, *The Usurpation of Richard III* ed. C. A. J. Armstrong (Oxford, 1969), 67–9; Bernard, 757.

30 Myers, 127; Smyth, I, 314.

31 English kings who had been born the sons or grandsons of reigning monarchs tended to form intimate and long-lasting friendships with those who were close to them in their youth.

32 *Paston*, xxxviii-xliii. Rather remarkably the activity of the second John Paston at court is a theme which still awaits proper examination.

33 ibid., nos 355, 397, 997.

34 Supplication to a social superior for a favour against someone who had interfered with your property did not necessarily lead to confrontation with the latter like a law suit would.

35 *Paston*, nos 392, 393, 464, 532. John Paston had been a client and servant of the duke of Norfolk in 1450: ibid., no. 121.

36 ibid., nos 407, 409, 411. Young people of upper-class blood, who were placed as servants in noble or even royal households at th end of the Middle Ages, were usually supported there financially by their families and did not expect reward from their masters: see R. F. Green,

Poets and Princepleasers (Toronto, 1980), 41. Their intent was often to obtain a permanent position in the upper reaches of the household. One attraction of being employed in the king's service was that it carried with it protection from being sued: see for example *Plumpton*, cxvi and *Paston*, no. 111.

37 *Paston*, nos 409, 410, 411, 465.

38 ibid., nos 572, 603, 604, 672.

39 ibid., nos 626, 654.

40 ibid., nos 570, 596, 703.

41 Sir John's selling of the manors of Saxthorpe and Titchwell and his borrowing from Roger Townsende, the judge, may have been on this account: *Paston*, nos 634, 694, 695, 696, 702, 708, 745, 746, 752, 754, 802. Gairdner saw Sir John as a failure: 'Thriftless, extravagant and irresolute, Sir John Paston was not the man to succeed either in money matters or in anything else': ibid., ccv-ccvi.

42 ibid., nos 717, 729, 750, 775.

43 ibid., nos 750, 753, 763.

44 ibid., nos 701, 703, 714, 762, 765.

45 ibid., nos 763, 764, 765, 768, 778, 779.

46 ibid., nos 512, 513, 514, 517, 518, 530, 533, 534. Saul has recently made the point that there was a relative absence of large-scale gentry violence in fourteenth-century Sussex and that the reason may have been the absence of 'overlapping spheres of magnate influence' (N. E. Saul, *Scenes from Provincial Life* (Oxford, 1986), 77). There is, however, no weighty evidence that the reverse was true of fifteenth-century Norfolk. The Pastons, we must remember, because of the nature of their landed interests in the period *c.* 1450–80 were particularly liable to be subjected to pressures of the land-war sort. Furthermore what is very evident from their correspondence and what has not been commented on is the fact that the family of John Paston was a swarm of legal tigers. They were very literate, very knowledgeable in the ways of the law, and very ready to make use of any opportunity in and out of the courts which their adversaries allowed them. Thus their correspondence can hardly be typical of that of a fifteenth-century gentry family. The very fact so much of it survives suggests it was preserved, indeed, for legal purposes. probably so that the strategic and tactical thinking behind land war moves and the nature of those moves should be remembered at a later date were particular quarrels to revive. The letters would also provide enlightening commentaries on the circumstances behind 'evidences' in the Paston deed boxes and thus be a source of invaluable and decisive information in the case of later law suits.

47 ibid., no. 579.

48 ibid., nos 600, 603, 604, 815, 817, 818. Sir John's delay in marrying amply demonstrates his appreciation of the strategic value of remaining in the marriage market while heavily engaged in the struggle for land.

49 The general content of petitions to the kind in the early fifteenth

century is discussed by J. L. Kirby in *Cal. of Signet Letters*, especially 8–9.

50   Stow, 342; *Chr. Ch. Letters*, 70; *Paston*, no. 612. There is a reference to Elizabeth I receiving bills (i.e. petitions) when going to chapel. She gave them to a master of requests attendant on her person: Leadam, xii.

51   Elton, 'Tudor government', 216; *Paston*, no. 410.

52   J. G. Bellamy, 'Justice under the Yorkist kings', *American Journal of Legal History* 9 (1965), 136–9; *Ingulph's Chron.* 484; *Paston*, no. 612.

53   J. Raine, *The Priory of Hexham, I* (Surtees Society, 44, 1864), cxiii–cxiv; *Paston*, no. 841.

54   *Paston*, nos 753, 764.

CHAPTER SIX THE END OF BASTARD FEUDALISM

1   J. A. Guy, *Court of the Star Chamber and its Records to the Reign of Elizabeth I* (London, 1985), 57–9; E. Skelton, 'The Court of Star Chamber in the Reign of Elizabeth' unpublished M. A. thesis (University of London, 1931), I, 194–6.

2   T. G. Barnes, 'Star Chamber litigants and their counsel, 1596–1641', in J. H. Baker (ed.), *Legal Records and the Historian* (London, 1978), 13; H. E. I. Philips, 'The last years of the Court of Star Chamber 1630–41', *Transactions of the Royal Historical Society*, 4th Ser., 21 (1939), 116.

3   See 'Staffordshire Quarter Sessions Rolls, 1581–97', ed. S. A. H. Burne, in *William Salt Archaeological Society*, 3rd Ser., 1929 (1931), 1930 (1932), and 1932 (1933), 'West Riding Sessions Rolls, 1597/8–1602', and *Minutes of Proceedings*.

4   *Minutes of Proceedings*, 44, 91, 98, 101, 109–10, 113; F. G. Emmison, *Elizabethan Life: Disorder* (Chelmsford, 1970), 119–24; BL. Lansd. MS 620f. 3v. In Elizabethan Wiltshire there was usually a single indictment for either forcible entry or riot at each quarter sessions, which suggests a token accusation by the grand jurors in response to the list of crime catagories which comprised the justices' charges.

5   *Acts of the Privy Council*, x, 325; *William Salt Soc.*, 3rd Ser, 1912, 206–7; *Les Reportes . . . Hawarde*, 34–5; HMC, *Salisbury*, v, 515–18, XII, 410–12.

6   I have dealt with these developments *in extenso* in my forthcoming book *Felony in England, 1300 to 1600*.

7   Notably Lord Dacre of the South in 1541 and Lord Stourton in 1557.

8   Probably not only because of the greater certainty of punishment for felony or misdemeanor than hitherto but because they might be left by their leader to pay their own fines: see *Smyth, I*, 310.

9   Philips, *'The last years'*, 116; BL. Lansd. MS 620f. 3v.

10   *Yorks. Proc.*, 50–6. The Sacheverell-Dorset case is noted by J. A. Guy in *The Cardinal's Court*, (Hassocks, 1977), 60–1.

11   The nature of the solutions attempted suggests the involvement of a person with legal expertise who had lived for some time abroad.

12   I have considered the employment of non-traditional criminal law
     procedures in this period at some length elsewhere. See Bellamy,
     Criminal Law and Society in the Late Medieval and Tudor England
     (Gloucester and New York, 1984), particularly chs 1, 2, and 5.
13   ibid., 11–13, 15–19, 46.
14   ibid., 17–18.
15   On attempts to get specific instances of felony rated as treason (by
     Act) see J. G. Bellamy, *The Law of Treason in England in the Later
     Middle Ages* (Cambridge, 1970), p. 125.
16   It can be argued that Henry VII's desire to remove the evils of
     bastard feudalism very nearly led to the development of a new criminal
     law procedure of a truncated or summary nature: see my remarks in
     Criminal Law, 4–6, 15–19.
17   See the statutes 25 Edw. III st. 5 c. 4 and 31 Hen. VI c. 2. There
     were objections raised to writs of privy seal in parliament in 1347,
     1363, 1377, 1384, 1401, 1402, 1406, 1421, and 1427.
18   *Bayne and Dunham*, lxiv; G. R. Elton, *The Tudor Constitution, Documents
     and Commentary* (Cambridge, 1960), 160. It is worthy of note that
     those who drafted the statute 5 Eliz. c. 9 on perjury by witnesses
     believed 11 Hen. VII c. 25 was still in operation.
19   Another statute worthy of notice is 8 Hen. VI c. 4, which allowed
     justices of assize and justices of the peace to attach those suspected of
     illegal livery and try them by examination. It was an obvious
     precursor of 8 Edw. IV c. 2.
20   Guy, *The Cardinal's Court*, 72. There must also have been some
     reliance, where offenders were of less prominent status, on
     indictments before the quarter sessions.
21   Eng. Reports, 5 Coke 51a. BL Harl. MS 6847 f.133 seems to have a
     rough draft of a bill to enlarge the jurisdiction of the Star Chamber
     to offences mentioned in 3 Hen. VII c. 1 and 21 Hen. VIII c. 20,
     such cases to have priority over private suits. This supports the
     view that there were very few criminal prosecutions in Star Chamber
     and that the act of 1529 was ineffective.
22   On the origins and early history of riot see Bellamy, *Criminal Law*,
     54–67.
23   Guy, *The Cardinal's Court*, 52–3; Guy, *Court of the Star Chamber*, 52–3;
     J. A. Guy, *The Public Career of Sir Thomas More* (Brighton, 1980),
     51. Guy does not explain in exact terms what he takes to be a 'title'
     case. There is evidence from the mid-fifteenth century that those who
     sought the indictment of foes who had entered on them sometimes
     saw to it that their title was stated in the indictment. Should the
     accused be convicted their title was then of record in the king's court:
     see PRO KB 9/267/12, 34.
24   In the later years of Elizabeth I, so it has been argued, Star Chamber
     suits were often brought for purposes of harassment or counter-
     attack, and were intended to put defendants to considerable cost.
     They were also intended sometimes to discover conspirators,
     secrets, and especially evidence relevant to a case already before the

common law courts. Such evidence 'could not readily be used elsewhere, thus effectively arresting proceedings in another court'. Another intent of the collateral action in Star Chamber was to impeach one's adversary's chief witness of perjury but most common was the impeachment of procedure, evidence, or verdicts, in other courts through the impugning of deeds, wills, or by charging perjury, fraud, maintenance, or embracery: see Barnes, 'Star Chamber litigants', *Historian*, 18–21.

25 We know very little about the very crucial matter of the percentage of winners and losers among complainants. Legal historians, like lawyers, are prone to emphasize such variables as choice of action, the role of counsel, and the facts of the case, and to underestimate the greater truth, which was that certain courts at certain periods gave the complainant a better chance of defeating the defendant than did other courts. We may speculate that Wolsey's Star Chamber was popular because it gave the complainant just such an edge. In litigation before Wolsey in chancery the success rate of plaintiffs is said to have been as high as 61 per cent in decided cases: J. A. Guy, *Christopher St German on Chancery and Statute* (Selden Society, Supplementary Series, 6, 1985), 68, quoting the findings of Dr F. Metzger.

26 BL Harl. MS 2143f. 1v; HL, Elles. MS 2652 f.17; BL Harl. MS 1226 f. 18b.

27 My estimates here are based largely on the Star Chamber cases in print. Although *cestui que usent* were complainants in relatively few cases a use was not infrequently behind the grievances of lessees and tenants in tail. I am not attracted by the argument that the title cases which came before the Star Chamber were those where there was genuine violence or complexity: c.f. Guy, *Public Career of More*, 57.

28 However, in theory, if one party, who had occupied land in contention, was suspected by the other of then enfeoffing others to his use in order to conceal his misdeed he was permitted by the statutes 1 Rich. II c. 9 and 4 Hen. IV c. 7 to bring an assize of novel disseisin against the disseisor claiming the enfeoffment was obstruction. On the inability of the *cestui* to bring an action of trespass see Eng. Reports, Keilway, 42 and 46 (referring to cases Pasch. 17 Hen. VII pl. 7 and Mich. 18 Hen. VII pl. 2). The attraction of the Star Chamber for *cestui que usent* does not seem to have drawn the attention of modern investigators nor does the plight of the lessee (see below).

29 *Spelman*, II, 181–2.

30 St German, *Little Treatise*, 341–2. Uses in tail were obviously common by the beginning of Henry VII's reign. Their rise, one imagines, may have been a response on behalf of senior land holders to the arrival of common recovery in the second half of the fifteenth century. Alienation by *cestui que usent* in tail was the issue in an important case in 1488 (*Year Books*, Mich. 4 Hen. VII pl. 9) and another in 1528 (ibid., Trin. 19 Hen. VIII pl. 11)

31 See *Spelman*, II, 195–200.
32 The Acts 1 Rich. III, c. 1 and 4 Hen. VII c. 17 both treated the use as an integral part of the common law. There had been statutes touching uses less directly in the reigns of Richard II and Henry IV.
33 See E. W. Ives, 'The genesis of the Statute of Uses', *English Historical Review* lXXXII (1967), 689–91, and especially *Year Books*, Pasch. 27 Hen. VIII pl. 22, which shows (7–10) counsel for the defendant argued that the jury's interpretation of the law was quite erroneous, that uses were well known at common law and had never been challenged until now, and that since the will had been declared nothing illegal had been done. The crown may have been particularly grieved that the Dacre will required money to be raised for the payment of the deceased's debts and when raised conveyed to the heir, and thus was collusive: see S. F. C. Milsom, *Historical Foundations of the Common Law* (London, 1969), 189.
34 What was remarkable about this judicial conference was that the opinion of Thomas Cromwell (at that time king's secretary and master of the rolls), was allowed to count on the matter at issue as being equal in weight to that of one of the puisne justices. Furthermore the latter had been obliged to attend the hearing in chancery as observers, and to give their opinions 'by appointment' of Chancellor Audley and Cromwell; procedure which seems quite novel. The best report is in *Spelman*, I, 228–30.
35 *St German's Doctor*, 223–4.
36 The two schemes were printed by W. S. Holdsworth (*History of English Law* (Boston, 1924–6), IV, 572–7).
37 The statute 19 Hen. VII c. 15 made *cestui que usent* liable to execution against them in regard to statutes staple and merchant.
38 38 Hen. VIII c. 36 decreed fines were to be a sufficient bar against persons claiming land by force or any entail or use. Fines were by their nature an agreement or compromise and thus those with a legal interest had already been consulted. Also worthy of notice is 34/5 Hen. VIII c. 5, which forbade a tenant in tail from discontinuing an estate tail by means of a will.
39 Holdsworth, *History of English Law*, vii, 546–7, for the socially revealing bill against perpetuities, which received one reading in the parliamentary session of 1598.
40 On the early history of witnesses see Bellamy, *Criminal Law*, 33–7.
41 On the incidence of these offences in the Star Chamber see Skelton, *Court of Star Chamber*, I, 194–6, and Guy, *Court of the Star Chamber*, 60.
42 As with perjury there are few forgery cases to be found in Elizabethan assize records. The small number there are concern the forging of licences to beg and for the purposes of cozening.
43 This was in fact the second statute specifically on forgery. The first, 1 Hen. V c. 3, was mild, simply permitting private suits at common law against a party suspected of forgery in order to recover damages.
44 Skelton, *Court of Star Chamber*, I, 194–6; Guy, *Court of the Star Chamber*, 58, 60.

45 It should perhaps be pointed out here in respect of the justices who presided in the criminal courts which employed juries (i.e. under the common law) that there is little evidence from the fourteenth or fifteenth centuries of particular justices who are able to influence the juries towards a level of convictions above the norm for the period and area where the trials occurred.

46 A recent contribution to the history of juries, *Twelve Good Men and True. The Criminal Trial Jury in England, 1200–1800*, ed. J. S. Cockburn and T. A. Green (Princeton, 1988), is very welcome. Unfortunately it does not deal specifically with the jury in the context of the segment of crime connected with the 'gentlemen's wars'.

BIBLIOGRAPHY

MANUSCRIPT SOURCES

British Library (BL)
  Harleian MSS 1266, 2143, 6847 (Harl. MSS)
  Lansdowne MS 620 (Lansd. MS)
Essex Record Office, Essex Quarter Sessions Records (ERO)
Huntington Library (HL)
  Ellesmere MS 2652 (Elles. MS)
Norfolk Record Office, Norfolk Quarter Sessions Files (NRO)
Nottingham City Library, City of Nottingham Sessions Files (NCL)
Public Record Office (PRO)
  Chancery Miscellanea (C 47)
  Common Pleas, Plea Rolls (CP 40)
  Gaol Delivery Rolls (JUST 3)
  Ancient Indictments (KB 9)
  Coram Rege Rolls (KB 27)
  State Papers, Domestic, Elizabeth I (SP 12)

LEGAL TREATISES

Britton, ed. F. M. Nichols, Oxford, 1865. (*Britton*)
Fitzherbert, A., *The Newe Boke of Justices of the Peas*, 1538. (Fitzherbert)
Fortescue, J., *De Laudibus Legum Anglie*, ed. S. B. Chrimes, Cambridge, 1949. (Fortescue)
Hudson, W., *A Treatise on the Court of Star Chamber*, in *Collectanea Juridica*, ed. F. Hargrave, London, 1791–2. (Hudson)
Lambarde, W., *Eirenarcha*, London 1581 (Lambarde)
  William Lambarde and Local Government, ed. C. Read, Ithaca NY, 1962.
Pulton, F., *De Pace Regis et Regni*, 1609. (Pulton)
Smith, T., *De Republica Anglorum*, ed. L. Alston, Cambridge, 1906. (Smith, ed. Alston)
  De Republica Anglorum, ed. M. Dewar, Cambridge, 1982. (Smith, ed. Dewar)

171

CALENDARS AND PRINTED SOURCES

Acts of the Privy Council of England, ed. J. R. Dasent, London 1890–1907. (*Acts of the Privy Council*)

Anonimalle Chronicle, ed. V. H. Galbraith, Manchester, 1926. (*Anonimalle Chron.*)

Brinklow, H., *The Complaynt of Roderyck Mors*, ed. J. M. Cooper, Early English Text Society, extra series, 22 (1874). (Brinklow)

Calendar of Assize Records: Home Circuit Indictments, Elizabeth I and James I, ed. J. S. Cockburn, London, 1975–85. (*Cal. of Assize Records*)

Calendar of Close Rolls. (*Cal. of Close Rolls*)

Calendar of Patent Rolls. (*Cal. of Patent Rolls*)

Calendar of Signet Letters of Henry IV and Henry V, ed. J. L. Kirby, London, 1979. (*Cal. of Signet Letters*)

Calendar of State Papers, Domestic, Edward VI, Mary, Elizabeth, ed. R. Lemon and M. A. E. Green, London, 1856–70. (*Cal. of State Papers*)

The Chronicle of Walter of Guisborough, ed. H. Rothwell, Camden Society, 3rd Series, 89 (1957). (*Chron . . . Guisborough*)

Christ Church Letters ed. J. B. Sheppard, Camden Society New Series, 19 (1877). (*Chr. Ch. Letters*)

A Collection of Ordinances and Regulations for the Government of the Royal Household, London, 1790. (*Collection . . . Royal Household*)

The Copie of a Leter Wryten by a Master of Arte of Cambridge, 1584. (*Copie of a Leter*)

Dudley, E., *The Tree of Commonwealth*, ed. D. M. Brodie, Cambridge, 1948. (Dudley)

English Reports, Full Reprint, 1220–1865 (1900–32). (Eng. Reports)

Historia et Cartularium Monasterii Sancti Petri Gloucestriae, ed. W. H. Hart, Rolls Series (1863–7). (*Historia . . . Gloucestriae*)

Historical Manuscripts Commission, *Calendar of the Manuscripts of the Marquess of Salisbury, London, 1883–1976*. (HMC, *Salisbury*)

Calendar of the Shrewsbury and Talbot Papers, London, 1966–71. (HMC, *Shrewsbury and Talbot*)

Report on the Manuscripts of Lord Middleton, London, 1911. (HMC, *Middleton*)

Report on the Manuscripts of R. R. Hastings, London, 1928–47. (HMC, *Hastings*)

Report on Manuscripts in Various Collections, London, 1901–14. (HMC, *Various Colls*)

Ingulph's Chronicle of the Abbey of Croyland, ed. H. T. Riley, London, 1854. (*Ingulph's Chron.*)

The Journal of Sir Robert Wilbraham, ed. H. S. Scott, Camden Society, 3rd Series, 4 (1902). (*Wilbraham*)

Lancashire and Cheshire Cases in Star Chamber, I, ed. R. Stewart-Brown, Lancashire and Cheshire Record Society, 71 (1916). (*Lancs. and Cheshire Cases*)

Letters and Papers, Foreign and Domestic, Henry VIII, ed. J. S. Brewer, J. Gairdner, and R. H. Brodie, London, 1920–32. (*Letters . . . Henry VIII*)

Letters of Philip Gawdy, ed. I. H. Jeayes, London, 1906. (*Gawdy*)

Mancini, D., *The Usurpation of Richard III*, ed. C. A. J. Armstrong, Oxford, 1969. (Mancini)

Minutes of Proceedings in Sessions, 1563 and 1574 to 1592, ed. H. C. Johnson, Wiltshire Archaeological and Natural History Society Records Branch, IV (1949). (*Minutes of Proceedings*)

More, T., *The English Works of Sir Thomas More*, London, 1557. (More)

The Paston Letters, ed. J. Gairdner, Edinburgh, 1910. (*Paston*)

Plumpton Correspondence, ed. T. Stapleton, Camden Society, Old Series, 4 (1839). (*Plumpton*)

The Political Songs of England, ed. T. Wright. Camden Society, Old Series, 6 (1839). (*Political Songs*)

Records of the Borough of Nottingham, ed. W. H. Stevenson, Nottingham, 1882–1900. (*Nottingham*)

Les Reportes del Cases in Camera Stellata, 1593 to 1609, from the Original MS of John Hawarde, ed. W. P. Baildon, 1894. (*Les Reportes . . . Hawarde*)

The Reports of Sir John Spelman, ed. J. H. Baker, Selden Society, 93–4 (1977–8). (*Spelman*)

'The rhymed chronicle of John Harestaffe', ed. J. C. Cox, *Derbyshire Archaeological and Natural History Society Journal*, X (1887): 71–147. ('Chronicle of John Harestaffe')

Rotuli Parliamentorum, ed. J. Strachey and others, London, 1767–77. (*Rotuli Parl.*)

St German, C., *Litle Treatise concerning Writs of Subpena*, London, 1787. (St German, *Litle Treatise*)

St German's Doctor and Student, ed. T. F. T. Plucknett and J. L. Barton, Selden Society, 91 (1974). (*St German's Doctor*)

Sale, A. de la, *Jehan de Saintré*, ed. J. Misrahi and C. A. Knudson, Geneva, 1965. (Sale)

Select Cases in Chancery, A. D. 1364–1471, ed. W. P. Baildon, Selden Society, 10 (1896). (Baildon)

Select Cases in the Council of Henry VII, ed. C. G. Bayne and W. H. Dunham Jr, Selden Society, 75 (1958). (Bayne and Dunham)

Select Cases in the Court of King's Bench, ed. G. O. Sayles, Selden Society, 55, 57, 58, 74, 82, 88 (1936–71). (Sayles)

Select Cases in the Court of Requests, A. D. 1497–1569, ed. I. S. Leadam, Selden Society, 12 (1898) (Leadam)

Smyth, J., *Lives of the Berkeleys*, ed. J. Maclean, Gloucester, 1883–5. (Smyth)

Statutes of the Realm, Record Commission, 1810–28. (*Statutes of the Realm*)

The Stonor Letters and Papers, 1290–1483, ed. C. L. Kingsford, Camden Society, 3rd Series, 30 (1919). (*Stonor*)

Stow, J., *Annales*, London, 1615. (Stow)

Tudor Royal Proclamations, ed. P. L. Hughes and J. F. Larkin, New Haven Conn., 1964–9. (Hughes and Larkin)

West Riding Sessions Rolls, 1597/8–1602, ed. J. Lister, Yorkshire Archaeological Society, Record Series, 3 (1888). (*West Riding Session Rolls*)

William Salt Archaeological Society, vols for 1927 (1929), 1929 (1931), 1930 (1932), and 1932 (1933). (*William Salt Soc.*)

Willoughby Letters of the First Half of the Sixteenth Century, ed. M. A. Welch, Thoroton Society, Record Series, XXIV (1967). (*Willoughby*)

Year Books of Edward II, The Eyre of London, 14 Edward II, A. D. 1321, ed. H. Cam, Selden Society, 85 (1968) (*Year Bks of Ed. II*)

Year Books (*Les Reports del Cases en Ley* (London, 1678–9)). (*Year Books*)

Yorkshire Star Chamber Proceedings, II, ed. H. B. McCall, Yorkshire Archaeo-logical Society, Record Series, XLV (1911). (*Yorks. Proc.*)

SECONDARY WORKS

Anglo, S., *The Courts of Europe*, London, 1977.

Barnes, T. G., 'Star Chamber litigants and their counsel, 1596–1641', in *Legal Records and the Historian*, ed. J. H. Baker, London, 1978: 7–28.

Bean, J. M. W., *The Decline of English Feudalism, 1215–1540*, Manchester, 1968.

Bellamy, J. G., 'Justice under the Yorkist kings', *American Journal of Legal History*, 9 (1965): 135–55.

    The Law of Treason in England in the Later Middle Ages, Cambridge, 1970.

    Criminal Law and Society in Late Medieval and Tudor England, Gloucester and New York, 1984.

    Robin Hood: An Historical Enquiry, London, 1985.

Bernard, G. W., 'The rise of Sir William Compton, early Tudor courtier', *English Historical Review*, XCVI (1981): 754–79.

Bulow, G. von, 'Journey through England and Scotland made by Lupold von Wedel in the years 1584 and 1585', *Transactions of the Royal Historical Society*, new series, IX (1895): 233–70.

Carpenter, C., 'The Beauchamp affinity: a study of bastard feudalism at work', *English Historical Review* XCV (1980): 514–32.

    'Law, justice and landowners in late medieval England', *Law and History Review*, I (1983): 205–37.

Chesters, G., 'John Daniel of Daresbury, 1544–1610', *Transactions of the Historical Society of Lancashire and Cheshire* CXVIII (1966): 1–17.

Chrimes, S. B., *Henry VII*, London, 1972.

Cockburn, J. S. and Green, T.A., eds, *Twelve Good Men and True. The Criminal Trial Jury in England, 1200–1800*. Princeton, New Jersey, 1988.

Cooper, J. P., 'Henry VII's last years reconsidered', *Historical Journal* 2 (1959): 103–29.

    Land, Men and Beliefs, ed. G. E. Aylmer and J. S. Morrill, London, 1983.

Coward, B., *The Stanleys, Lord Stanley, and Earls of Derby 1385–1672*, Chetham Society, 3rd Series, 30 (1983).

Cowell, J., *The Interpreter*, Cambridge, 1607.

Dobson, R. B. and Taylor, J., *Rymes of Robin Hood*, London, 1976.

Dunham, Jr, W. H., *Lord Hastings' Indentured Retainers 1461–1483*, Hamden, Conn., 1970.

Elton, G. R., *The Tudor Constitution, Documents and Commentary*, Cambridge, 1960.

'Henry VII: a restatement', *Historical Journal* 4 (1961): 1–29.

'Tudor Government: the points of contact, III. The Court',
Transactions of the Royal Historical Society, 5th series, 26 (1976): 211–28.

Emmison, F. G., *Elizabethan Life: Disorder*, Chelmsford, 1970.

Fortescue, J., *The Governance of England*, ed. C. Plummer, Oxford, 1885.

Given-Wilson, C., *The Royal Household and the King's Affinity*, New Haven, Conn., 1986.

The English Nobility in the Late Middle Ages, London, 1987.

Goheen, R. B., 'Social ideals and social structure: rural Gloucestershire, 1450–1550', *Histoire Sociale/Social History* 24 (1979): 262–80.

Green, R. F., *Poets and Princepleasers*, Toronto, 1980.

Guy, J. A., *The Cardinal's Court*, Hassocks, 1977.

The Public Career of Sir Thomas More, Brighton, 1980.

Christopher St German on Chancery and Statute, Selden Society, Supplementary Series, 6 (1985).

The Court of the Star Chamber and Its Records to the Reign of Elizabeth I, London, 1985.

Hanawalt, B. A., *Crime and Conflict in English Communities 1300–1348*, Cambridge, Mass., 1979.

Harding, A., 'The origins of the crime of conspiracy', *Transactions of the Royal Historical Society*, 5th Series, 33 (1983): 89–108.

Hicks, M. A., 'Restraint, mediation and private justice: George, Duke of Clarence as "Good Lord" ', *Journal of Legal History* 4 (1983): 56–71.

Holdsworth, W. S., *History of English Law*, Boston, 1924–6.

Ives, E. W., 'The genesis of the Statute of Uses', *English Historical Review* LXXXII (1967): 673–97.

The Common Lawyers of Pre-Reformation England, Cambridge, 1983.

Jackson, J. E., 'Longleat Papers, No. 4', *Wiltshire Archaeological and Natural History Society Magazine*, XVIII (1879): 258–78.

Jefferies, P., 'The medieval use as family law and custom: the Berkshire gentry in the fourteenth and fifteenth centuries', *Southern History* I (1979): 45–69.

Kaeuper, R. W., 'Law and order in the fourteenth century: the evidence of special commissions of oyer and terminer', *Speculum* LIV (1979): 734–84.

Lehmberg, S. E., 'Star Chamber, 1485–1509', *Huntingdon Library Quarterly* 24 (1960–1): 189–214.

Leyser, K. J., 'K. B. McFarlane', *Proceedings of the British Academy* LXII (1976): 485–506.

Long, C. E., 'Wild Darell of Littlecote', *Wiltshire Archaeological and Natural History Society Magazine* IV (1857): 209–32.

M. I., *A Health to the Gentlemanly Profession of Servingmen* (1598).

McFarlane, K. B., 'England: the Lancastrian kings, 1399–1461', in *Cambridge Medieval History*, ed. C. W. Previté-Orton and Z. N. Brooke, Cambridge, 1911–36, vol 8: 362–417.

'Bastard feudalism', *Bulletin of the Institute of Historical Research* 20 (1943–5): 161–80.

'William Worcester, a preliminary survey', in *Studies presented to Sir Hilary Jenkinson*, London 1957: 196–221.

The Nobility of Later Medieval England, ed. J. P. Cooper and G. L. Harriss, Oxford, 1973.

England in the Fifteenth Century, London, 1981.

Maddicott, J. R., *Law and Lordship: Royal Justices as Retainers in Thirteenth and Fourteenth-Century England, Past and Present*, Supplement 4 (1978).

Maitland, F. W., *The Collected Papers of Frederic William Maitland*, ed. H. A. L. Fisher, Cambridge, 1911.

Merriman, R. W., 'Extracts from the records of the Wiltshire quarter sessions', *Wiltshire Archaeological and Natural History Society Magazine* XXI (1883): 75–111.

Miller, H., *Henry VIII and the English Nobility*, Oxford, 1986.

Milsom, S. F. C., *Historical Foundations of the Common Law*, London, 1969.

More, T., *The History of Richard III*, ed. R. S. Sylvester, New Haven, Conn., 1963.

Myers, A. R., *The Household of Edward IV*, Manchester, 1959.

Newton, A. P., 'Tudor reforms in the royal household', in *Tudor Studies*, ed. R. W. Seton Watson, London, 1924: 231–56.

Nichols, J., *The Progresses of James I*, London, 1828.

Palmer, R. C., *The Whilton Dispute, 1264–1380: A Social Legal Study of Dispute Settlement in Medieval England*, Princeton, 1984.

Philips, H. E. I., 'The last years of the court of Star Chamber 1630–41', *Transactions of the Royal Historical Society*, 4th Series, 21 (1939): 103–31.

Pilkington, J., *The History of the Lancashire Family of Pilkington and its Branches 1066–1600*, Liverpool, 1894.

Pollock, F. and Maitland, F. W., *The History of English Law before the Time of Edward I*, Cambridge, 1911.

Powell, E., 'The administration of criminal justice in late-medieval England. Peace sessions and assizes', in *The Political Context of Law*, ed. R. Eales and D. Sullivan, London, 1987: 49–59.

Pugh, R. B., *Imprisonment in Medieval England*, Cambridge, 1970.

Putnam, B. H., *Early Treatises on the Practice of the Justices of the Peace in the Fifteenth and Sixteenth Centuries*, Oxford, 1924.

Proceedings Before the Justices of the Peace in the Fourteenth and Fifteenth Centuries, London, 1938.

The Place in Legal History of Sir William Shareshull, Cambridge, 1950.

Raine, J., *The Priory of Hexham*, I, Surtees Society, 44 (1864).

Richmond, C. F., *John Hopton. A Fifteenth Century Suffolk Gentleman*, Cambridge, 1981.

Roskell, J. S., *The Knights of the Shire for the County Palatine of Lancaster (1377–1460)*, Chetham Society, New Series, 96 (1937).

Sargent, R. M., *At the Court of Queen Elizabeth*, Oxford, 1935.

Saul, N. E., *Knights and Esquires: The Gloucestershire Gentry in the Fourteenth Century*, Oxford, 1981.

Scenes from Provincial Life, Oxford, 1986.

Skelton, E., *The Court of Star Chamber in the Reign of Elizabeth*, unpublished M.A. thesis, University of London, 1931.

Stone, L., *The Crisis of the Aristocracy*, Oxford, 1965.

Storey, R. L., *The End of the House of Lancaster*, London, 1966.
    'Lincolnshire and the Wars of the Roses', *Nottingham Medieval Studies*
    XIV (1970): 64–83

Stubbs, W., *The Constitutional History of England*, Oxford, 1898.

Sutherland, D. W., *The Assize of Novel Disseisin*, Oxford, 1973.

Tout, T. F., *Chapters in Administrative History*, Manchester, 1920–33.

Willard, J. F., Morris, W. A., Strayer, J. F., and Dunham Jr, W. H., *The English Government at Work, 1327–1336*, Cambridge, Mass., 1940–50.

INDEX

179